RUGB

Rugby has been a major part of Derek Wyatt's life for the past thirty-five years, first as a player which saw him represent Oxford University, Bedford, Bath, the Barbarians and England, and latterly as a coach, selector, journalist, publisher and television producer.

In his spare time he is a local Labour Councillor for Haringey, and will contest the next General Election in the UK as the prospective parliamentary candidate for Sittingbourne and Sheppey.

RUGBY
DisUnion

DEREK WYATT

VISTA

First published in Great Britain 1995
by Victor Gollancz

This Vista edition published 1996
Vista is an imprint of the Cassell Group
Wellington House, 125 Strand, London WC2R 0BB

A catalogue record for this book is
available from the British Library.

ISBN 0 575 60015 2

Printed and bound in Great Britain
by Cox & Wyman Ltd, Reading, Berkshire

96 97 98 99   10 9 8 7 6 5 4 3 2 1

Contents

To John Chandler and his wonderful staff at the
Ocean View Hotel, Hastings, Barbados, who gave me
the space to complete this book

Acknowledgements

Grateful thanks are to the following.

In South Africa: Ross MacDonald, Donald and Ann MacDonald, John Robbie, John Dyer, Rian Oberholzer, Craig Jamieson, John Holmes, Jonathan Goslett, Ian Kirkpatrick, Gilden Huys.

In Australia: Sir Nicholas Shehadie, Norbert Byrne, John Howard, Dr Roger Vanderfield, Michael and Diana Bray, Nick Farr-Jones, Peter FitzSimons, Greg Campbell, Ross Turnbull, David Lord.

In New Zealand: Cheryl Watt, David Kirk, Ray Cairns, Bob Stuart, Ivan Vodanovich, John Hart, Ted Turner, Paddy Finnigan, George Verrey, Liz Davison, Ian Robson, Dick Littlejohn, Ces Blazey, Laurie Mains, Wynne Gray, Lindsay Knight, Keith Quinn, Eddie Tonks.

In America: Karl and Kathy Laucher.

In France: Bernard Lapasset and Henri Bru.

In Wales: Vernon Pugh QC, Denis Evans and Jonathan Price.

In England: Dudley Wood, Stuart Barnes, David Hinchcliffe MP, Paul Farrelly, Peter Berlin, Keith Rowlands, Neil MacDonald, Jack Rowell, John Hopkins, Sir Ewart Bell.

In Argentina: Carlos Guarna.

Many others who have helped me remain anonymous – they prefer it that way.

Jo Willett, my wife, and our children, Daisy and Jack, who allowed me the freedom to travel, which I did not always choose to do at the most convenient of times. Thankfully, they were able to join me in Barbados.

My editor, Caroline North, and my publisher, Richard Wigmore, who had the courage to take me on board and the strength to see the book through.

Finally, my employers at United Artists, especially Joyce Taylor, Nigel Haunch and Sarah Simpson, for coping with my absence and supporting me, too.

A special fund has been established for Max Brito, the Ivory Coast player paralysed for life as the result of an injury sustained in the 1995 World Cup match against Tonga. Donations can be made to the First National Bank, Johannesburg: branch number 25:13:05; account number 9000129801.

Introduction

We were five minutes into the fourth period of the third rugby World Cup final, the first to have gone into overtime. The All Blacks had taken an early 12–9 lead. Then Joel Stransky kicked his third penalty goal of the match after Josh Kronfeld had stupidly fallen offside. At 12–12 the 62,000-strong crowd were informed that if there were still no tries at the end of extra time, then New Zealand would win on the basis of their superior disciplinary record. For the World Cup to be settled in this way might be acceptable according to the rules but it would cause an outcry.

How much this was on the minds of Joost van der Westhuizen and Joel Stransky was clear. 'I said to Joost, "I'll try a drop, give it to me straight,"' said Stransky. South Africa won the scrum and Van der Westhuizen duly gave the ball to his half-back partner, but by then the scrum had wheeled slightly to make Stransky's angle for the drop even more difficult – it was bad enough that it was on the right side of the posts. The pressure must have been enormous, and the drop could have gone over or just as easily have cleared the dead-ball line. Stransky took aim and the goal was true. It sailed high and through the posts to the left-hand side. Stransky, the man left out of the Springboks' tour to New Zealand in 1994, had done it. South Africa led 15–12.

The crowd found it hard to contain themselves, and the poor All Blacks, the pre-final favourites, found the pressure too much. They fumbled 22s; they knocked on for no reason. They knew they had lost at the last. Ed Morrison, the referee, turned 10 metres from the All Blacks' line, pointed to the centre and whistled for the end of the game. South Africa, the pariahs of the rugby World Cups of 1987 and 1991, had won it at their first attempt. Ellis Park went bananas.

François Pienaar, the captain and player of the tournament, sank to his knees and made the sign of the cross on his body. Within ten seconds he had gathered his team together in a huddle and, extraordinarily, asked them to kneel. In front of an audience of 1.2 billion, he said a prayer of thanks. The cynics whispered about rugby being the new religion of white South Africa. Only when the prayer was finished did the celebrations really begin.

Meanwhile, the All Blacks, uncertain of quite what had happened to their dream, were trooping off the field, already pondering the reaction at home in New Zealand, where a huge wake would be about to begin. Pienaar, interviewed live, claimed that the victory was not just for the 'sixty-two thousand here but for the forty-three million that make up our country'. All along he had controlled the emotional strings to perfection.

President Nelson Mandela, wearing Pienaar's number 6 Springbok jersey and cap, came out to present the William Webb Ellis Trophy to the captain. Three sky-divers arrived perfectly on cue. One had a 'Congratulations South Africa' flag attached to his body, another 'See You in Wales 1999'. The Springboks went on a lap of honour. The crowd was ecstatic, the whole country on meltdown. This was more than they could have imagined, even though the game itself could not equal another magical day only four weeks earlier, when South Africa had turned over Australia in the opening match of what had become a quite amazing World Cup.

The final brought to an end the best-organized World Cup in the short history of the tournament. Yet it was not all sweetness and light: there were negative aspects to the 1995 tournament, as there had been with its predecessors. Did the Springbok players receive a private allocation of tickets for the final beyond the needs of their closest families? We should be told. Did Jannie Engelbrecht have a contract to manage the Springbok side through to the World Cup? Perhaps the high court would decide. And why did the final dinner end in such disarray? The tournament was sullied, too, by the domination of one man, Dr Louis Luyt, president of the South African Rugby Football Union. He made life difficult at the best of times, but over the citation of Pieter Hendriks by the Rugby World Cup directors for kicking a Canadian opponent, his public disagreement with the

RWC was a downright disgrace. The RWC directors should make public the correspondence that passed between Sir Ewart Bell, their chairman, and Dr Luyt on the subject.

This, then, was modern rugby. In France, Australia and New Zealand, players were contracted by their unions for the first time. If a player could not bring himself to sign he was left out of the World Cup squad. Soon, all players would be contracted to prevent them from moving between the two rugby codes, Union and League.

All this was completely beyond anything that could have even been imagined in the parochial rugby world of twenty years ago, when the seeds of the idea of a World Cup had yet to be sown.

PART 1: 1987

1

Prelude

Twenty years ago, the idea of a rugby World Cup would have seemed like the product of a fevered imagination. Playing rugby at the top in the mid-seventies meant playing for your country, every now and again being carded for the British Lions and, if you were lucky, being picked. The Lions selectors determined the composition of the touring side, and naturally they favoured their own home players, irrespective of their ability. Clubs in Ireland did not play clubs in Scotland or, for that matter, Wales or England, except on rare occasions. Likewise, the Scottish clubs kept themselves to themselves. Only a smattering of English clubs, and those mainly in the west country, had regular fixtures with the Welsh. There were no leagues at all. Various newspapers tried promoting their own, but these were half baked and essentially meaningless.

I can remember many a conversation turning towards what we needed as players: formal leagues that gave our fixtures bite. The older players resented us young 'uns – 'You'll wreck the spirit of the game,' they would curse, and mean it. It just seemed logical to me. What didn't seem so obvious was the need for a World Cup, for either clubs or countries. Our thinking was cocooned by our culture and understanding of the game's potential, or lack of it. In my wildest dreams, I had seen rugby back in the Olympic movement because it had been there before and therefore could be again, or so I thought. Besides, that was the only organization that sponsored a true world competition. But rugby just didn't think like that. We were, at least in England, happy in the tradition of the game. Coaching was still a dirty word; training was largely unscientific and progress something that happened in America.

At international level, the only side that put the fear of God into us was New Zealand. Some things don't change. Australia was still perceived as a second-rate country, despite the thumping the national team gave England in the two-Test series in 1975. South Africa had been hounded out of making visits, although the country welcomed visitors with an armful of krugerrands, and France, the only other member of the International Board (or International Rugby Football Board, to give it its more pompous title), was content to play in the Five Nations Championship. French rugby also suffered from isolationism (nothing changes), but it was buoyed by the amount of cash available from local resources.

The nearest we came to a top-level knock-out competition was in 1976. In 1975, an unworldly rugby club in England called Bedford had beaten a then fashionable Rosslyn Park in what was the John Player Cup (it's now called the Pilkington Cup) by 28–12. The following season, the club committee thought it would be a good idea if Bedford, the English champions, challenged Llanelli, the Welsh champions, to a home-and-away fixture in what was branded the British Championship play-off.

Bedford duly travelled down to Llanelli for a midweek game that saw Stradey Park packed to the hills and back again. The Bedford squad were told to assemble at Paddington Station in London to catch a lunchtime train to Swansea, where they could switch to a local service to Llanelli. Lunch was booked in the restaurant car, seats were reserved, albeit in economy (then still quaintly called second class), and taxis were waiting at the station to take us up to Stradey, which was quite a hike. As it was an evening fixture under lights, the committee had had the foresight to book sleeping accommodation for the players for the return journey on the midnight train. Nothing could have been simpler.

Good intention was a byword of the Bedford club of which I was then a playing member. When we arrived at Paddington, there were no reserved seats; no restaurant car; no buffet, no taxis at Llanelli. Taxis in Llanelli? Get real, man. We walked to the ground. We all lived within fifty miles of the London hinterland, and I doubt that any of us had seen before such a landscape of terraced dwelling after terraced dwelling; an austere urban landscape where the local spec

18

builder of the nineteenth century had simply raped the ground and left it treeless.

We were angry when we got to the ground only because we thought, if we were honest with ourselves, we were about to be crowned world champions. Events didn't quite go according to plan. Llanelli won the toss and elected to receive the kick-off. We waited for Neil Bennett, our England fly-half, to do the honours. He was nowhere to be seen. He'd been accidentally locked in the changing rooms.

We came a close second, losing by 40–6. The walk back to the station was at least twice as far as the journey to the ground. I was then a naive young player on the fringe of the England team. Rugby was my life. The match against Llanelli changed my views of the game. Why? Because the crowd must have been 12,000 or more; the car park, which had a capacity of perhaps eight hundred cars, was full; the programmes were sold out; the bars were packed. Where, I pondered, was the money going?

The train back to Paddington appeared to travel via Land's End and John o'Groats and I finally reached the school in Ipswich where I taught by breaktime the next day. My head of department took me to one side. 'Just remember, Derek, that ninety-nine per cent of the world's population get by without rugby, and, after all, you were only chasing a piece of pigskin around a paddock for eighty minutes.'

The return match was not one to which we were looking forward. Aside from the verbals we gave the committee for the total lack of organization, none of us had been on the receiving end of such a hiding as we'd had at Llanelli. Phil Bennett and the boyos had beaten us at their leisure. Incredibly, when it came to the night of the second leg, the referee advised us that the game would have to be delayed for twenty minutes on the instructions of the police. The queues of people wanting to come in to the match were so long that traffic had ground to a halt in Goldington Road. I don't know what the official attendance was, but it felt like 6,000 squashed into a ground that could take no more than 2,500. It was some night, and when the Llanelli visitors broke into song, a condition which then slowly, like the wretched Mexican wave nowadays, took hold of us all, it was as if the fairies and hobgoblins had come out to play. Magic was one of the most overworked clichés in sports journalism that year but magic it was. Bedford lost 28–12, but it was an electric evening and I can still see in my mind some of the plays and tries of the game.

In the context of today's controversies over amateurism and the money swilling around the game, what constituted a breach of the amateur regulations in the 1970s and 1980s is scarcely credible. I was very nearly banned by the Rugby Football Union on three separate occasions. In 1979–80, in addition to my teaching duties, I started up, with Mike Beese, a sports consultancy. Mike had captained Bath in 1978–9 and earlier, when playing at Liverpool, had been capped by England. We ran sports medicine conferences and events and frankly did anything that could make us a few bob, including selling cricket ties and rugby T-shirts and designing notepaper for sports clubs. Someone reported us to the RFU and after some correspondence with Bob Weighill, the secretary, we agreed to curtail our operation.

In 1981 I was awarded a place to read for an M.Sc. at Oxford. Awarded is hardly the most appropriate word because I had to raise £10,000 to cover my tutorial and accommodation expenses. I opened a small trust fund through my solicitor, David Gay (Bath and England), and I wrote to hundreds of organizations who had charitable funds and many rugby clubs, asking for donations to go to my trust. Someone else reported this letter to the RFU and I was given a severe warning. We returned the money and closed down the trust.

But it was while I was studying at Oxford that my amateur status came closest to being ended. I was called before a small RFU panel at the East India Club one afternoon. On the morning of the snow-bound centenary Varsity Match in 1981 I had written an article for Nicholas Keith, sports editor of *The Times*. He liked it and asked me to do some more. I wrote about rugby but also about sports coaching, sports medicine and sports psychology. In March 1982 I began to cover rugby matches for the *Observer*. All I was trying to do was to find a less painful way of meeting my fees than extending my already over-extended overdraft.

The upshot was that the RFU found me guilty of infringing my amateur status by writing and receiving money for articles and reports on rugby. I could keep the payment for those pieces that were published but were not on rugby. I contended that, as writing was my full-time occupation while I was a student receiving no income, I had not infringed the amateur regulations. It was clear that I had not, because otherwise the RFU would have banned me. Instead I agreed to pay back only the money I had received from the *Observer* for match reports, which I did. In return the RFU were happy to let me off with yet another severe warning.

It struck me as delightfully and deliciously ironic that one of the first stories I had to cover in depth for *The Times* was the Adidas boot scandal, in which it was revealed that leading players of the day had accepted money for wearing Adidas boots in international matches. J. V. Smith, the president of the RFU, kept us waiting in the freezing cold outside the East India Club in early December 1982 for three or four hours. Then, suddenly, the doors opened and he ran out faster than at any time since his Varsity Match performances of 1948, 1949 and 1950. He legged it down to Pall Mall to catch a taxi, dodging the press and the cameras. No statement was forthcoming. That was how good the RFU was at press relations.

I had to smile when the Old Farts v Will Carling affair erupted at the beginning of May 1995. As far as I was concerned, all non-players were Old Farts, and as it had been a decade since I had put on a jersey, I was definitely eligible for life membership of the Old Fartonians (sponsored, naturally, by Heinz Baked Beans) myself.

It seemed to me that nothing had changed. Rugby World Cup '95 was to alter this landscape once and for all.

In many ways the first rugby World Cup, held in Australia and New Zealand in 1987, was a benchmark for the game. That it took place at all was some kind of minor miracle, given the animosity that existed between the Four Home Unions – England, Ireland, Wales and Scotland – and the other four members of the International Rugby Football Board (IB), South Africa, Australia, France and New Zealand. The acrimony was not confined to these two factions: indeed, frequently the Four Home Unions so loathed each other that it is hardly surprising they have agreed on only two major administrative matters over the past hundred years or so – the Five Nations Championship (which was quietly superseded by a Five Nations Cup in 1993) and the British Lions tours. Now both of these institutions are under threat as the game moves relentlessly on to the fourth World Cup in 1999, to be hosted by Wales.

This book began with a conversation I had with Brendan Mullin, the Oxford University and Irish centre, in Grosvenor Square in Mayfair in May 1987. Brendan was still wondering whether he would be picked for the Irish athletics team in the 110-metre hurdles for the Seoul Olympics in 1988. He had already been chosen for the Ireland rugby squad for the first rugby World Cup in Australia and New Zealand. Ireland had a reasonable draw – Wales, Canada and Tonga – and only needed to beat the last two to qualify for the quarter-finals. With typical understatement, Brendan suggested that the first game against Wales would be 'a tough one'. He added: 'We must beat them if we are to progress.'

The Irish squad had no real understanding of how a World Cup worked, and in this they were on a par with the rest of the rugby-playing countries. What worried me was that Ireland's most important match was not their opener with Wales, however much they fancied themselves, but their quarter-final, which was likely to be against Australia. The Irish, if Mullin was a typical representative, were greener than green. Their representatives on the IB had never been in favour of the damn thing in the first place. They feared that it would expose them to the world game, for which they were not ready and which they did not want.

The problem for the Old Guard, as I shall refer to the Four Home Unions, is that they believed they owned the game lock, stock and barrel. They acknowledged that combinations of people, usually of Welsh farmers and Scottish railway émigrés, introduced the game throughout the latter half of the nineteenth century as the British empire expanded, or, as in the case of the dominions, took root. But that was the extent of their understanding. Yet, the record books show that in 1984, when the IB agreed to evaluate the possibility of a World Cup, South Africa had the most successful international record against all countries; that New Zealand were next, and that coming up fast in the outside lane were Australia. The latter did not host a Lions tour of their own until 1989 (the Lions won 2–1) and had always been the junior partner to both New Zealand and South Africa.

This is the account of a journey, and it was not always a straightforward one. I was unable to access the minutes of the administrators

22

of the 1987, 1991 and 1995 World Cups, and the IB minutes pertaining to the three tournaments were also unavailable.

One day I hope they will understand that if the game is to retain its sanity, these minutes should be placed in the public domain.

2

Wizards of Oz

It is not surprising that Rugby Union in Australia was seen as a poor relation since in terms of wealth and popularity it was overshadowed by Australian Rules (dominant in southern Australia, particularly in Victoria), by Rugby League (the main Aussie game in New South Wales and Queensland) and latterly by soccer. But Rugby Union is no longer the poorest nor necessarily the weakest team game in Australia. In December 1994, the International Management Group (IMG), one of Mark McCormack's companies, paid A\$52 million for the television rights to the game, a quantum leap of such huge dimensions that some insiders wondered if IMG would go under as a result. We shall see.

Ten years earlier almost to the day, Mark Ella and David Campese were putting Scotland to the sword by 37–12 at Murrayfield and in so doing creating history for the Wallabies. This was their first-ever Grand Slam, although they had previously beaten Wales 28–9, Ireland 16–9 and England 19–3. Australia, a driven team under their mercurial coach, Alan Jones, were now the hottest Rugby Union property in the world. This precipitated, at the end of 1984, a fundamental changing of the guards. Australia, who really should have won a Grand Slam in 1981, had finally come of age. They had joined the elite.

New Zealand and Australia represented the 'new guard'. South Africa and France only ever represented themselves: they did or followed or agreed only what was good for them. They put up a front that might suggest they were a party to this or that, but this was pure pragmatism.

Meanwhile, in Britain there was a background of deep hostility between England and Wales. At Twickenham they believed that as they had 'invented' the game, they were the true and only governing body, irrespective of the origins of the International Board. In Wales they knew they were the guardians of the game, a fact that had been borne out by their total domination on the playing side in the 1960s and 1970s, which resulted in outright Grand Slams in 1971, 1976 and 1978 and Championships in 1964, 1965, 1966, 1969, 1970, 1975 and 1979.

Into this cauldron stepped Neil Durden-Smith, a very English sports entrepreneur, who in 1982–3 had the temerity to suggest a rugby World Cup and gave the notion of such a competition its first nudge. In a past life, he had also been an aide-de-camp to the governor general of New Zealand, so although the Old Guard dismissed his efforts out of hand, the idea struck a chord down under.

Ivan Vodanovich, the former All Black full-back and a member of the 1987 NZRFU World Cup committee, suggested to me: 'I think the originator of the idea for a World Cup was a guy called Pat Gill who was a NZ council member. My memory's not great, but I have a feeling that there was a players' committee at the time and that Pat was its chairman. I believe the pressure came from the players and through Pat to the council of the NZRFU.'

Sir Nicholas Shehadie, the former Mr Everything in Australia, was more to the point. 'If you ask me, the instigator of the idea of a rugby World Cup was a man by the name of Harold Tolhurst, who had been an international threequarter and referee back in the 1950s, I think 1957–8. He'd wanted it.'

My own research yielded no serious discussion about either rugby in the Olympics or a World Cup, not even an article in the UK press, until Neil Durden-Smith's excursion. The playing horizons of most British and Irish international players were limited to selection for the British Lions or, failing that, the Barbarians.

So who really started the first World Cup? Until further research proves otherwise, I will plump for Bill McLaughlin, president of the Australian Rugby Union in 1979, who with an eye on his country's own bicentennial celebrations in 1988, suggested that year that the ARU should organize a World Cup, by invitation, as part of this important event. Unfortunately, for reasons best known to himself, Bill McLaughlin was not talking to his New Zealand counterpart, Ces Blazey. Consequently, the ARU was unaware that the NZRFU had their own plans for such a tournament. So it was that the International Board received two separate and discrete applications to run the inaugural World Cup.

In the meantime, Sir Nicholas Shehadie had become president of the ARU, and in 1982 he managed to herd Ces Blazey and Russ Thomas of the NZRFU into a hotel room in Auckland to bash some heads together. Shehadie was fast becoming a desperate man. He had just come from a weekend at a favourite Sydney retreat of his.

It was no ordinary weekend. The Australian press had seized upon a story from another sports entrepreneur, this time an Aussie by the name of David Lord. Lord, it was to be alleged, had signed up 212 of the leading 217 rugby players in the world to create a rugby circus similar to the Packer cricket circus of 1978–9. Even in a good year Sir Nick could ill afford a stream of defections to Rugby League, and this was something else altogether. What Lord was suggesting would create a double whammy. Six elite Aussie internationals spent that weekend with Sir Nick, and if they didn't actually show him contracts they'd been offered, he nevertheless became aware of the seriousness of the situation. Only a rugby World Cup in Australia would save his bacon, or, failing that, at least a rugby World Cup shared with New Zealand.

Sir Nick's head-banging session in Auckland was to reap a fruitful harvest. It wasn't too long – March 1984 – before the IB, conscious that they had to give some kind of reaction to the requests for a World Cup, decided to ask the representatives of Australia and New Zealand to come forward with some recommendations for their next meeting, due to take place in March 1985. The decision was helped somewhat by the fact that the 'Buggins' turn' chairman of the IB was Dr Roger Vanderfield, a former international referee who represented Australia. 'It was a mistake by the Four Home Unions to ask for a report. The stay of execution was only their stay of execution,' said Vanderfield. 'What I didn't know was how the sixteen members would vote come 1985, and so we undertook some discreet lobbying.'

The ARU had put in its bid for the World Cup at an IB emergency meeting on 25 June 1983; the NZRFU at the IB meeting in March 1984. The two unions were quick to appoint a joint working committee. The ARU nominated Sir Nick Shehadie, John Howard (treasurer) and Norbert Byrne of the Queensland Union; the NZRFU reciprocated with Dick Littlejohn (chair). The first feasibility study for a World Cup was commissioned by them on 1 December 1984.

In the meantime, a small fishing expedition had been at work back-stage in Ireland during Australia's Grand Slam tour. The IRFU was a problem. It was totally against a World Cup. Then, during the 1985 Five Nations Championship, Sir Nick Shehadie and Dick Littlejohn tried again to extract promises from the Four Home Unions and France.

When they arrived in England no one from the RFU showed up at Heathrow and there were no messages at their hotel. Aware that they were being cold-shouldered, Dick Littlejohn rang John Reason, then the leading rugby correspondent in the UK, and he agreed to meet them the following day. But Reason was the *Sunday Telegraph*'s correspondent and the story couldn't wait for the Sunday newspapers. Somehow, Terry O'Connor, rugby correspondent of the *Daily Mail*, was inveigled to turn up too and he broke the news. Shehadie and Littlejohn, through the offices of Bob Weighill, then secretary of the RFU, did then learn that a loose schedule had in fact been agreed with Ireland, Wales and Scotland, but interestingly, not England.

The importance of the vote in March 1985 was absolutely critical to the whole process. The only year the World Cup could conceivably take place was 1987: the Seoul Olympics were scheduled for 1988 and the FIFA soccer World Cup was due to be held in Italy in 1990. A first Lions tour to Australia had been pencilled in for 1989. If the March 1985 IB meeting did not agree to a World Cup, then the earliest it could be held would be 1991. Shehadie and Littlejohn were aware of the mounting pressures. There were sixteen votes to be cast and a simple majority would suffice – England, Ireland, Wales, Scotland, France, South Africa, New Zealand and Australia had two votes apiece.

The unknown quantity in 1985 was South Africa. That country's two votes would be crucial, especially as it was unlikely that they would be allowed to participate in a World Cup in either Australia or New Zealand. Indeed, the governments in both countries, then both Labour administrations under Bob Hawke and David Lange respectively, had strong anti-apartheid leanings. Yet it was possible that Dr Danie Craven and Fritz Eloff would hold all the cards.

I put this possibility to Dr Roger Vanderfield over lunch at a delightful seafood restaurant in Rose Bay in Sydney. He told me:

I was very worried about South Africa. I saw their vote as being crucial to the whole matter, and as chairman I couldn't afford for them not to vote in favour. At that time there were no direct flights to South Africa and trade and contact with the country was severely restricted. I took it upon myself – and not one member of the IB knew this – to go against government advice, and I travelled to South Africa to see the South African Rugby Board [the whites only rugby union].

I saw Eloff in Johannesburg and Craven in Cape Town to ask for their support. Luckily, they both wanted in, but they both probably knew that even if they voted in favour they would not be allowed to participate. I have to say I'm glad I went, for I recognized on the same flight none other than David Lord.

The critical part to Vanderfield's work had already been undertaken by Shehadie and Littlejohn. First they travelled to Cardiff to meet the WRU committee. They made a point of addressing the executive committees wherever practical, rather than the two nominated IB members, because they wanted to put their case to the largest audience. Over dinner, Shehadie presented the case for a World Cup to be shared between Australia and New Zealand and to be held in just over two years from then. Sir Nick takes up the story.

I finished my speech and there was a stony silence. I thought we had lost it there and then. I think Alun Turner spoke first, and he was vehemently against it. Thankfully, Ken Harris, the Welsh treasurer, spoke for it and his speech was followed by a lot of 'hear, hears'. He turned the atmosphere around. We left Cardiff thinking we had two votes in our pocket.

We were due next to fly to Ireland to meet the Irish executive on the morning of the Ireland–England game. It wasn't our week. There was snow and the game was cancelled. We had to wait a further two weeks for the Scotland–Ireland match at Murrayfield before we met them both. The Scots were against a World Cup. They believed it would herald the end of the Lions tours and of the amateur game. The Irish – well, Ronnie Dawson and Tom Kiernan – were totally opposed too. Typically, they said that if it was to happen, it should happen in six years. Six years was a nonsense as far as we were concerned. We understood the Scots' fear of professionalism, but we were heartened by a poll taken of the Scottish players published on the morning of the match which said they were very much in favour.

In spite of Sir Nicholas Shehadie's optimism, the omens were not good. For the ARU, the most junior of the eight IB countries, it was a tense time. They had met Neil Durden-Smith and his partner, Gideon Lloyd, in 1982 and given a firm commitment to their proposals for a World Cup. Three years on, with less than two weeks to go before the critical vote, they were still uncertain as to whether they would have enough.

The French Fédération de Rugby's president at this time was Albert Ferrasse, who ran French rugby as an autocrat. France had applied to be a member of the IB in 1978. The Scots abstained and the decision was deferred a year, but by 1979 they were full members. Even though the French had always had their own agenda, it still came as a surprise to the IB when Ferrasse made yet another proposal for a World Cup – to be held, naturally, in France.

It is at this point that memories start to become hazy. Ces Blazey and Bob Stuart were the NZRFU IB members in 1984–5. Blazey, arguably the foremost rugby intellect in the world, had been a member of the IB since 1963.

I'm not sure whether Ferrasse's paper was ever tabled. I have to admit, though, that initially I was firmly against a rugby World Cup. Bill Ramsey, a former president of the RFU, had told us of a discussion he had had with Sir Stanley Rous about the soccer World Cup in England in 1966. 'If we had any brains at all,' Rous had commented, 'we wouldn't get involved in a World Cup of any description. It provoked an unhealthy regard for nationalism.'

The notion of a World Cup had been raised at IB meetings well before 1982. In 1985 I thought it unwise to dismiss it outright and I began to accept that it wasn't a case of we may have one;

rather, we would have one. If that was the reality, better, then, to vote for it.

He might have added better, then, to ensure that if it was going to happen, it happened on your own doorstep.

New Zealand's other IB member, Bob Stuart, reminded me one day in Wellington: 'There were definitely three bids for the World Cup tabled in 1984 – New Zealand's, Australia's and France's. I was against; someone, possibly Sir Matt Busby [he meant Sir Stanley Rous], told us not to have a World Cup because if we did, we would lose control of the game for ever.' Gradually, though, Bob Stuart was won over too. But even this meant that as the IB delegates met in Paris over two days, on 20 and 21 March 1985, Dr Roger Vanderfield, its chairman, could count on only votes from New Zealand and his own country (his other IB member was Ross Turnbull).

Shehadie had last met Ferrasse in 1982, when the Frenchman had said he was in favour of a World Cup. The ARU phoned Ferrasse; he was 'duck shooting in Agen', but they were confident of the French votes. That made six. Four more were needed.

Just before the trip to France, the IB members from the southern hemisphere met their Four Home Unions counterparts at a dinner at the East India Club in St James's Square. There was a difficult and tetchy discussion about the Australian players' out-of-pocket expenses at the Hong Kong Sevens. They had allegedly been paid more than the IB daily allowance. The ARU were in a tight corner and the last thing they needed was a confrontation that would provoke the Four Home Unions into voting against their proposal in Paris a few days later.

Bob Weighill, meanwhile, was quietly penning a short note to Sir Nick Shehadie. It said something to the effect that a similar situation had occurred on England's tour to America in 1982. Shehadie, without giving the game away, alluded to this. His neck was saved, an apology was offered to the ARU about the out-of-pocket expenses, and the rugby World Cup was back on the rails.

It seems only sensible to allow Dr Roger Vanderfield, the chairman of the IB over those two critical days in Paris, to recount the mounting tension:

I remember the second day, the day we had given over to the discussion on the World Cup, as though it was yesterday; it is so vividly etched in my memory. We had all done so much hard work, so much talking, so much pleading, but we were still unsure which way it would go.

The morning session began around ten-thirty. The discussion ebbed and flowed. Sometimes I thought we would lose it, other times I thought we'd win it. At three-fifty p.m., with ten minutes to go to tea, I'd had enough. It was time to bite the bullet. I asked for a vote. Ten voted in favour. We were home – we only needed nine votes. We'd done it.

And who voted for it? Vanderfield was not so forthcoming. My research suggests the voting might well have gone as follows:

Australia (Vanderfield and Turnbull) FOR (2–0)
New Zealand (Blazey and Stuart) FOR (4–0)
South Africa (Craven and Eloff) FOR (6–0)
France (Ferrasse plus one) FOR (8–0)
England (Kendall-Carpenter) FOR (9–0)
Wales FOR (10–0)
Scotland AGAINST (10–2)
Ireland (McKibbin and Dawson) AGAINST (10–4)
Wales AGAINST (10–5)
England (Alf Agar) AGAINST (10–6)

It is possible that the English and Welsh IB members who voted for the World Cup did so against the wishes of their own executive committees.

No doubt there was the odd smile on the faces of the Australian and New Zealand IB members as they took a break. The decision to hold the World Cup had finally been made, but there was more to it than that: the Old Guards' power base had been routed once and for all. It was a victory for the pragmatism of Shehadie and the sensibilities of Blazey and Stuart. Vanderfield, too, deserves his fifteen minutes of fame.

3

Decision Made

Once the decision to hold the tournament had been taken, a working committee was needed to take the World Cup forward. Ronnie Dawson, now that the vote had been carried, was keen to ensure that he was elected to that committee and successfully lobbied over tea. All eight countries insisted that they should all be formally invited to play in the finals and that the remaining eight should be chosen by the sub-committee. Eventually, the other eight invited were Italy, Romania, Canada, Argentina, USSR, Japan, Fiji and Tonga.

South Africa were invited but sensibly declined. The invitation to the USSR to attend was, it appears, never accepted. They had a host of demands. The IB gave a place to Zimbabwe, not because it was a major rugby country, but to give 'white' Africa a place in the finals.

Two weeks before the opening game was due to start there was an army coup in Fiji which caused some doubt about whether their team would turn up. Understandably, this gave rise to some consternation back in New Zealand. Dick Littlejohn recalls:

> Western Samoa was our reserve side. I thought I'd better order up their jerseys, but the problem was we didn't know what their logo looked like. I saw a picture in one of the rugby journals in which a New Zealand boy had on a Western Samoan jersey. I called him, and he agreed to swap it for an All Black one.
>
> I could not get through to the Fijian Rugby Union and so I had no idea whether some of them had been imprisoned or what. Eventually, I called Air New Zealand to ask if the players had boarded their scheduled flight and I was relieved when they told me they had.

So Fiji's fortune was Western Samoa's loss, and the Samoans' colour-ful debut in the World Cup was delayed for a further four years.

In a sense that was that. The IB meeting in Paris broke up, the press reported the decision to go ahead with the first World Cup and the players waited in an anticipation which was heightened further when Dr Danie Craven withdrew, under extreme pressure, the invitation for the Lions to tour South Africa in 1985.

In another sense, though, that wasn't it. The first World Cup still had to be organized, the venues agreed, sponsors signed up and broadcast facilities to be shared. The IOC in its infinite wisdom ensures that the host city for a summer or winter Games has six years to prepare; the IB had just over two years to get everything into shape. It was a tall order, and in retrospect a huge round of applause is due to the thousands and thousands of volunteers in South Australia and New Zealand who made it happen and made it such an outstanding success.

In essence, this is where the story really begins. No one in rugby, of course, had the experience of organizing a World Cup, and it was felt that a professional company should be engaged. It was also clear that Australia and New Zealand were following their own agendas. The Australians knew they had the wherewithal to organize the event; they were also aware that New Zealand expected to arrange it all. A compromise would lead to cock-ups – both unions wanted control. Both initially went their own ways. The actual order of the following events is not altogether clear to me, but they illustrate some of the thinking current at the time.

Those members of the ARU whom I met at Darling Harbour Hotel in September 1994 – Shehadie, John Howard, Philip, Norbert Byrne – recalled a meeting with Cliff Morgan, the great Welsh fly-half of the 1950s and then at the BBC, and, they thought, Jonathan Martin, head of sport at the BBC. They gave the BBC first refusal on the broadcast rights to the World Cup. The asking price was US$6 million. That meeting was not with Jonathan Martin, however, but more probably with Keith Owen of BBC Enterprises. Owen never saw the deal even when it got off the floor and slapped him in the face. He turned it down.

Meanwhile, there was another meeting going on at the BBC. In 1985 TVNZ had only two outside broadcast trucks geared to providing a world-class television picture and not enough hardware to do the job. It was this sort of detail that the IB members failed to ask at that Paris meeting. Consequently, Ces Blazey and Bob Stuart met Harold Anderson at the BBC (he was later to head up TVNZ and briefly Star in Hong Kong) and then, they think, Hugh Greene, director general of the BBC. There was some enthusiasm shown by the corporation, but it led to nothing.

It is doubly ironic when you consider that both Australia and New Zealand tried to broker a deal with the BBC in 1985 and that, when the opportunity came for them to bid for Rugby World Cup '91 on their home patch, they lost it to ITV, their fiercest rivals.

It would not be an over-estimation to conclude that in 1985 the IB and its World Cup sub-committee were out of their depth. They began to appreciate their problems themselves: they needed tax advice, insurance cover, agreement about who took the gate money and a solution as to how the whole thing was going to be funded before a ball was kicked. And this was at a time when the IB was meeting only once a year. (It still meets only twice a year, though fundamental change is in the air.)

When the ARU agreed to fund the whole exercise, the NZRFU quickly agreed to co-fund it with them. The underlying tension within the IB was the Four Home Unions' desire for substantial profits to be paid to them first. As one IB member put it, 'Scotland voted against the 1987 World Cup yet showed unmitigated greed when it came to sharing out the spoils.' Eventually, on 16 September 1985, Rugby World Cup Pty Ltd was formed in Australia to handle the money from the tournament and a tender document was put out to the commercial world asking for companies to bid for the rights to Rugby World Cup '87. In all there were ten or eleven formal inquiries and a shortlist of three was drawn up. At least, that's the story from the Australian camp. New Zealand's Bob Stuart remembers it differently. 'There were eight formal presentations, including one from Ireland and one from the BBC. The worst bid was easily from the BBC. It was an absolute shocker.'

Before the rights were dealt with, however, there needed to be agreement about the dispersal of the potential losses and profits. On 21 March 1985, a committee comprising John Kendall-Carpenter, the chairman, Dawson, Keith Rowlands, Stuart and Turnbull was agreed and they met in London on 16 June, in Hong Kong on 21 and 22 September, Los Angeles on 23 and 24 November and Sydney on 20 and 21 March 1986.

The bone of contention between the organizing committees and the IB was how the dosh should be distributed. The minutes confirm the following:

10. Finance. Whereas the Board [IB] at the 1985 Annual Meeting laid down the administrative framework for the 1987 Tournament, it only by implication provided the financial commitment to see the matter through. It was agreed but not minuted that the IB underwrite its own Tournament.

This point was pursued at the Tournament Committee Meeting in London on 16 June 1985, where it was confirmed that the IB stood by its agreement to bear and share any loss. Distribution of any surplus would recognize:

major share for the Host Unions
share to the IB
share to Member Unions and possibly
share to Other Unions.

The Chairman confirmed this in writing with South Africa, who, despite being rendered, by reason of visa regulations, ineligible to participate, had accepted their share of any putative loss and so certainly deserved a share of any surplus.

At their Meeting in Sydney on 21 March 1986, the Committee unanimously confirmed their view set out in the Minutes of 22 September 1985 in Hong Kong that the distribution of monies should be

1. Net gates accrue to Host Unions for distribution as they see fit
2. All income derived through the Tournament representatives to be divided
    (a) 50% for Management
    (b) 50% for distribution
3. The IB receive 10%, i.e. one-fifth of the sum available for Management

4. The Host Unions receive 40%, i.e. the remainder available for Management
5. The 50% for distribution to be divided into 25 parts
    (a) 16 parts to the 8 Member Unions
    (b) 9 parts to the 9 Other Unions.

In these early stages of the administration of the Tournament there have been financially embarrassing moments.

(a) There was no money available to fund air fares and accommodation en route for Meetings
(b) The Executive Director had been unable to furnish his office
(c) The Executive Director had not been able to take his salary.

As there was no money available via the Interest of the Guaranteed Tournament Revenue to pay (a), (b) and (c) above, and barely sufficient to pay the legal fees, the bulk of the operation to mount the Tournament was being borne by the two Host Unions to the tune of $100,000 each of their own currency. The Tournament Committee expressed their gratitude to the Australian and New Zealand Unions for shouldering for the time being this very considerable burden.

What all this boils down to is that the NZRFU finally won their demands for the gate receipts over which they had dug in their heels. The territory was conceded for RWC '87 and that set a precedent for RWC '91. (For RWC '95, South Africa was allowed to keep only 50 per cent of all gate receipts.)

That meeting's minutes also confirmed the appointment of West Nally to act as the tournament representative, tenders having been sent out as early as May 1985. There were three runners for the rights to organize the 1987 event: West Nally Ltd (London) run by former sports commentator Peter West and Patrick Nally; Mark McCormack's International Management Group (Cleveland, Ohio); and a consortium put together by the NSWRFU and headed by Ross Turnbull, an IB member.

The ARU had insisted on a down payment of US$5 million for the rights, and only West Nally Ltd appeared to have the loot. IMG prevaricated about how much would be earned and in the end seemed happy to agree to provide the down payment, but then they wanted a substantial portion of the profits. The NSWRFU bid was altogether more intriguing. It was being financed through an intermediary company owned by Rupert Murdoch. No one on the IB or ARU (except Turnbull) was aware of this connection. However, the Australian bid was never really seriously considered as a bid from a 'neutral' country was preferred.

So it came down to a straight choice between West Nally and IMG. There was a feeling that IMG presented a real threat to the game. As the company also handled sporting professionals such as tennis and golf players the fear was that giving them an entrée into rugby would provide them with the chance to professionalize the game. (They were eventually to gain their foothold and to move rugby nearer to professionalism anyway, initially in Australia.) Because Patrick Nally seemed the most plausible candidate, and because he had the down payment, he was awarded the contract. He had less than two years to deliver.

The ARU, to their eternal credit, insisted that the monies were paid in instalments and that the final payment was made before a match had been played. In this they were well briefed and soundly advised – West Nally Ltd was shortly to disappear from the scene.

4

Go West, Young Man

Peter West and Patrick Nally teamed up in the 1970s. Peter had been the voice of sport on BBC Radio in the 1940s and 1950s and had transferred across to television, acting as the front or interval commentator at Lord's or Twickenham or Wimbledon in the 1960s and 1970s. He was a genuine all-rounder and lover of sport. In his spare time he was rugby correspondent of *The Times* and his sure touch is missed. He was the perfect foil for Nally, a young and effervescent entrepreneur. West Nally Ltd essentially functioned as Nally's toy. Peter West had the contacts, Nally had the vision thing.

In 1982, Patrick Nally fell out with Adidas supremo Horst Dassler. Dassler was the charismatic son of Adolph (Adi) Dassler, the founder of a boot manufacturing company that serviced Hitler's armies in the 1930s. After the Second World War, Adi Dassler created the Adidas leisure shoe company. Until 1982, Patrick Nally's reputation was such that in the sports marketing business he was perceived to be one of the sharpest thinkers and a match for Mark McCormack, ProServe's Donald Dell or Horst Dassler. That year proved to be his nemesis.

In many ways those sports marketing entrepreneurs were frontiersmen and women, creating a new global marketplace. Often it must have seemed as if they were pushing water uphill. Horst Dassler was simply dazzling. He created a company called International Sports Licensing (ISL Marketing) in Lucerne, Switzerland, if not exactly the centre of the universe, at least a tax-free zone. He had one partner, the Japanese communications company Dentsu, which was and still is, despite the protestations of the old Saatchi & Saatchi, the largest advertising agency in the world. Dassler held 51 per cent and Dentsu 49 per cent of ISL. Into ISL went the most prestigious sports licensing

38

rights ever assembled – those to the soccer World Cup, which Dassler managed to own alongside the winter and summer Olympic Games; the International Amateur Athletics Federation's World Championship, equestrianism and basketball and other high-rolling sports with high-rolling dollars attached.

When Dassler died prematurely of cancer on 10 April 1987, his company had a turnover thought to be in excess of US$2 billion. Unbelievably, the four surviving Dassler sisters were persuaded to sell their company almost before Horst's ashes had reached their three-striped destination, a decision they now deeply regret. Once sold, the company lost itself and the sparkle went out of both Adidas and, more importantly, ISL, where the vultures continue to circle on a daily basis.

Patrick Nally had a smidgen of Dassler's talents, and though they had a business relationship, they fell out over the 1982 FIFA soccer World Cup in Spain. West Nally survived, even though one of their most able lieutenants, Karen Earl, left to create her own company, Karen Earl Ltd. Nevertheless, there was still some lead in the company's pencil, for in 1985 West Nally was appointed the tournament organizer of the first rugby World Cup.

The jury is still out as to whether West Nally had already peaked as a company in 1985. Whatever the truth, the critical element of their pitch to the ARU and NZRFU was that they were able to put their hands on US$5 million, a substantial sum then, as a down payment. In my interviews with the ARU RWC '87 committee, they were not able, apparently because of confidentiality clauses, to tell me with whom they actually signed the RWC '87 contract. It doesn't appear to have been West Nally Ltd. Michael Gray, the solicitors to the ARU committee, would not answer my faxes or telephone calls.

Thwarted, I spent some time in Sydney checking back over some newspaper cuttings concerning RWC '87. There was the occasional mention of a company called Strathmore Holdings, a New Zealand-based firm, and I determined to find out more about them. My time in New Zealand in September 1994 was short – just six days, and those made up of a flight to Wellington from Sydney, two days in Wellington, a flight to Auckland, the game between Auckland and Otago, a day with Dick Littlejohn in Whakatane, an hour's flight from Auckland, and a Monday in Auckland, when I met Ian Robson and Liz Davison of the Auckland Warriors, John Hart, Paddy Finnigan

QC and Justice Thomas, and which had to end by 6 p.m. as I had to catch a flight to Los Angeles. Every remaining spare minute of Monday 19 September was spent at the records office of the Auckland Stock Exchange looking for Strathmore Holdings. My research was not as straightforward as I had hoped.

The records office clerks were incredibly helpful – they knew time was limited. The problem was that their records were not fully computerized and not available on microfiche. Worse, the records of the Auckland Stock Exchange for the years 1985, 1986, 1987 and 1988 were stored on handwritten cards stacked neatly in some deposit archive a million miles from the records office I was in. I had neither the time (I was already late for my John Hart interview), nor the up-front cash, to persuade one of the clerks to assist me.

You know that saying, 'I was feeling downhearted and a voice came to me and said, "Cheer up, things could be worse," so I cheered up and, sure enough, things got worse'? Well, that's how it was for me. Until, until, a neat little Auckland records office clerk turned to me and said: 'You're the rugby fellow from London, aren't you? My husband read me out your quote in the paper this morning, when you said the best rugby you'd ever seen was the Auckland–Otago game but you couldn't for the life of you understand why the national team couldn't play in the style of either side. He said to me, "That's exactly how I feel" – how can I help you?'

We had breakthrough. For the next six hours the Records Office pulled out all the stops. At ten minutes to four we found what we wanted. During the day we came across a number of different Strathmore companies: Strathmore Management Ltd (dissolved 3 September 1990), Strathmore Group Ltd and Strathmore Group Ltd 1993. As the last was a 1993 company, it couldn't have been connected to RWC '87.

Knowing that the ARU RWC '87 committee banked the last of the up-front monies before the first game kicked-off meant probably a combination of factors. Factor one was that Strathmore company was created specifically to hold the marketing rights to RWC '87 in 1985. Into that account was placed US$5 million. Factor two was that the Strathmore funds came from the holding company which appeared to have an interest in Breeding Horses. Factor three was that the personnel inside Strathmore saw the huge potential of the RWC '87 and its likely profits. Factor four was that they did not have the expert-ise to go to the ARU RWC '87 committee to win the rights but they knew someone who did. Factor five was that they knew or were put in touch with Patrick Nally. Factor six was that Strathmore went bottom up not just because the 1987 World Cup failed at almost every level to raise the funds it thought it would, and therefore no profits accrued from their relationship with West Nally, but because of Black Thursday, October 1987, when the bottom fell out of the world's stockmarkets.

As we gave a round of applause to the thousands of helpers who made RWC '87 happen on the ground, we ought to pause here and give a standing ovation to the ARU RWC '87 committee for ensuring that they got it mostly right, because the last instalment of the US$5 million was banked before a ball had been kicked. Take a bow, gentlemen.

West Nally did their utmost to make RWC '87 work. They needed this break and they needed to be able to dine out on it in London. They were severely handicapped in that they were dealing with two organiz-ing bodies, one in Sydney and one in Whakatane–Wellington. Worse, the IB itself met only once a year, a recipe for disaster.

There was another problem which impacted on the revenue side: it was absolutely vital to the success of RWC '87 that the stadia where the games were going to be played were 'clean', that is, that whatever contracts had previously been signed with whatever sponsors, brewery or bank or Japanese trading company, by the owners of the stadia, they could not apply to RWC '87. But contracts are contracts, and some of the nitty-gritty details involved to ensure clean grounds were tiresome, unrewarding, time-consuming and even occasionally bloody. The IB had agreed to a World Cup without knowing 1 per cent of the full implications of their decision.

Unlike those of the RFU, SRU and WRU, the international grounds in Australia and New Zealand were not owned by their unions. And the one ground that should have played host to the RWC '87 final didn't in the end stage any of the games. The Sydney Cricket Ground was owned by the Sydney Cricket Ground Trust, who would not agree to cleaning their stadium and thus the chance to see the final at what was then the best venue in Australasia was lost. Since the final was eventually held in New Zealand, at Eden Park in Auckland, it also resulted in a substantial loss, perhaps as much as A$3 million, in gate money to the ARU.

As if the mechanics of trying to secure a platform for RWC '87 were not hard enough, there were rumblings of dissatisfaction within the IB and an attempt was made to hijack the tournament. As there was some suspicion about the level of commercialism for the World Cup, RWC Pty needed a front man to reassure the Four Home Unions. They appointed Sir Desmond Sullivan QC as their chief executive officer, although he aspired to the role of secretary of the organizing committee. He was hardly ever available, and, thankfully, the New Zealand government called him out of retirement to head up an investigation. In a slight panic RWC then appointed Jim Campbell, a man who had expertise in this arena. This, too, was a grave error, as Campbell, jokingly described by Ivan Vodanovich as a 'cow on a bike', could not deliver. Indeed, at an RWC '87 interim meeting in Bangkok, Ces Blazey and Bob Stuart, the two New Zealand representatives on the IB, had what amounted to a stand-up fight in which doubts were cast on Campbell's parentage. For what it is worth, Vodanovich thought that the NZRFU may have paid out up to NZ$150,000 just to cover Campbell's fee and expenses.

Meanwhile, the ARU RWC '87 committee, nervous of both West Nally and Jim Campbell, had appointed an unofficial consultant called Wilf Barker, who had been responsible for the Rothmans sports account in Australia.

In either June or July 1986, Norbert Byrne made a phone call to Ivan Vodanovich. He had heard that the IB wanted to take over the control of the tournament and appoint their own organizing committee from the Four Home Unions to administrate it. Ivan called Dick Littlejohn, who in turn rang Russ Thomas, chairman of the NZRFU council. There then appears to have been a number of conversations between Thomas, Shehadie and Littlejohn before John Kendall-Carpenter, chair of the RWC '87 IB committee, was contacted at his home at Wellington School, Somerset.

The rumour had an element of truth in it. Ross Turnbull, the New South Wales IB representative, wanted to take over the organization of the tournament, that is, to take it away from Shehadie, chairing the ARU RWC '87 committee, and Littlejohn, chairing the New Zealand equivalent. Matters came to a head at an IB special meeting

42

in Los Angeles on 18 July 1986, less than one year before the World Cup kick-off. Turnbull spoke to a brief that wanted to create a new and dynamic organizing committee to run the event (in other words, let's fire the current lot, they're effing useless).

There were eight representatives present at the meeting: John Kendall-Carpenter, Nick Shehadie, Dick Littlejohn and Ray Williams, plus Ross Turnbull, Bob Stuart and Ronnie Dawson, and one other whom I have been unable to identify. The most crucial vote of the many crucial votes between 1985 and 1987 ended in a draw, four all. As chairman, John Kendall-Carpenter had the casting vote, and he used it against the Turnbull Four (Turnbull himself, Stuart, Dawson and one other).

Ross Turnbull is another one of rugby's more colourful characters and one for whom I have a soft spot. When I was selected for my one and only England tour to Australia in 1975, Turnbull was the manager of the Australian side and saw to it that although matters on the field – four losses in eight games including both Tests (with Mike Burton being sent off at Brisbane) – could have been happier, we had a full social calendar off it. He was Mr Generosity to me.

I had breakfast with Turnbull at a friendly Bellevue hostelry during my visit to Sydney in September 1994. I suspect that he was right to try to hijack the organizing committee and the more I reflect on the demise of West Nally and the Strathmore Group, the more sympathy I have for those companies. The administration for RWC '87 was amateurish in the extreme. Shehadie ran the show, but in the final analysis he could not deliver the Sydney Cricket Ground. Yet without Shehadie there would have been no RWC '87, but I digress.

Turnbull made one tactical error in Los Angeles. He had brought with him the ex-director of the NSWRFU, who either bumped into Dick Littlejohn in the Beverly Hills Hotel lift or was spotted by him. Turnbull was so confident of winning the vote that he'd brought his former director to LA to swear him in as the CEO of RWC '87. You've got to admit the man had balls.

Between 1975 and 1987, Turnbull immersed himself in New South Wales rugby. Indeed, he was into many projects, including the ill-fated Oval at Concord. I'm surprised no one has written a book about the shenanigans in national and provincial government regarding the

Oval. Having read some of the correspondence, I would suggest it would make a fascinating TV docudrama.

The Turnbull case was essentially the Old Farts v the New Farts in Australian rugby. Sadly, Shehadie and Turnbull did not see eye to eye. They did their level best to block one another whenever it was convenient. Both wanted to be Mr Rugby Australia; both came from Sydney and both were high-profile players. Turnbull ultimately played poker; Shehadie played smart.

5

Bring on the Players

Fourteen teams arrived in Australia and New Zealand to join the host countries during the third week of May 1987: England, Ireland, Wales, Scotland, France, Italy, Romania, Canada, USA, Argentina, Zimbabwe (replacing USSR), Japan, Tonga and Fiji, at the last minute.

The competition was held in two stages. Teams were divided into groups of four, with every team in each group playing each other once; the top two teams in each group then advanced to the second stage, the quarter-finals, which was based on a knock-out format. It had already been tacitly agreed that those countries reaching the last eight would automatically qualify for the finals of RWC '91. The groups were:

Pool A: Australia, England, USA, Japan.
Pool B: Wales, Ireland, Canada, Tonga.
Pool C: New Zealand, Fiji, Italy, Argentina.
Pool D: France, Scotland, Romania, Zimbabwe.

The opening ceremony was modest in comparison with those of the Commonwealth Games, which New Zealand had hosted twice since the war (and were to do a third time in 1990). The organizers were short on cash and short on ideas. They were not best helped by the fact that across the Tasman Sea what amounted to another rugby World Cup was about to begin as well.

When the ceremony on 22 May 1987 was finished, New Zealand, one of the two hosts, were pitted against Italy. It was an unfair beginning for the Italians, who were only just awakening to the true potential of the game within their own country. The power and authority of the All Blacks' 70–6 win sent shivers up and down the collective backs of all the teams. It was awesome. John Kirwan scored a simply outrageous try to bring their score up to 50 points, bobbing and weaving his way over the line from all of 60 metres. It brought the house down.

The reality was that in 1987 there were only three teams capable of winning the World Cup: New Zealand, Australia and France. Scotland were the dark horses. The rest were there simply to make up the numbers. New Zealand raced through her pool with wins over Fiji, by another extravagant score of 74–13, and Argentina, by a more modest 46–15.

Elsewhere, England, a side made up of hopefuls, were beaten by the referee as much as Australia in their opening encounter. David Campese scored a try not dissimilar to Diego Maradona's Hand of God goal, but although the ball was never grounded – it bounced off a knee – in the morning's papers was proof that Campese had been credited with a try and England with a loss by 19–6. It was embarrassing to watch the appallingly low standard of the English play. Australia, who had decided they were the favourites, didn't look like it after this game. They lacked the power and authority of the All Blacks. Andrew Slack's side would need to increase their effort if they were to reach the final.

Meanwhile, Jonathan Davies was making sure that Wales qualified as the winners of Pool B. In another wretchedly poor match, they beat Ireland by 13–6. In Pool D, which was the hardest to call, France and Scotland provided the best game of the tournament up to that point, which ended in a 20–20 draw. France were to go through as winners on a higher try-scoring factor, which meant they played Fiji rather than New Zealand in the quarter-finals. That signposted the end of the road for the plucky Scots. Had their try tally been higher, they would have reached the semi-finals, where they would have played Australia.

Fortunately, the Four Home Unions countries all made it to the second stage, the quarter-finals. England played like a side with the collective IQ of 1 – and that was being generous – and lost to the old enemy, Wales, by 16–3. England's thinking at the top, within Twickenham, was light years away from where the action was. The management were simply appalling, and sadly the side matched them for ability. The game itself was of the most stultifying quality which did justice to no one. Wales, however, deserved their place in the semi-finals, even though they, too, showed how far they were behind the standards being demonstrated by New Zealand from the outset and France as they warmed up. Australia were winning, but they lacked something. It was hard to put your finger on it, but this was certainly not the Grand Slam side of 1984.

Scotland were comprehensively outplayed by New Zealand in their quarter-final and were 2 metres off the pace. They simply did not have the players or the nous to combat a rampaging All Blacks pack and lost by 30–3. The All Blacks were in the semi-finals without having broken into a sweat. 'They play at a higher level,' opined Scotland's Colin Deans. 'They're so athletic, even when it comes to their second rows.'

Ireland had fumbled their way through to this stage and, as is often the case with them, when we least expected it, they would give a performance that can only be described as 'typically Irish', harrying the opposition, competing for every ball, chasing every up-and-under. It's part of their psychological make-up: for most of their international rugby life they've been at the bottom of the pile (a single Grand Slam was won as far back as 1948), and when the big occasion comes they seize it with two hands. So the stage was set when they came to play Australia at the Concord Oval on 7 June.

By 4.30 p.m. on 8 June, only four teams had survived – New Zealand, Australia, France and Wales. No one had predicted Wales would get this far – except one-eyed Welshmen and women, of course – but the others had all been odds-on to reach the semi-finals. Semi-finals are beasts. They're beasts because getting so near and yet so far is no joy at all. That's why frequently they are games best forgotten. There is simply too much at stake. In this case it was a place in the final, not just any final, but that of the first-ever rugby World Cup. It's probably a truism, but it seems to me that the first championship was the easiest one to win because there was no history and therefore no expectations, unless you were the favourite. It helped, then, if you were not.

Coming into RWC '87 Australia had played New Zealand fourteen times in the 1980s and had won six of the fixtures, including the previous Bledisloe Cup series in 1986 by two Tests to one. The edge was just with the Wallabies. In addition to the slight disadvantage this brought them, Australia suffered because in Alan Jones, their coach, they had a media-friendly personality. In 1986 and 1987, when I was a publisher, I was occasionally in contact with Jones, whose autobiography I wanted to publish. It seemed to me that he might go all the way to being prime minister if he could win a safe Liberal seat. Indeed, he had worked for a former prime minister, Malcolm Fraser, and his after-dinner speeches were uplifting. On that circuit he was in constant demand. How wrong can you be? Alan Jones turned down a safe seat and my enthusiasm for his book waned. Moreover, Jones himself changed too.

Several of the players associated with him in 1984 spoke out against his methods, particularly Mark Ella. Some, notably Nick Farr-Jones, even went as far as to commit their comments to print.

As usual, the Wallabies gathered in the Camperdown Travelodge, which was to be their headquarters for the next four weeks with only a brief foray to Brisbane. This time, though, there was something different. And it wasn't just that it was a World Cup and the Wallabies were going to try to beat fifteen nations instead of one [New Zealand]. Instead of training in the mornings, as they used to, beginning the day with hard work, they would only train in the afternoons. The reason, Alan Jones said, was because he had an 'unbreakable commitment' to keep broadcasting on Radio 2UE, which meant his working on the morning shift.

This seemed odd to the players, because Jones's commitment to the station definitely hadn't been unbreakable when the Wallabies had to go away on tour. Why was it unbreakable now?

I'm no psychologist, but from a distant shore it seemed to me that Alan Jones had got too big for the game of rugby and had his eye elsewhere. He had lost his focus, and this was becoming obvious to all but the ARU. (A later illustration of this came when Jones chose not to turn up to the tenth anniversary of the 1984 Grand Slam in Sydney.) Notwithstanding this friction, the even money was on the dream-ticket final, New Zealand against Australia; a final everyone would savour and which would at last resolve the question of who was the strongest of them all.

The 1984 Grand Slam side was kept together, save for the Ella brothers, through to RWC '87. Indeed, this was due to exactly the same thinking that had been behind the Australians' demands for a world rugby tournament for 1988 to coincide with the bicentenary. It was felt that the prospect of a competition of this importance would reduce the likelihood of the players being tempted to defect to Rugby League. In fact, if anything, the team was stronger. Farr-Jones and Lynagh had emerged as the best half-back partnership in the world, Campese was at the top of his form; the back row of Poidevin, Miller and Tuynman were no slouches, either. Yet they were a team of fits and starts. Some of their handling was quite superb, some of their forward play was out of the top drawer, and yet doubts were expressed as to whether they really had enough strength up front to take the All Blacks in the final.

France were the team who had the potential to upset the favourites wherever they played. Their problem was that they were the menopausal XV of the decade, any decade, they were so, so unpredictable. Worse, they had a poor record Down Under – indeed their tour record anywhere overseas had been abysmal. But they had achieved the Grand Slam in the 1987 Five Nations Championship, and since we in the north thought that was all there was to rugby, they carried our hopes – even though, if you put the average member of the Four Home Unions committee against the wall, he would never have admitted it. The French played more international rugby than anyone else by virtue of their inclusion in the Fédération Internationale de Rugby Amateur (FIRA), which they founded because they felt that the IB favoured the old WASP countries. They were right, too. Nevertheless, under pressure, the French were thought to be too ill-disciplined and too hot-headed to be capable of playing controlled football for more than one game.

In the semi-finals at home at the Oval on 13 June, against France, Australia blew it. Serge Blanco's dramatic try in the final minute won the game for France by 30–24. It was an epic match, quite the best of the tournament, and once again the French were effervescent and deserved their win. Lagisquet's and Sella's tries were beautifully worked. Normally semi-finals are tense and taut matches, and to witness five tries in one is a rarity. Here was proof of the overall beauty of the game. Two sides almost seduced themselves into playing what for both of them was their toughest match of the tournament.

For Australia the world fell in – or at least, the world fell in for their ebullient coach, Alan Jones. It was then that matters turned nasty within the Aussie camp. The distaste for Jones, which had quietly been festering, became apparent. Their behaviour afterwards, particularly when they failed to pick up their fourth-place award in Christchurch (where it remains) was a disgrace, and the demeanour of Jones himself was scarcely savoury. The game itself was a great game which Australia could and should have won. It was not the end of the players, five of whom would contest and win RWC '91. It was, though, the end of Alan Jones. I suppose it is a comment of some sort on the situation that the highest-profile individual of RWC '87 was not David Kirk or Grant Fox of New Zealand, or Serge Blanco of France, but Alan Jones: not a player, but a coach.

As for France, they were a joy to behold and, frankly, saved the day for the northern hemisphere. Moreover, they had improved bit by bit and stood a real chance in the final.

In the other semi-final, held at the Ballymore Oval, Brisbane, New Zealand cast aside a desperate Welsh team by 49–6. This was the result which was to signal the end of the road for Wales as a major rugby-playing nation, but I'm not sure they realized that at the time. New Zealand simply destroyed Wales. They had reached the final without having to play a hard game. For the All Blacks, who had been on special fitness programmes and diets, there was some consternation at the low standard of the opposition. Maurice Trapp, an Auckland coach, summed it up: 'If the Four Home Unions only want social rugby, then they shouldn't bother coming to the World Cup.'

There was a week's respite between the semi-finals and the final. The only other game of note was a meaningless third-place play-off between Wales and Australia, which was embarrassing to watch, even though 20,000 turned up to do so at the Rotorua International Stadium in Christchurch, the tip of the South Island. Australia lost in the last minute to a try by Adrian Hadley, converted by Paul Thorburn from the touchline to give Wales victory by 22–21.

Play-off games mean nothing unless they act as a qualifying bonus for the next World Cup. The IB took another six years to work that one out. In the 1995 World Cup, France, the winners of the third-place play-off, qualified automatically for RWC '99. They will join the winners, South Africa, and runners-up, New Zealand, and Wales, who qualify as the host nation. If anything, Wales's third position in RWC '87 gave a false view of their strength which cannot have helped when they slid into decline between 1987 and 1992.

France did not have the strength to play another hard game within a week. Even so, they gave New Zealand, as you would expect in a final, a tough ride until half-time. New Zealand captain David Kirk remembers:

I had no doubts we'd win once we reached the quarter-finals. We beat Scotland comprehensively, by 30–3. They offered nothing. Our semi-final against Wales was our only game held outside New Zealand. We were never tested – it was so easy. As for the final – well, I guess most of New Zealand expected us to be there, but it was still a thrill to know we were there for sure. It was a different day. There was a huge build-up; there were helicopters and cameras everywhere. We had to meet the governor general; we had to stay focused.

Before the match I told the team that we would fail if we did not take the opportunities offered. I had some small doubts at the back of my mind because it was wet and slippery. At half-time we led 12–3. I told the boys we needed to score first after the break and that whoever did would win the game. However, we still needed to add to that score and remain single-minded.

When we broke down the right-hand side of the field and I went over for a try I knew we'd won. It was the toughest game in the tournament, but I felt all along we were the best side.

The smiling David Kirk, the captain of the side only because Andy Dalton had been injured in training, took the cup and New Zealand partied for forty-eight hours.

For those of us in Britain, RWC '87 was a bit of a damp squib, and not only because of the poor performance of our teams (Wales excepted). It was also a damp squib because in order to watch it on television or listen to it on the radio, you had to be up in the early hours of the morning. Sydney and Brisbane were twelve hours ahead of London; Auckland and Wellington fifteen hours ahead. Moreover, listening to Nigel Starmer-Smith's commentary at that hour was enough, apparently, to put most people back to sleep. The BBC marginalized their coverage of the World Cup and as this was the only way to follow the game, save by reading the newspapers, the impact of the tournament on rugby followers in the Four Home Unions was lessened. Sometimes, it seemed as though we were also guilty of marginalizing it because it was happening over there and not, as it should have been, over here.

In Australia, where, as I have indicated earlier, rugby struggles to find media space (and still does in 1995, despite the tickertape welcome laid on for the victorious RWC '91 side on their arrival back in Sydney after the tournament), RWC '87 registered only as a blip. In New Zealand, where rugby was the national religion, it was front- and back-page news for four weeks. There, the television and radio coverage was virtually wall to wall.

In every sense RWC '87 was a marker. It confirmed the All Blacks as the best in the world and acted as an incredible spur to them as they thrashed just about every team on earth for the next two and a bit years. It confirmed many other things, too: the need for a professional referee association; the potential for a professional playing circus; how far the IB was from the game. It would not be an overstatement to suggest that the IB was ten years behind where the game was then. Specifically, it wasn't so much the IB itself that was ten years behind, it was most of the IB members from the Five Nations.

The essential problem of the 1987 World Cup was that the senior members of the IB had strangled rugby. They had fought against democratizing it for fear that they would lose control or that other countries would beat them at their own game. All these things will, of course, happen. There was neither a true world body nor an acceptance of the idea of one member one vote. Consequently, the first World Cup was in one sense a major disappointment, yet maybe my judgement is awry. For in the interviews I carried out in Australia and New Zealand there was a feeling that, despite everything that went on beforehand, the actual games were a triumphant success.

It was widely accepted that the Four Home Unions' decision to allow the inaugural tournament to be held outside their own territory put them at a distinct disadvantage. In Australia the grounds were harder and faster; in New Zealand the crowds and the media enthusiasm were no match for them and the winter grounds could be heavy and difficult to play on. Given that Romania, Italy, Tonga, Fiji, Japan, Zimbabwe, Ireland, Canada, the USA and Argentina were there only to make up the numbers, the final was only ever going to be contested, in my view, by France from the northern hemisphere and by the two host countries from the southern hemisphere. And I thought Australia would walk it. From a televisual point of view, and wearing a slightly biased northern-hemisphere hat, it was vital for the future of the game worldwide that the final was contested by countries from each hemisphere, something which did not seem possible when the teams met for the opening dinner.

As to the administration of RWC '87, it was held together by John Kendall-Carpenter in England, Nick Shehadie in Australia and Dick Littlejohn in Whakatane. This was not an ideal solution. The recommendations from the ARU RWC '87 committee included a suggestion that RWC '91, whenever it was destined to be held, should take place in one country.

Yet in a way RWC '87 proved nothing. The IB countries selected themselves and took most of the money; the invited countries had at that time no real sense of their positions in the game. The World Cup helped them to define themselves. The hidden agenda was to be found in those countries not present – those on the periphery – the Western Samoans, the Namibians, the Russians, the South Koreans, the Paraguayans and the Dutch. They now had an inkling of what they needed to do to qualify for 1991.

Both Australia and New Zealand were used to hosting major sporting occasions – Melbourne had staged the 1956 Olympics, and Auckland (1950), Perth (1962), Christchurch (1974) and Brisbane (1982) the Commonwealth Games. The Five Nations had managed one Olympic Games (London, 1948), one soccer World Cup (England, 1966) and two Commonwealth Games (Cardiff 1958 and Edinburgh 1970). On balance, Australia and New Zealand had proved themselves adept at winning political kudos among the world's sporting bodies. So it should not have been a real surprise that the 1987 World Cup in New Zealand was such a staggering success. Dick Littlejohn and his committees up and down both islands knew that this event had to galvanize a new generation of rugby supporters, and so they used venues that weren't necessarily the most obvious choices.

Look at the success of this policy. The crowds seemed bigger than the populations of some of the towns. The nation became caught up in the event and was, it is no exaggeration to say, in love with the tournament. The enthusiasm generated a rugby bonhomie the like of which has never been seen before, and for those lucky enough to have been there, it was a thrill to be part of it. The country gave its heart to RWC '87. After the ructions of 1981 (the flour-bomb Tests against South Africa), the Finnigan court case in 1985 (in which a private individual succeeded in stopping the proposed All Blacks tour to South Africa) and Andy Haden's mischievous and ultimately disgraced Cavaliers tour in 1986, the World Cup healed the nation. It was as well, then, that they also won it.

Yet the first rugby World Cup was undoubtedly too one-sided an affair. New Zealand, a country that loves to win and hates to lose – or as John Gallagher, their full-back, said, 'Rugby is New Zealand; New Zealand is rugby' – were far too strong. They took every other side by surprise with their outright mental and physical fitness. The world now knew how far it had to climb to match them. How far up that mountain the other countries had reached would be revealed in England some time in October 1991, when the second World Cup was due to commence.

PART 2: 1991

6

Game On: The Business of Rugby

It was announced in 1988 that RWC '91 would take place in England, Wales, Scotland, Ireland and France. You will recall that the major recommendation of the ARU to the IB was that the second World Cup should take place in one country. The IB, in its infinite wisdom, decided not to take on board this recommendation and instead agreed to hold the competition in five countries with four different legal systems, three different currencies and two different languages. It was a recipe for disaster.

If the players – now more demanding, better organized and aware of the power vacuums that exist – were even half up to speed with the story of RWC '91 that is about to unfold, I am certain they would have called for the replacement of the IB by their own player-management organization, had such an organization existed then.

In 1988, the only common denominator between RWC '87 and RWC '91 was the former Oxford Blue and England forward John Kendall-Carpenter. John was the chairman of RWC Pty Ltd in 1987 and frequently kept the show on the road. He was also to be nominated chairman of RWC in 1991. It was a sensible decision, though quite how he was able to give time to being headmaster of Wellington School in Somerset as well is difficult to fathom. I would guess that between 1985 and 1990 (when he died, quite suddenly), he was on an aeroplane going somewhere every two or three weeks. His workload was phenomenal and went largely unrecognized because, I suspect, while he nominally represented the RFU on the IB, in truth he largely represented himself. The RFU found this irksome at the best of times.

Kendall-Carpenter's premature death was a setback in solving the IB's ills. The board desperately needed a professional, full-time chief executive who was not at the mercy of the Four Home Unions. Most major sporting bodies – the IOC, FIFA, the IAAF, for example – were either resident in Switzerland or Monte Carlo, or on their way there. Both countries offered tax-free havens for sports organizations. In the world of Rugby Union, on the other hand, only three countries – Ireland, South Africa and Italy – offered tax-free havens, or, in the case of Italy, tax incentives, for sport. The IB chose to locate its brand-new headquarters not in Geneva, Zurich, Lucerne, Lausanne, Monte Carlo, Dublin, Cape Town or Venice, but in Bristol, England.

There were three overriding reasons why Bristol was chosen. The first was that the new full-time secretary (the IB baulked at calling him a chief executive) of the IB, Keith Rowlands, lived in Cardiff, a short distance away. The second was that the RWC '91 chairman lived in Somerset, not a million miles from Bristol. And the third? The man who was put in charge of organizing RWC '91 was Ray Williams. Ray, too, lived in Cardiff. The main reason, the IB will tell you, why they re-located to Bristol was that they wanted independence from the RFU. Before Keith Rowlands was appointed, Bob Weighill had acted as secretary of the IB, albeit in an honorary capacity, during the interregnum of the mid-1980s. Bob had been a former secretary of the RFU. Until their wholesale move to Bristol, the IB administration, such as it was, had been housed and serviced at Twickenham. The RFU was keen for this to continue and offered a number of ideas as to how it might be achieved. Their helpful suggestions clearly fell on deaf ears. The result was 5 College Green, Bristol.

In 1988, I was a director of a company called Television Sport and Leisure Ltd (TSL), a small but thriving London-based independent television production and sales company run by Mike Murphy and Brian Venner, two former stalwarts of the BBC sports department and, in Brian's case, IMG Europe as well. Mike loved his soccer and Brian loved messing about in boats. Sadly, they have since fallen out in spectacular fashion. When TSL made a pre-emptive bid in December of that year to run RWC '91, the IB was still at Twickenham. Communications were hampered because Keith Rowlands, though appointed secretary by this stage, lived in Wales and ventured to Middlesex only when he had to.

We at TSL had put together an experienced team. Robin Courage from the Rowland Company (Granard Rowland, as it was then), which was part of the global Saatchi & Saatchi empire, apparently had a client (DHL) who wanted to sponsor RWC '91, all things being equal, for £10 million. Our second team member was Peter Lush of the Test and County Cricket Board. Cricket was the only sport in the UK to have organized, in recent times, two World Cups. The third player was Alex Fynn, then a senior executive, or 'veep', as they liked to be called, at Saatchi & Saatchi's UK agency. Though soccer was his acknowledged field of expertise, he came at problems, to use a baseball term, from a left-field perspective; from the most difficult angle. TSL's Mike Murphy and I brought up the rear.

We made our pitch to John Kendall-Carpenter and Keith Rowlands on the morning of the 107th Varsity Match at the East India Club in St James's Square, the unofficial second headquarters of the IB and Four Home Unions. We did not believe that anyone else had a £10 million sponsor ready and willing to commit to the 1991 World Cup at this early stage. The brilliant element about DHL was that the company had an office in every rugby-playing country in the world. We left the meeting unaware that there were others waiting in the wings – ISL, IMG, Neil Durden-Smith, and the RFU itself (taking a leaf from NSWRFU's RWC '87 bid). Keith Rowlands promised us a response in January.

January passed, February passed, and then, out of the blue, it was announced that a company called Keith Prowse Associates (KPA) had been awarded the contract for RWC '91. Further inquiries elicited that they had made no financial guarantees. Their bid was successful because they suggested that what was required was a 'broking house'. A partnership would be created between KPA, RWC '91 and the IB. In other words, KPA would receive an administration fee from the IB for organizing the 1991 tournament and a percentage for the business it brought in.

To understand this apparently extraordinary decision, before examining the background to it, we need to look in detail at the complex structure devised by the IB in 1989 to handle future events. The reason for its complexity is that they wanted to avoid paying taxes on the turnover of the 1991 tournament and subsequent World Cups.

The IB ceded all the television and marketing rights to and the organization of the tournament to Rugby World Cup Limited

(RWCL), an Isle of Man-based company. RWCL was ultimately responsible for the income and the costs of the World Cup and reported to the IB.

RWCL in turn vested responsibility for the selling of rights and generating income to Rugby World Cup (Licensing) BV (RWC BV), a Rotterdam-based company, which later appointed the commercial adviser CPMA (formerly KPA) to handle the sale of the rights. In fact, CPMA had a number of companies. For the 1991 event it held the rights in a company called CPMA Communications Ltd, which was ultimately to cede the rights to the CPMA Group Ltd. It then created a company called Hiposa Ltd, into which various assets from CPMA Communications Ltd were transferred. Eventually, though, Hiposa was put into liquidation. Then, the original CPMA Communications Ltd was recreated.

The current directors of RWC BV are: Marcel Martin (chairman, IB vice-chairman), Keith Rowlands (secretary of the IB), Sir Ewart Bell (Ireland), Leo Williams (Australia), Dr Nic Labuschagne (South Africa), Anton Wotterbeck (Netherlands), Jan de Jong (Netherlands). The directors of RWCL are identical, the only difference being that Sir Ewart Bell is the current chairman (he is due to stand down at the end of 1995). In Rotterdam, Dutch national Jan de Jong handles financial matters on a day-to-day basis for RWC BV.

To complete the picture, surpluses from the Cup are distributed to rugby projects around the world via the International Rugby Settlement, an Isle of Man-based discretionary trust. Marcel Martin said at the first RWC '95 press conference in Cape Town that over £6 million had been awarded to over forty countries from the fund. RWCL, however, first set aside reserves to finance the following World Cups, the qualifying rounds, the World Sevens (the inaugural tournament was to be held in 1993) and other activities under its ambit. Interestingly, RWC '91 has not yet paid any tax. It hasn't paid any tax because although the World Cup took place in the UK and France, the company organizing the event, while clearly operating from London and Bristol, was registered in Holland. Since its tax-avoidance scheme has yet to be challenged, the organizers have also kept a substantial sum, thought to be £1.9 million, in reserve in case either the UK or French tax authorities (there's no tax on sport in Ireland) challenge the structure of companies set up by the IB under advice from tax specialists.

In May 1995, I was told by a senior rugby source that the tax position for RWC '91 was indeed under investigation. The International Rugby Settlement is based at Barclays Bank in the Isle of Man. The official trustees are Ralph Thomas and Colin Jones. Conveniently, it thus shares no common personnel with the IB. Power, though, lies with the IB and a formal advisory committee of members to the trust.

'An organization like RWC was set up to be non-profit making. All the money was to be for the benefit of rugby,' one senior RWC source said. 'Such organizations were not recognized by the UK. Therefore we had to be careful not to carry on activities in the UK and not pay taxes. Of course we have a reserve, because we are prudent.'

The diagram below may help to clarify the labyrinthine structure of the companies.

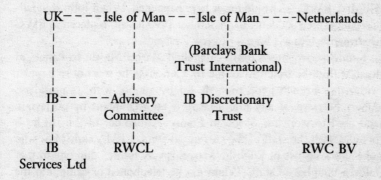

The settlement and RWC structure are entirely separate from the IB's own commercial arm, IB Services Ltd. This was incorporated in November 1989, and provides 'technical, promotional marketing, development, administrative and other services to the IB and to other rugby organizations'. The company is the IB's attempt to put its own administration on a commercial basis after its move to Bristol. Keith Rowlands is the only paid director and all its income comes from outside the UK. After tax, all profits are paid out to the IB. The firm operates from short-leasehold premises and owns none of its own. In

1990, £25,000 was spent, however, on refurbishment of the East India Club.

RWC sources say that the RWCL–RWC BV structure evolved from an organizing committee set up after the 1987 event (which had been handled by Rugby World Cup Pty, a company formed in Australia for the purpose), to handle arrangements for 1991. That organizing committee comprised John Kendall-Carpenter, Russ Thomas of New Zealand, Marcel Martin of France and Keith Rowlands, and was responsible in early 1989 for appointing the commercial adviser, Keith Prowse Associates.

When the new structure was in place, Kendall-Carpenter, Thomas and Martin became directors, while Rowlands initially became board secretary, 'attending for convenience purposes'. The other key figure in 1991 was Ray Williams, the former secretary of the Welsh Rugby Union, who was appointed tournament director. Many independent observers judge that without Williams (and Nigel Rushman at CPMA), RWC '91 would never have happened. When John Kendall-Carpenter died suddenly in September 1990 he was replaced as RWC chairman by Russ Thomas of New Zealand.

Kendall-Carpenter's death catapulted Marcel Martin to fame – at least, within the fraternity of the IB. Curiously, he was not so popular within the French Fédération de Rugby, or not with its president, Albert Ferrasse, at any rate. Martin is an accountant by profession and used to work for Mobil in France. A member of the IB, he is popular with the staff of the current advisers, CPMA and IMG, who joke about his use of English. 'Marcel is very funny,' said one former CPMA member of staff. 'Whenever he telephoned or came into the office, we would teach him new English phrases – but using the wrong words. We'd teach him things like "the bucket stops here" and "it's as fat as a pancake".'

Martin visits the Rotterdam office regularly and stresses the full-time, though unpaid, nature of the RWC directors' roles: 'All the directors are working in honorary positions, drawing only their legitimate expenses,' he has said. He himself retired early to devote himself completely to RWC duties. At the age of sixty-one, he feels he still has quite enough energy to go on until 1999, and is willing to do so if the IB votes to allow him to continue. If the IB should decide to create two chief executives, one for the IB and one for the RWC, the betting is on Martin to succeed to the latter position, for which he is quietly canvassing.

7

Enter CPMA

Given that Patrick Nally had provided RWC '87 with its only source of profits, it would have seemed sensible to have given him and his new company the opportunity to bid for RWC '91 – especially as West Nally had taken such a financial hit on its own bottom line as a consequence.

In the aftermath of RWC '87, Patrick Nally was trying to extricate himself from a disastrous alliance with ex-Carlton Communications chief Mike Luckwell and David Ciclitira, formerly of Sky Television. The marriage, in which West Nally became Parallel Media Group, foundered on personality clashes and disputes over strategy and, inevitably, money.

One of Nally's new ventures was with the Keith Prowse Group. The proposal, known by the code name Project Nanouk, was to put together an international sponsorship group. Sources close to Nally said that he was stunned when Keith Prowse failed to come up with the £800,000 promised from the Royal Bank of Scotland to complete their part of the deal. Keith Prowse chairman Ranjit Anand and managing director Paul Burns fronted the talks, during which their company gained a great deal of information about West Nally, rugby and RWC '87. Enter Alan Callan. A colleague of Nally's explains:

Alan Callan was also part of those negotiations. We were dealing mostly with Ranjit Anand and Paul Burns and didn't pay too much attention to Callan. With hindsight, maybe we were wrong.

When we came to have talks about 1991, there was an awful lot of jiggery-pokery involving Kendall-Carpenter and friends. You'll have to ask them what went on behind the scenes. We weren't actually invited to bid. We had one meeting, but came away with the impression there'd been a stitch-up. We smelled a rat.

The 1987 tournament had been assured from the start – it wouldn't have gone ahead without guarantees. We actually invested to create the thing. Then we were ousted by some interesting manoeuvring by Kendall-Carpenter.

The man responsible for RWC '91, Alan John Callan, now in his late forties, is the founder, owner and managing director of the CPMA Group. When John Kendall-Carpenter was considering how to proceed with the commercial side of the second World Cup, he approached Paul Burns, then CEO of the Keith Prowse Group, to ask for advice. Burns suggested he talked to Alan Callan, managing director of Keith Prowse Associates, their main trading company.

Callan has often protested his new-found regard for tomato juice but has a liking for champagne when it takes him. 'He was a strange character. He had a fondness for alcohol, but then went on the wagon. We'd seen it all before in the music business,' said one sports promoter who dealt with Callan in the late 1980s. 'One of Alan's favourite stories was about when he was stopped by the police and asked the last time he'd had a drink. Ten or eleven or twelve years, went the reply,' confirmed a former CPMA employee.

Callan originally started in the music business where he was once a roadie for the rock band Led Zeppelin. By the early 1980s, he was running his own music firm, Simran, as well as being involved in the MCA music label and design and event marketing in general. Callan became a director – and, later, a shareholder – of the Keith Prowse Agency in July 1984, when it first started trading under that name with a brief to develop the Keith Prowse Group's activities in music, sport and event marketing and licensing. In parallel, he also dabbled in events privately from home (then in Cobham, Surrey) via IGP Limited. His work included the development of the Glasgow Open, soon to be renamed the Scottish Open Golf Championship.

Almost a year after he became the commercial adviser to RWC '91, in February 1990, Callan bought control of what had been Keith Prowse Associates. Striking out with sports marketer Ged Palmer and former Wales fly-half Cliff Morgan, he renamed the company CPMA Communications. The involvement of Morgan was in a way a coup de grâce. For £40,000 a year and car, he brought to the company a legendary rugby name of the 1950s to add authenticity to Callan's empire. In another way, it was a kind of coup de disgrace, because it tarnished Morgan's name for ever.

Callan's £35 million earnings forecast for RWC '91 quickly proved wildly over-optimistic, especially with no guarantees, and publicly quoted estimates would return to haunt the Rugby World Cup organization. None the less, the organizers appeared so deeply impressed that, it seemed, they lost no opportunity to trumpet the predicted earnings in 1989 after Callan's appointment. Furthermore, 'estimates' became 'firm predictions' and, in a sloppy shorthand, 'income' became 'profits', which was later to exacerbate the confusion and embarrassment.

CPMA sources say the contract was drawn up by Callan's lawyer, Stephen Townley, another figure brought on board from West Nally days – he had also been Patrick Nally's solicitor. Some time before early 1991, when Callan publicly stated that he had already been 'guaranteed' the tournament for 1995, sources confirm that the contract was extended to include rights over contract renewals and first negotiating options up to the year 2003.

Fortunately for us at TSL, we had just helped KPA (soon to become CPMA) out of a major golf hole which they had dug for themselves. They held the European rights to the USPGA tour, having paid over £1 million for a three-year licence, but couldn't sell them. TSL's Mike Murphy, with one phone call, sold them to the pan-European satellite sports channel Screensport, and KPA's skin was saved. Thus TSL, or at least, Mike Murphy, was flavour of the month with KPA. So, although we had to submit all the official tender documents to bid for the TV rights for RWC '91, we knew from Alan Callan that we would ultimately be appointed.

Rugby World Cup '91 sub-contracted various aspects of the organization and packages of rights to the following firms: Rushman Communications (media facility and accreditation managers), Keith Prowse Hospitality (corporate hospitality), Television Sport and Leisure (sales of TV rights), Telemundi (merchandizing and licensing rights) and Hill & Knowlton (PR). Travel packages were first awarded to the Keith Prowse Agency but eventually were won by Gullivers Travels, for reasons that remain unclear.

In each case, CPMA sources say, RWCL was presented with a shortlist of firms, details of bids and company accounts on which to make its choice. In each case, it chose the firm recommended by Callan and CPMA. Some of the awards caused controversy, notably the selection of Keith Prowse Hospitality, which prompted a suspicion of nepotism because of Callan's close links with the group. In 1995, IMG were to be careful to avoid similar charges by rejecting their own South African unit in favour of an outside bid. One of the best-kept secrets was the bid Jeffrey Archer made for RWC '91, '95 and '99. He had a meeting with Alan Callan and Cliff Morgan in his penthouse suite just opposite the Tate Gallery, and offered £30 million for the rights. According to Archer, Callan and Morgan accepted his bid. However, the next day Archer received a letter from Callan in which an absurd number of prerequisites were laid down. Archer brought this to the attention of the IB. Nothing was done. Whatever occurred at the meeting, there was a great deal of irritation at CPMA about Archer's action in writing to the IB. There was a strong feeling among people in 1991 that Alan Callan and CPMA were a maverick organization, according to John Mason in the *Daily Telegraph*. This was certainly the feeling in the rugby fraternity and the commercial sporting world. It was rooted in the way the contracts had been awarded for RWC '91.

8

Missed Opportunities

Alan Callan was a clever operator, but in 1989 he was completely out of his depth when it came to television rights. He hid his weakness from the IB and the RWC '91 committee because they knew little better.

The deal with TSL was instructive. The television rights we were awarded to RWC '91 excluded Japan. Although Callan did not have an office in Tokyo, he thought that Japan was the one country in which he would hold all the rights to the 1991 World Cup. It is unclear whether the IB or the RWC '91 committee understood this. Callan was right.

In the sponsorship of the Olympics, FIFA soccer finals and IAAF World Championships, Japanese companies were to the fore, a state of affairs brought about by ISL Marketing in Lucerne. ISL Marketing's junior shareholder (49 per cent) was a Japanese firm called Dentsu. The Dentsu office in Tokyo housed the Japanese arm of ISL Marketing. Dentsu's clients included major blue-chip Japanese companies – the TDKs, Sonys, Mitsubishis, Toyotas and Nissans of this world. In Japan it didn't matter if an advertising agency held the accounts of rival companies.

I went to Tokyo in May and June of 1991 (I had severed my links with TSL in December 1990) to find out, among other things, why Japanese companies were not to be a major part of RWC '91, especially as at that time rugby was second only to baseball as the biggest team game in Japan (the J League in soccer was still to be officially launched). While I was there I spent a day or two in various offices within the Dentsu organization.

The problems were due to two errors made by CPMA. The first

and most important was that CPMA had sold the Japanese television rights for the 1991 tournament to NHK, the most bureaucratic of any of the national television stations in Japan. Worse, it was owned by the state. It had originally modelled itself on the BBC, and, like the BBC, it took no advertisements and would not countenance any sponsored programming. CPMA's decision lost them face in Tokyo. They had become, inadvertently, a laughing-stock.

The second mistake they made, given that the first one cost RWC '91, in revenue terms, £20 million, was that they overpriced the sponsorship packages at £2.2 million. When none were sold, they were reduced to £2 million and then to £1.5 million. Of course, the advertising and sponsorship agencies in Tokyo realized that if they waited long enough they'd get them for £1 million or less. But to them that wasn't the point: the point was, what sort of professional organization was putting these packages together without a fuller understanding of local conditions?

CPMA, in their defence, would counter that they did try to form a relationship with a Japanese media company, Daiko Shuwa. The main contact there was a Mr Fujio Okatani. Having seen some of the correspondence that passed between them, it comes as no surprise to me that nothing was accomplished. CPMA demanded a £100,000 non-refundable advance from Daiko Shuwa, plus a US$1 million guarantee and the customary 7.5 per cent agent's fee.

The cock-up in Japan had severe repercussions on the profitability of RWC '91. At one stage, Alan Callan was quoted as saying that he could foresee a revenue stream of £35 million. This was palpably absurd: Japanese companies may have American or European headquarters with grand notepaper and grander addresses, but these are always subsidiaries and every major decision has to be referred back to Tokyo or Kyoto or Nagasaki. When Ricoh (Europe), for example, became an RWC '91 sponsor, a decision was requested from Japan. Headquarters was not enthusiastic and preferred to leave the responsibility with Europe. So although Ricoh (Europe) did in the end sponsor the tournament, their contribution was made mainly in kind, in the form of donations of photocopiers and faxes and so on.

The critical contract was television. Because the live audience for RWC '87 had been so small, the television rights package was tiny.

Europe, where the audience for rugby was, was not going to pay much for a championship in 1987 whose matches were played between 3 a.m. and 5 a.m. Part of the problem was, of course, that so few stadia in Australia or New Zealand had floodlights, and so even the midweek games had to kick off in their afternoons. Had the stadia had lights, they could have kicked off at 8 p.m. in Sydney (8 a.m. in London) and the live TV package would have been worth buying.

RWC '91, on the other hand, was to take place in Europe, and not only were the Five Nations hosting it, but Italy and Romania had qualified and there had also been a veritable sea-change in the multi-channel broadcasting environment. Europe now had three dedicated sports channels: Eurosport (part of Sky), Screensport and the Sports Channel (part of BSB). By the RWC '91 kick-off Sky and BSB had merged, but fortunately, satellite rights had been sold to Screensport which, along with Eurosport, was a pan-European channel reaching a wider audience.

In the UK, the conventional or terrestrial TV rights were auctioned. The BBC had always held the rights to the Five Nations Championship and were arrogant enough to assume that they would be the broadcaster for RWC '91. ITV, their rivals, comprised fifteen network stations, an altogether more complex arrangement, and saw rugby as a way of boosting their ABC1 audience share. As they were commercial stations, able to take advertising and the sponsorship of programmes, they were in a much stronger position financially to bid for the tournament than were the BBC, who had to rely on the tradition of the sport, their knowledge of the technical problems of covering rugby and their status as one of the premier broadcasting companies in the world.

The BBC blew it. It was an illustration of the lack of thought they had given the matter that their tender document arrived at TSL's offices in a plastic folder which still had the £1.99 price tag on the back. They had not weighed up the opposition accurately enough and their opening offer of just over £1 million was well below the price at which the rights had been valued. ITV, on the other hand, if they were to be successful, had to persuade the RWC '91 committee not only of their gravitas (some of their coverage of boxing and soccer had been quite appalling), but also that they could persuade all of their fifteen network stations to adhere to a schedule of potentially thirty-two live games occupying a minimum of forty-eight hours of television time.

The RWC '91 committee were not bothered with the niceties of the contract for the Five Nations Championship, which they believed was undervalued in any case. Their job was to maximize profits for the game at large and therefore for the companies who were specific rights holders.

In the end, Jonathan Martin, head of sport at the BBC, could not match the bid from Greg Dyke, head of the network sport committee at ITV. ITV bid just over £3 million and also successfully secured the rights to the first RWC Sevens, to be held in Edinburgh in 1993. They also acquired options on the UK rights to RWC '95 (for which they paid £5 million, well below their commercial value), and, apparently, RWC '99 as well (for which a fee of £12 million is currently doing the rounds, even though a pay-per-view UK-only rights deal would net about £45 million).

Dyke – with the help of colleagues John Bromley, David Elstein and Richard Dunn – had seen the importance of having the first major sporting world championship exclusive and live on ITV since the 1966 soccer World Cup. It was a major coup for ITV. Channel 4 (who had originally planned to support and complement ITV's coverage) must have kicked themselves at the chance and the revenue they missed. Indeed, so clever were ITV that they also secured (I don't actually think this was in the original contract) the broadcast sponsorship rights, which they sold to Sony (UK) for over £2 million, according to *PR Week* of 26 September 1991, and so essentially paid only £1 million for the broadcast package. When you consider that RWC '91 easily attained its audience share and set all-time records for rugby on UK television, you can guess that ITV's network companies, particularly their shareholders, were very happy with the deal. Moreover, after some initial hiccups, ITV's coverage was more assured, friendlier and less class-based than the BBC and talked to, rather than at, the viewer. It was one of their great success stories.

Unfortunately, RWC '91 did not share in it. Having dined out for months on the amount of money they had screwed out of ITV, they failed to notice the small print. ISL Marketing had consistently shown with countless Olympics and world championships that the television and sponsorship rights to a tournament like the World Cup have to be sold together. In America, where the National Football League, baseball, National Hockey League and National Basketball Association were continually setting new records and finding new ways to split television revenue, there had already been discussions about the sports bodies and the major television companies taking a percentage of the advertising revenue in lieu of a rights fee. But UK thinking was still rooted in the 1970s.

All RWC '91 demonstrated when it came to the packaging and selling of rights was that no company in the UK possessed the necessary expertise and that no one on either the RWC '91 committee or the IB understood this crucial area. By establishing a £3 million floor for the UK television rights, Mike Murphy at TSL had done better than anyone could have reasonably expected. It gave him a stick with which to beat the French – they had to come pretty close to that mark. Again, to his credit, and after expending much energy running from room to room in the George V Hotel in Paris, where all the bidders and decision-makers were separately holed up, he pulled off a similar coup. Like the UK rights, the French rights did not go to the company which held the rights to the Five Nations Championship, which in France was Antenne 2 (now France 2), but instead to TFI and Canal Plus. Once again the old cartel had been broken.

Two deals and £6 million in the RWC '91 bank put TSL very much in the driving seat. CPMA's sponsorship packages, however, remained unsold. Although there were small deals elsewhere, for most of 1989 the only good news coming from RWC '91 was the fees from the TV rights.

There were to be some further complications. The Sony deal to sponsor ITV's coverage caused some discomfort among the main sponsors, who had been given the opportunity to buy into the TV package, but had declined. It was heightened by the discovery, late in the day, that EC legislation coming into force at the beginning of October 1991 would bar the sub-licensing of TV rights. Heinz executive Mike Sargent was quoted by John Reason in the *Daily Telegraph* as saying: 'ITV are very embarrassed about this because it does seem incredible that we were only told about the problem a few days before the tournament is due to start.' Heinz were then engaged in a Golden Try of the Tournament promotion. 'Obviously legislation of this kind must have been public knowledge for some time, and we certainly feel we should have been made aware of it.' Apparently, under this EC legislation there could be no on-screen or verbal branding by what was defined as sub-licensee because the programme itself already had a sponsor in Sony. To overcome this, Heinz expanded outside the UK by buying a television package in France.

After the 1991 tournament, Sony announced that their sponsorship had been a huge success in viewing terms. 'The reason we went after the sponsorship is the same as why ITV went after the rugby – to reach the notoriously light-viewing ABC1 males, our core audience,' said Paul Campbell, Sony project sponsorship manager, in *Broadcast*, a television trade paper. In the UK, 13.6 million had watched the England–Australia final.

In October 1989, CPMA attempted to buy TSL. Indeed, in the Cannes MIPCOM 1989 catalogue, Alan Callan erroneously appears as a director of TSL, but fortunately, although the directors of TSL voted 3–2 in favour of a takeover, it never happened.

Part of the problem for the World Cup was the way in which CPMA worked with TSL. I was told that our mark-up for the sales of the TV rights was, once we had achieved our pre-set financial target, 17.5 per cent. The difficulty here was that we had to reallocate half of this profit, that is, 8.75 per cent, to CPMA. In other words, there was a deal within a deal. I have talked to other rights owners who have confirmed this arrangement. As one of them put it, 'Better half a cake than none at all.'

The most significant problem for the tournament, however, was the original valuation placed on the target eight sponsorship packages by CPMA. Sums of £16 million, or £2 million for each package, were being bandied about in 1989. Even when it was reduced, the valuation was still too high. This was to dog the company for the whole of the RWC '91 campaign.

CPMA originally appointed advertising agency Young & Rubicam to help them find sponsors, but that relationship quickly hit the rocks. So it was that, some time in October 1989, Alan Callan of CPMA and Mike Murphy of TSL paid their first joint visit to 80 Charlotte Street, London W1. They were probably as gobsmacked as most visitors were when they arrived at the offices of the UK arm of what was then one of the great advertising agencies in the world, Saatchi

& Saatchi. In the cavernous foyer, whose size was on a par with the collective egos of the owners, were TV screens highlighting the scale and scope of the clients S&S represented around the world – Mars, British Airways, Proctor & Gamble, BP, Famous Grouse and Rover, to name a few. Saatchi's boasted that they were the largest advertising agency in the world. In reality they were dwarfed by Dentsu of Tokyo, but it was a myth that was popularly repeated as a truth, not least by themselves.

Callan and Murphy had come to see Alex Fynn, one of the company's many deputy chairmen. Fynn, you will recall, had also been part of the original TSL bid for RWC '91 in December 1988.

The advertising business in 1988–9 was uncertain of quite what it was and where it should be. The Saatchi brothers' whirlwind success story, which had seen them bid, quite outrageously, for the Midland Bank (later acquired by the Hong Kong & Shanghai Bank), had blazed a trail in hoovering up all sorts of companies on the fringes of their core interests. Terms such as 'global communicators' and 'global server' punctuated the hype that filled the bars off Charlotte Street and Berkeley Square.

In October 1989, Saatchi's wanted an in to the lucrative world of sports sponsorship. Or, to be accurate, Alex Fynn wanted an in to the market – not every deputy chairman at Saatchi's shared that ambition. But Fynn had the vision to anticipate how companies needed to expand their communication antennae.

The meeting led to CPMA bringing Saatchi's on board. Perhaps because their experience of rugby sponsorship was slight, their recommendations were ignored, and CPMA overvalued the packages. Consequently, when Cliff Morgan finally persuaded Tony O'Reilly, the CEO of Heinz and a former Irish international himself, to sign the first sponsorship package, the critical aspect was not that it was the first such deal, but that everyone agreed the amount should be £1 million to set a benchmark for other sponsors. But O'Reilly was no fool. It could be argued that Heinz was hardly a brand which could gain from sponsoring the tournament, but O'Reilly knew that if Heinz were in first, his PR team could annex the Rugby World Cup. And so it proved. RWC '91 was known, until the Sony boys ambushed everyone with their UK TV sponsorship, as the Heinz World Cup.

I find it incredible Heinz's sponsorship amounted to £1 million in cash – that would have priced the other seven packages at an average of £380,000 (the total revenue was £3.7 million). My hunch is that whilst Heinz (UK) agreed to pay £1 million, as publicly announced, they may have reduced their contribution to around £800,000 in light of the other sponsorship offered.

So sponsorship in 1991 turned into a fiasco and the public accounts are not clear as to how much actual cash was eventually raised. The furthest Marcel Martin is prepared to go is to say that sponsorship accounted for around 25 per cent of the total income of £19.5 million to £20 million. This appears to be an exaggeration, but it is impossible to be accurate since the public documents do not make clear whether the figure of £3.7 million includes the value of benefits in kind, such as the provision of equipment. Whatever the truth, there is no question that the sponsorship income scarcely compares favourably with the figures that were being quoted publicly in 1989 on the basis of CPMA's bid: £2 million to £2.2 million – a total of £16 million plus – for each of the eight packages, you will recall.

CPMA and RWC BV gave all sorts of reasons for the shortfall, blaming, among other things, the world recession and the Gulf War. 'At least one major sponsor withdrew because of the war, and it's not the best of times for the world's airlines,' Callan said in February 1991. IMG argued: 'Rugby never realized the asset they were sitting on in 1991. CPMA set expectations which were unrealistic.'

By the time RWC BV began a series of meetings in Rotterdam on 19 February 1991, only one – Tony O'Reilly's Heinz – of the target eight commercial sponsors had been announced, to the consternation of the sixteen participating rugby nations. Crucially, none of the original 1987 sponsors, which included Coca-Cola and Rank Xerox, had signed up. A CPMA source explained: 'We spoke to Coca-Cola, to Mike Steele there. We lost them. They were interested, they'd seen what we were doing, but they offered less than the others. And, quite frankly, we couldn't sell it for less than Heinz had paid.' Yet Coke's offer of £600,000, which was dismissed by CPMA, exceeded the price for which some packages must eventually have been sold, as we shall see later. Moreover, there is some evidence to suggest that the computer company Commodore were prepared to commit to £1.5 million in cash and kind. This potential deal also appears to have evaporated.

Japan's Ricoh was the next sponsor to come on board, in March 1991. A figure was not revealed, but estimates doing the rounds at the time calculated that the deal was worth £600,000 to £850,000, depending on the value placed on the equipment and services element. The whisky company Famous Grouse signed up at the end of the month and Lionel Nathan's New Zealand Breweries followed, in April 1991, in a move to promote their Steinlager brand, again for an undisclosed sum. Famous Grouse owner Matthew Gloag added to CPMA's embarrassment at the time, happily putting a £1 million figure on the total cost of its promotion while CPMA were refusing to disclose such information. The £1 million floor was again illusory, however, as RWCL actually received far less – Famous Grouse is thought to have paid some £250,000. The French bank Société Générale came next, followed by Glass South Africa in September, just three weeks before the kick-off. Cathay Pacific and British Steel were added to the list of 'global sponsors' to formally complete the eight, but again how much they actually paid is uncertain.

Somewhere in the middle of all this, CPMA were awarded the rights to three more successive World Cups – the 1995, 1999 and 2003 tournaments.

9

It Doesn't Quite Add Up

If the IB were completely out of touch with the game in 1987, by 1991 they were completely out of their depth. There was an answer: the IB needed its own impartial secretariat in a neutral, preferably non-rugby-playing country with a full-time president on a par with someone like Juan Antonio Samaranch, president of the IOC. And pigs might fly.

The question that still needs to be satisfied is why did RWC '91 cost £14.5 million to run? Let's backtrack to 1988, when the decision was made by the IB to hold RWC '91 in the Five Nations. Remember that in 1987, the New Zealand Rugby Football Union had fought resolutely to keep the gate income. As both the Australian Rugby Union and New Zealand Rugby Football Union were putting up the development monies for RWC '87, this was not an unreasonable request, and it was granted.

For the 1991 tournament, the major problem on the ground was again the demand by RWC '91 committees for clean stadia (that is, you will recall, that existing sponsorship contracts at stadia were suspended for the duration of the World Cup). In the end, the five unions agreed to this, but on the condition that they kept the gate monies. Given the nature of the crowds – there were sell-outs at Twickenham, Lansdowne Road and Murrayfield – the Five Nations probably banked, after costs, at least £1 million each. And their costs for the second World Cup were minimal: each country agreed to pay all the expenses of those nations it was hosting, and that was it.

In mid-July 1992, provisional figures were finally released to the media by Russ Thomas in Wellington, New Zealand, putting profits at some £5.5 million (excluding, of course, the gate money). Total income was given as £20 million. Television brought in £11.6 million; sponsorship raised only £3.7 million – and, as I have said, it was unclear to me whether this included the value of donations of material and equipment. The rest totalled a meagre £4.7 million: licensing a paltry £800,000; hospitality, £1.4 million; tours, £800,000 and miscellaneous, £1.7 million.

In effect, this means that the eight sponsorship packages were eventually sold for an average of £460,000. But the sums that really caught my eye were not the figures in the income column but those relating to expenditure.

In the world of marketing, companies work on a percentage. The original literary agents, for example, tended to charge authors between 10 and 15 per cent for their services. In advertising, the percentages have always been higher but usually range between 16.5 to 20 per cent of the budget. Because sports marketing is a newish business area, the percentage has been higher still: more in the area of 20 to 25 per cent, although some companies, such as ISL Marketing and IMG, have surpassed even those figures. Within the organizational costs, £3 million was said to have been spent on nineteen media centres and Cup accreditation. They are also understood to have included undisclosed management fees to the Five Home Unions. The profit figure given in the RWC '91 accounts of £5.5 million on a revenue of £20 million means, in short, that the cost of organizing the event was £14.5 million. And don't forget that so far no tax has been paid. Remember the contingency fund, thought to contain £1.9 million, set aside in case the tax position was challenged? If my analysis is correct, RWC '91 appears to have been the most expensive amateur sports tournament run this century.

The final figures were never announced, despite the publicity surrounding the provisional estimates. Marcel Martin, however, puts the final surplus at between £4 million and £5 million, after reserving his unspecified amount for tax.

The marketing brochure issued by CPMA and RWC BV after the 1991 World Cup is an instructive read. It begins: 'Rugby World Cup in 1991 had two prime objectives. The first was to use the event as a means of spreading the image of rugby to recruit new players and viewers to the game. The second was to raise at least £20 million in commercial revenue.' While both objectives were achieved, the second assertion is palpably economical with the truth. Although the heady £35 million estimates were quickly revised, in February 1991 Alan Callan was still hoping for more than £20 million. 'We are still within an income band of £25 million, but whether we extend that I don't know, because I believe we will still be negotiating contracts with people like suppliers as late as July,' he was quoted as saying. And in March 1991, at Cardiff Arms Park, Cliff Morgan revealed to the press that £18.9 million had been contracted so far, but he stuck to the £25 million target, which was achievable, he said, via possible new deals. More than half, £10.5 million, had come from twenty-four TV contracts in fifty-eight countries, said Morgan. That included £3.5 million from ITV, while poorer nations such as Czechoslovakia, Yugoslavia and the USSR would get free coverage.

By that stage, only two of the sponsorship deals had been announced, indicating that Famous Grouse, Steinlager, and certainly Société Générale, Glass South Africa, Cathay Pacific and British Steel, came in for relatively small amounts. Yet in November, after the tournament, CPMA was still predicting to *The Financial Times* income of £23 million, including nearly £12 million from broadcast rights and £1.5 million from Telemundi's merchandizing.

By January 1992, however, RWC had started to release income estimates of £20 million, but no profits. Surprise was reported among RWC officials at the scale of the costs involved. Income from the six main sponsors was put at just £3 million. 'Royalties on certain items are continuing to come in, but when we say £20 million, we really mean that and very little more,' an RWC spokesman told *The Times*. In the same article, Peter Bills wrote: 'RWC officials were taken aback at the costs of the event. They did their best to cut back on expenditure, but they concede that they found it difficult budgeting for the enormous variety of costs.'

Overall, on the income front, the result is remarkably close to reported English RFU proposals to run the sponsorship and marketing, which had provisional agreements for £20 million of income. Alan Callan, however, vigorously defended the result, claiming that other bidders had suggested possible incomes of only £9 million to £14 million. In the *Independent* he headed off renewed criticism of the handling of the sponsorship. 'Commercially, we think we have delivered an extraordinary programme. The objective was to try to create a platform of stability where Rugby World Cup could go forward. Its bank balance was zero, its labour force was zero. It was all done from a standing start.' And in the *Daily Telegraph*, 'The 1987 inaugural World Cup left no commercial legacy, but the players created a playing vehicle to be supported.'

Balderdash.

Despite CPMA's performance, RWC BV confirmed in April 1991 that the company would continue to sell rights for 1995. And as the decision on the venue was not due to be taken until October, no financial guarantees would be sought.

Callan was fearful of publicity after 1991 and took a close interest in inquiring reporters, which added to the edgy atmosphere. Leading British rugby journalists were once invited to a lunch arranged to set the record straight. Unsure of the tactics he should adopt for the function, Callan resorted to wall charts and tried to explain to the company present the reality of the problems of organizing the event. It was a PR disaster. The press left nonplussed.

In the end it was difficult to find anyone who supported CPMA. For reasons that are still not entirely clear, they became the *bête noir* of the companies and rugby organizations with which they worked, despite the sterling efforts of managing director Nigel Rushman. Perhaps it was because, over a very short time, the rugby world took deep offence at the man at the centre of the events, Alan Callan. I'm not sure we'll ever know. It certainly seems as if Callan has managed to fall out with or rub up the wrong way most of those he has worked with, including Marcel Martin, Keith Rowlands, Ray Williams, Mike Murphy of TSL and, most spectacularly, Nigel Rushman.

'Alan is very clever, but arrogant, always right and abrupt. Very often he'll tell someone where to go and walk out of a meeting,' one former CPMA employee said. 'They all call him "the strategist". He's very good at thinking ahead, but bad with dealing with the immediate.'

The mood was also soured by RWC's realization that Callan 'stuffed them with the options in the contract', CPMA sources say. Few people know the contents of that contract. Many would like to know. There are, it appears, two contracts: one for Callan's management services and one for the actual event. The contract, referred to as the Master Licence Agreement, gave CPMA the rights to the Rugby World Cup until 2003. Quite a few companies and rugby unions have coveted that agreement. At one stage, Callan, thinking it might be the subject of a renegotiation, had two leading counsels look at it. He was reassured that it was valid. Nevertheless, under pressure from the IB, it was ultimately to be reassessed. However, the IB finally grasped the CPMA nettle at their meeting in New Zealand in 1992. Callan was told that for South Africa he had to find an international partner to act as co-adviser to CPMA. The second company would be assigned the rights for RWC '95 on a fifty–fifty basis. Throughout 1992 and early 1993, confidential talks began with Interpublic, the New York-based advertising conglomerate, and specifically with Frank Lowe of Lowe, Howard & Spink, an international subsidiary, and Andrew Croker and Paul Smith of Academy, which was then a sponsorship sports marketing company within LH&S.

Unbeknown to Lowe, Croker and Smith, Callan was also conducting separate talks with IMG. He took the wind out of Interpublic's sails by signing a deal with Mark McCormack's company. Callan was backed into a corner. He badly needed a partner but he couldn't let his position be made public. His natural cunning won out and he agreed terms with IMG for 1995. IMG have an option clause in their contract for 1999, and they believe that, as they have performed well without ruffling any feathers, it will be exercised in their favour.

Working with CPMA has never been easy. The key figures left at CPMA include Richard Dorfman, exiled from Howard Marlboro at Saatchi's but being paid a salary of £75,000 a year, Charles Perring and Nick Chesworth. Chesworth, the 34-year-old account manager, is the key RWC figure at CPMA. He is popular with Marcel Martin and RWC personnel and is now their front man for the Rugby World Cup.

Meanwhile, there was, in spite of all indications to the contrary, a second World Cup, in October and November 1991, and it's about time we addressed that issue.

10

The Other Game: The Real RWC '91

The rugby World Cup in 1991 was the biggest sporting occasion to hit the UK, Ireland and France since football's World Cup in England in 1966. It gave the Five Nations a chance to show the sport to the world through the biggest window ever offered to the game. Already, the world governing body for soccer, FIFA, had seized a similar opportunity in Rome the previous year by staging the spectacular concert which united the world's leading tenors, Carreras, Pavarotti and Domingo, and brought a popular version of opera to the masses. It was a stunning success.

RWC '91, meanwhile, dithered about what type of opening ceremony they should have. The first game, between the holders, New Zealand, and the main hosts, England, had already been scheduled for a Thursday afternoon at Twickenham. It was hardly the most appropriate time to launch the biggest event for twenty-five years, but only France and Wales had floodlights so the match had to kick off during daylight hours. In the end, the organizers settled on a short welcoming ceremony before the opening match, as in Auckland in 1987. It was a shambles.

What was needed was something of the order of a concert comprising the world's finest choirs representing each of the sixteen countries, led by Dame Kiri Te Kanawa, but the last thing we had come to expect by the start of the tournament proper was anything creative to stir the blood. Instead, we had rugby's Cliff Morgan, now of CPMA, droning on about this great game. Here was an opportunity to show the new world audience for rugby that the sport had changed and was still changing. Instead we had old 45s and a ceremony organized on the cheap. It was not the way to launch the World Cup and it once again demonstrated how far off the pace the UK was in international sporting terms. In short, a collection of yesterday's men had been charged with arranging an opening ceremony that was excruciatingly embarrassing and left an international audience wondering if this was the sum of the imagination that existed in the game. It was barely a year later that Barcelona was to mount a sensational prelude to the Olympics, culminating with an archer 'lighting' the famous torch.

Fifty-seven thousand spectators made it to the opening shoot-out between England and New Zealand, and as it turned out, the match was a major disappointment as well. England had won the Grand Slam earlier in the year and New Zealand, though not playing as well as they had between 1987 and 1990, were still considered to be the team to beat. England had Ackford and Dooley as their twin pillars in the second row; New Zealand had Ian Jones and captain Gary Whetton. Guscott, Andrew, Carling and Rory Underwood were in the backs, although Chris Oti on the left wing was some way from full match fitness. They were matched against Grant Fox, John Kirwan, Craig Innes, John Timu and Terry Wright. No wonder so much was expected of the game.

Yet the players seemed to be badly affected by the occasion and the match was played in fits and starts. England led at half-time by 12–9 through three Jon Webb penalty goals and a Rob Andrew drop to three penalties from the metronome himself, Grant Fox. Ten minutes into the second half, a smart move involving Bachop, Innes and Kirwan led to a try by Michael Jones, which Fox converted. And that was that. It was uncertain whether either team would reach the final on this form. The All Blacks, victors by 18–12, did not dominate as expected and they did appear beatable. England were still at sixes and sevens and they were a long bet to go much further than the quarter-finals.

Undoubtedly, the people I took to the opening event were deeply unimpressed with it. It just seemed like any other game. 'We wanted some razzmatazz. We'd paid enough to be there; we wanted entertainment and entertaining. We didn't want it to be like every other visit to Twickenham,' said one of them.

The teams who had qualified for RWC '91 were those who had finished in the last eight in the previous tournament, namely New Zealand, France, Wales, Australia, England, Scotland, Ireland and

Fiji. Yet by 1991, Wales, Ireland and Fiji would hardly have ranked in the top eight in the world. To them were added eight countries who had pre-qualified, seven of which had played in RWC '87. From the Americas came Canada, USA and Argentina; from Africa, Zimbabwe; from Asia, Japan; from Europe, Italy and Romania; and from Australasia, Western Samoa, who had beaten off the challenge from Tonga to win a place in their first World Cup.

The tournament followed exactly the procedures laid down in 1987: four groups of four playing each other with the top two from each pool qualifying for a quarter-final. The groups were:

Pool A: New Zealand, England, Italy, USA.
Pool B: Scotland, Japan, Zimbabwe, Ireland.
Pool C: Wales, Australia, Argentina, Western Samoa.
Pool D: France, Fiji, Canada, Romania.

Once again, those finishing in the last eight would automatically qualify for 1995. I suspect that the reason for this was that the Five Nations were frightened they might not pre-qualify automatically and therefore might have to run the gauntlet of preliminary rounds for the next tournament.

You didn't need to be a brain surgeon to come to the conclusion that the four qualifiers from Pools A and B would be New Zealand, England, Scotland and Ireland. Pools C and D were harder to predict, but the likelihood was that Wales, with home advantage, would qualify with Australia from Pool C and France and Romania would progress from Pool D.

While Wales might not have been rated among the top eight rugby nations in the world, few of the 45,000 who made it to the Arms Park on 6 October would have dreamed that by the end of the game they had come to see, Wales would lose their status as a major rugby-playing country altogether. Their opponents that day were the friendly Western Samoans, the tournament's newcomers. Little was known about their players before the match. Afterwards, of course, we were to learn that all fifteen had had some kind of club or provincial experience in New Zealand. Indeed, it was becoming commonplace to find Tongans, Western Samoans (Michael Jones, Graeme Bachop and Va'aiga Tuigamala) and Fijians playing for New Zealand and occasionally, as in the case of Willie Ofahengaue, Australia too. This flexibility in qualification for national sides was weakening the value of playing for one's country.

It was a tough uncompromising game with no quarter given and none asked. Going into the last twenty minutes, Western Samoa were leading by thirteen points (two tries, a penalty and a conversion) to nine (a penalty, one try and a conversion). Neither side seemed able to break the deadlock. Then, almost on full-time, Vaea kicked a penalty goal to seal the game – or so it seemed. But back came Wales, and in the dying seconds Ieuan Evans touched down. It was a valiant effort, but the conversion could take them only as far as within one point of the Samoans and they were out of time. Ring's unsuccessful kick was therefore rendered somewhat academic by the sound of the final whistle moments later. Western Samoa had won 16–13.

Western Samoa had created a sensation. They had beaten one of the seeds. It was not only the upset of the tournament; it was the biggest upset in the brief history of the World Cup. For Wales the consequences in World Cup terms would be suffered until 1995; the psychological effects would be felt for much longer. Coming three days after the disappointment of the clash of the Titans at Twickenham, this result caught the imagination of the public and set the media alight. The tournament had got the kick-start it needed.

Of course, to qualify for the next stage, Western Samoa still had to beat either Argentina or Australia. In the last game of the round they duly accounted for Argentina by 35–12 in a brutal match in which each side had a player sent off. In between, Australia compounded Wales's misery by thrashing them 38–3 in front of 54,000 spectators.

Australia were beginning to emerge as a favourite to reach the final. Elsewhere, the other side of the tournament was emerging, too, but because they were doing so out on a limb in France, their potential was not gaining the recognition it perhaps deserved. The team was unfashionable Canada. They only just lost to France, by 19–13, and although the results of their matches against Fiji and Romania were also close, the vital factor was that Canada had the edge. Whereas in the past they would have lost them, this time round they were the winners, by 13–3 and 19–11 respectively.

There was much joy to behold in some of the first-round matches and people began to understand how the country of New Zealand had been touched by the tournament four years earlier. Not much of it emanated from Twickenham, however.

I went to all the games involving England there and I cannot recall, four years on, one single piece of brilliance or real excitement from their matches against Italy or the USA, which they won, as expected, by 36–6 and 37–9 respectively. Perhaps of more interest were the attendances: for the Italy game 30,000 turned up; three days later, 45,000 spectators went through the gate to see England face the USA. Both games were on weekdays. The World Cup was beginning to catch the public's imagination, helped no doubt by the friendlier coverage of the game from the ITV team, down in their Teddington bunker, and Twickenham's improving image. Perhaps it was about to become a major attraction, like Ascot or Wimbledon; perhaps it was about to become the place at which to be seen.

The Machiavellian methods of the host countries could be divined from the allocation of some of the venues. England hosted matches in Otley (hardly a rugby hotbed), Gloucester and Leicester; Ireland gave Japan and Zimbabwe the two-fingered salute by making them play in Belfast in an era when other rugby nations would not have played there. Both countries acquitted themselves well, however, Japan emerging as 52–8 victors. Zimbabwe gained some consolation by winning the Fair Play Award for 1991. France, sensibly, rotated their games – Béziers, Bayonne, Grenoble, Toulouse, Brive and Agen – which created enormous interest.

Scotland remained at Murrayfield, England at Twickenham, Wales at the National Stadium and Ireland at Lansdowne Road. It was not difficult to guess who had their minds on maximizing gate revenues.

The whole nature of the tournament changed as the pool matches ended. The early rounds lacked the knock-out element which arrived with the quarter-finals. The eight countries with their sights set on the Webb Ellis trophy were: England, New Zealand, Australia, Western Samoa, Scotland, Ireland, France and Canada. Looking at it coldly, New Zealand were certain to beat Canada to go through to the semis; Scotland might be run close by Western Samoa, but looked to have too much power up front and too much nous to succumb as Wales had done; Ireland could not match the resources of Australia, now

86

firm favourites for the Cup. France versus England at the Parc des Princes was a hard one to call.

But it was the Ireland–Australia quarter-final at Lansdowne Road that was so very nearly the shock of the tournament. Incredibly, with barely six minutes to go, Ireland led 18–14 after flanker Gordon Hamilton raced away to score in the corner. Lansdowne Road went berserk – you could touch the excitement. Except, except, behind the goal-line Michael Lynagh was marshalling his troops. 'We'll kick long, win the ball and run it wide and score.' It didn't go quite as smoothly as his instructions, but none the less, with two minutes left on the clock, Lynagh did precisely that. He moved the ball wide and, as a good fly-half should do, he followed his pass. When David Campese was caught just short of the line he flung a pass inside and Lynagh was there to catch it and score. Poor Ireland had been just two minutes from the most sensational victory, but it was Australia, having gone to the wire and back, who were now in the semis against their old rivals, New Zealand.

Meanwhile, in Paris, France and England were departing from the script as well. France are rarely beaten at home. Neither Wales, Scotland or Ireland had ever won at the Parc. England, though, were beginning to enjoy the cauldron-like atmosphere and its power to intimidate them, not to mention that of the French, was fading. It was just as well – the match was the most physical of the tournament. But the English pack would concede neither space nor territory. It was England's finest hour, and they won a bruising encounter by 19–10, much to the chagrin of Serge Blanco, captain of France, the rest of the French team and management and the hostile crowd. But the right team had triumphed, albeit by a narrow margin. It was a massive victory for England, and the team finally began to believe that they could win the World Cup.

The All Blacks encountered major problems in disposing of Canada by 29–13, and the result did scant justice to the power of the Canadian scrum, which had the legendary New Zealanders struggling. The remaining quarter-final did go according to plan as the Scots accounted for Western Samoa 28–6. The four sides which lined up for the semi-finals were therefore England, New Zealand, Australia and Scotland.

Australia stayed in Dublin for their semi against New Zealand, and

England travelled away again, this time to Murrayfield. The whole of Ireland turned out to support Australia. The Aussies had been adept at milking the media there with well-publicized visits to schools and hospitals. It was as though they had a political spin doctor in their camp. By contrast, New Zealand's cause was probably already lost before a ball was kicked. The squad was bedevilled by insurrection, if the reports coming from their camp were to be believed. The two coaches, Alex Wyllie and John Hart, were at loggerheads. Grant Fox was not fully fit. Nevertheless, the All Blacks were not going to relinquish their crown without a heroic fight, regardless of their off-the-field tribulations.

What followed was yet another truly great match. Indeed, some observers felt it was the 'real' final as the All Blacks had already beaten England. It was Campese's game. He was everywhere. He was at his menacing best, scoring one beautiful try and making another with a basketball pass of such outrageousness it simply took the breath away. Here was a truly great talent. How many teams could boast a match-winner on the wing? It was as if he established the position as the equivalent of the Olympic 100-metre gold medallist. Here was somebody unconventional and unbending who was adored by the crowds. Campese had become the first rugby superstar. Australia overcame New Zealand by 16–6 and had at last made the final. Their style of play was a joy to watch. They were everybody's favourite to take the coveted trophy.

Meanwhile, England's encounter with Scotland was a tense affair and at the end only three points separated the teams. Two penalties and a dropped goal gave England nine points; all the Scots could manage in reply were two penalty goals. It was desperate stuff, but in that respect it was more typical of semi-finals in general than the scintillating game at Lansdowne Road.

So rugby got the final it deserved; the dream final (unless you're a one-eyed Scot or a one-eyed All Black): England versus Australia. A northern hemisphere country against a southern hemisphere country; a forward-driven side against a total-rugby side; a side scared to win against a side knowing it would win. And all this at the citadel of rugby, Twickenham, in front of a huge global television audience.

The final score of 12–6 does not fully explain the majesty of the day. It is only looking back that one realizes that this was the biggest sporting occasion in the UK for twenty-five years – since England lifted the soccer World Cup at Wembley in 1966, in fact. The Queen met the teams and the anthems were sung lustily. We had come to love the Aussie colours of ripe gold and green. It was a pity there was no closing ceremony to end the second World Cup in style. In terms of imagination, the RWC '91 committee was a dismal failure.

The game itself seemed to be over before you could blink. The Wallabies scored the only try in the first half from a movement which started with Tim Horan in the Australian 22 and stretched the length of the field. It ended in a line-out, from which Willie Ofahengaue and the aggressive Aussie forwards hustled to take Ewen McKenzie and Tony Daly over the line. Daly got the nod, but it was anyone's guess from the stands.

Earlier, the great Campeso, as he would surely have been known in another age when circus was our major entertainment, had caught a ball, chipped in his customary fashion ('let's get physical' was never a part of his Italian armoury), and suddenly, as happened so often, he was clear. All the ball had to do was pop up and a try was his. The crowd rose to claim him as theirs. Cruelly, the ball appeared and, moving off the seam, bounced away from him and he was enveloped by the despairing cover. We were denied the chance to adopt him as our hero. Life's like that sometimes. Later in the second half we booed him for what seemed like a deliberate knock-on which prevented what could have been a good try for England. Most people would have done just the same thing in his position; we'd be fooling ourselves if we thought otherwise. And Australia would still have won the Cup. There were some heroes on this day, but second-rower John Eales stood out. His line-out catching was a revelation. Here was the best forward on duty, and he proved it with a last-ditch tackle on Rob Andrew which saved a certain try.

England, however, were a disappointment. The selection had been wrong from the outset: Halliday and Guscott were the two best centres in the Five Nations, but the young Carling was captain and so Halliday had to fit in on the wing. England failed to score two tries – one by Simon Halliday in the first half and, funnily enough, another by Simon Halliday in the second. Playing on the wing, he didn't quite have the pace to score on the right-hand touchline. The first was a forty–sixty chance, the latter was a seventy–thirty. Yet it would be quite wrong to blame Halliday for England's loss. The back row of Skinner, Teague and Winterbottom was destructive; a more creative trio, which should have included Dean Richards, fit or not, was badly needed. The forwards were short on brain power.

The game was lost because England forgot their script. This was their Achilles' heel: they could never read a game. They made the mistake of thinking that they could play a tight game against the best defence in the world. They tried running the ball, something they had singularly failed to do throughout the tournament, and in this, the most important game in their history, all they ever did was run it sideways across the pitch.

So at the last England bottled it, and the West Car Park experts were unanimous in their view that Australia fully deserved their victory.

For the victors there was a tickertape welcome back in Sydney (which, considering the status of rugby there, was a magnanimous gesture by the Australian people). It was a great tribute to their coach Bob Dwyer, and Nick Farr-Jones, a fine example of the complete captain. Of course, the British papers were full of what might have been, but everybody knew that the right side had won.

The England–Australia showdown put rugby on a new pedestal. This was the essential difference between the 1987 and 1991 World Cups. Rugby had been a small-time sport played by a few; after this tremendous final, the game would never be the same again. The players emerged in their own right; indeed many paid homage to John Lennon by appearing in their own write. The players' columns in newspapers, appearing before and after matches, were a brand-new initiative which was welcomed by most.

11

It's All Over . . . It Is Now

The 1991 World Cup, then, ended in euphoria, but we might never know how close the tournament came to being called off. Three weeks before it was due to start, thousands of newspaper column inches were devoted to the dramatic demise of Keith Prowse, the corporate hospitality agent for the World Cup.

Controversy had dogged the hospitality programme from the start. Some 42,000 tickets were earmarked for Keith Prowse Hospitality Ltd within the commercial programme, a huge allocation which drew criticism from fans as well as the RFU. Including media and other complimentary tickets, 9 per cent of the total 1,128,000 tickets went to the commercial programme, rising to 16 per cent for the final. Rugby World Cup rebutted such criticism strongly: 'It's crucial to the expansion of rugby as a world game that it produces finances from the jewel in its crown,' said tournament director Ray Williams in *The Times*.

Interestingly, if a proper audit had been carried out on the relevant Keith Prowse accounts, Rugby World Cup would not have been left as an unsecured creditor of an already uncreditworthy group. Let me try to explain. The Keith Prowse Group encompassed some fifty individual companies grouped under the ownership of Keith Prowse Holdings (KPH). In addition, there were overseas satellites, owned by the directors, which played a significant part in the group's downfall. The main trading company, the ticket agency, was Keith Prowse & Co. Ltd (KPC). Keith Prowse Hospitality Ltd provided corporate hospitality packages and held the Rugby World Cup 1991 contract. CAP International, trading as Keith Prowse Agency, was the sports promotion arm. CPMA's Alan Callan was a director of this company.

KPH was incorporated in November 1974 as Expotel Group Limited, a hotel reservations and conference business, 95 per cent of which was then owned by Ranjit Singh Anand.

In the 1970s, Ranjit and his brother Devinder built Expotel into the UK's largest hotel reservations company, largely by focusing on smaller business accounts ignored by large travel agencies. By the 1980s they were booking 300,000 beds a year, turning over some £75 million, half of the group's annual sales. In 1980, the Anands bought Keith Prowse, joining forces with managing director Paul Burns. They renamed their top company Keith Prowse Expotel Group Ltd in October 1985, then Keith Prowse Holdings in October 1987.

KPH went into receivership on Monday 9 September 1991, less than a month before RWC '91 began on 3 October, with a deficiency of assets against liabilities of some £18.3 million, which included a net £4.63 million owed to the Royal Bank of Scotland, £1.18 million to factoring company Kellock and £11 million to unsecured creditors. Even the secured creditors were to recover little of what they were owed. The key directors, who sat on the boards of all the main trading companies, were the Anand brothers and Paul Burns. A three-month-long effort to sell the group, urged on by the Royal Bank of Scotland, had failed when prospective buyers for the ticketing and hospitality businesses pulled out the previous day. The directors asked the RBS to appoint administrative receivers Grant Thornton after being advised of their legal responsibilities under the Insolvency Act of 1986.

Yet from the examination of filed accounts, however – which were available to Rugby World Cup and their advisers – it is quite clear that Keith Prowse's problems started long before 1991 and that a series of warning signals were either not spotted or ignored. The group's reported profitability was not exceptional, yet KPH went through enormous expansion from 1986–7, increasing the number of employees by two hundred to just over six hundred. By 1988, stripping out a £175,000 exceptional profit, the group was barely operating at break-even. By 1990, exorbitant interest charges were more than eating up all the reported profits. The real story, though, is told in the balance sheet:

£	Year to 31/12/87	Year to 31/12/88	18 months to 31/6/90
Net assets	893,288	957,514	1,122,268
Borrowing	4,179,469	6,976,953	7,701,389
Cash	46,900	225,095	362,292
Total creditors	13,943,087	17,501,083	24,763,745
Total debtors	10,264,847	14,189,827	20,438,551

In June 1990 KPH revalued group properties by £912,419. After losses that year, without the revaluation net assets would have been just £209,849. Furthermore, the debts included sums, noted under 'transactions with directors', owed by companies owned by Ranjit Anand and Paul Burns.

To any competent adviser it would have been clear that KPH was in cashflow difficulties as early as 1988, if not before. Certainly by 1990, the group was facing a major liquidity crisis. From a very narrow equity base, KPH was financing an ever-inflating balance sheet via overdraft, loans and trade creditors. Worryingly, too, a growing proportion of the balance sheet was accounted for by amounts due from Anand–Burns companies, and with no fixed repayment dates or terms.

In 1988, the company raised a new loan of £1.5 million, which effectively financed the increased debt due from these companies. By 1989, however, new loans seem to have dried up and KPH resorted to financing the growing overseas debts directly by deferring trade creditors – a recipe for ruin. Cash was thus haemorrhaging from the group as early as 1988.

Indeed, in that year, when interest paid out jumped from £260,000 to nearly £600,000, some £368,000 of interest due from the Anand–Burns firms was capitalized on top of the amounts already owed, begging the question of whether these companies would or could ever repay the loans. It remains to be discovered what assurances the directors gave to the auditors to prevent the overseas debts from being written off, which would have confirmed KPH's straits much earlier. In addition to all this, at key times KPH revalued properties and changed its year-end accounts – further classic warning signals of a company in difficulties.

In spite of the fact that this information was available to the Rugby World Cup directors, RWC BV were caught hook, line and sinker. They were owed £500,000 by a group whose creditworthiness was suspect. As the commercial adviser, Alan Callan had – or should have had – the details to hand to enable him to warn RWC BV. The question is, was any advice or warning given, and if so, when? If not, why not? And if it was given, why was it ignored? Keith Prowse's problems could not be blamed on the Gulf War: the company was insolvent long before that. The only relevance of the war was that it prevented the group from trading out of the mire it was in already.

A comment at the time from Brian Bailey, managing director of credit reference firm Infolink, summed up in hindsight what could have been catered for with basic commercial foresight in *Accountancy Age*: 'Keith Prowse makes a mockery of facts which were open for all to see. Technically, they were bankrupt as early as 1987.'

The key point, though, is that all the subsidiaries had given cross guarantees in favour of KPH's debt, which meant that if the top company fell, so would all the others. Keith Prowse Hospitality, then, also went into receivership on 9 September 1991, with 175 unsecured third-party creditors left in the lurch to the tune of £1.8 million. RWC BV, with their £500,000 debt, were by far the biggest trade creditor. Until then, like its parent company, KP Hospitality had grown rapidly, but was not especially profitable. Indeed, the subsidiary was scarcely a good credit risk in its own right, even before the £12.3 million debt it had cross-guaranteed for group companies at the end of June 1990 (up from £6.98 million in 1988). KP Hospitality's business – the goodwill and certain assets – was sold to Wembley plc for £300,000 eight days later after the administrators received numerous inquiries, including one from CPMA (who failed to come up with the cash in time, suggesting that they had liquidity problems themselves).

Keith Prowse & Co. Ltd, the ticket agency, went into receivership at the same time, owing £3.94 million to some 235 unsecured creditors and £11.89 million to other companies within the Keith Prowse Group (including £2.44 million to KP Hospitality). The largest creditor was Wimbledon's All-England Lawn Tennis Club which went down for £500,000, the same amount as Rugby World Cup. Like those of KP Hospitality, the goodwill and certain assets were sold to Wembley plc, which took on around 150 KPC staff. Again, up to receivership,

KPC's profit record had been uninspiring and the firm had long been technically insolvent. Creditors included most of London's theatreland – the Palace Theatre Shaftesbury Avenue lost the most – £116,450 – and even the Prince of Wales's Symphony for the Spire Appeal for Salisbury Cathedral was affected, being owed £27,516. Many London hotels also suffered.

This desperate situation left the holders of twenty thousand tickets sold by Keith Prowse, but not paid for, wondering whether they would get to see a match, let alone enjoy the packages for which they had stumped up an estimated £5 million. It eventually cost Rugby World Cup £500,000, the sum they were owed, to honour those tickets. The tournament also lost valuable revenue from the hospitality part of the commercial programme. Perversely, they could count themselves lucky that Keith Prowse had sold only half of their 42,000 ticket allocation.

Under the deal struck with Grant Thornton, Wembley agreed to allocate £1 million, or £50 a head, to honour the hospitality commitments, though not necessarily to the original standards. 'Where someone has ordered a dozen bottles of Dom Perignon champagne, for example, they may get something a little different – but not just bottles of brown ale,' a Wembley spokesman said at the time. Wembley chairman Sir Brian Wolfson, quoted in *The Times*, was more direct: 'We have not been generous, but fair. Wembley is pleased with the transaction. Our first event is the Rugby World Cup, where an outstanding commitment by KP Hospitality was in place.' Wembley eventually sold the 4,500 RWC hospitality packages they had been allocated at £350 a time (before, some of the packages with multiple tickets had cost £3,000 each). Another 4,500 packages were allocated elsewhere, which salvaged at least something from the wreckage.

During the Wembley deal, Alan Callan adopted an uncharacteristically high profile in the face of mounting criticism. Wembley had 'demonstrated great willingness and co-operation to ensure that rugby's greatest international celebration would not be marred by the collapse of Keith Prowse', he said, without any hint of irony or self-blame. Meanwhile, Townley's, CPMA's solicitors, threatened to issue a writ against the RBS demanding the return of ticket-holders' money, which had been swallowed by Keith Prowse's overdraft. The deposits, they argued, were held on 'constructive trust': the RBS were effectively trustees and should not have mixed clients' money with their own when they knew of Keith Prowse's problems. This gambit was not new, but it had no basis in law. In fact, separation of funds had been proposed secretly by auditors Coopers & Lybrand in 1990 but the suggestion had been ignored by Keith Prowse. The rival Ticketmaster agency already ran their operation in this way on a voluntary basis. Yet the solicitors' warnings amounted to shutting the door after the horse had bolted. Neither they nor Callan had implemented safeguards against Keith Prowse's lack of creditworthiness, such as insisting on the separation of funds or obtaining a bank guarantee.

Rugby World Cup, already stung by accusations that they had given too many tickets to the commercial side, were all too ready to leap to Callan's defence. 'I am sick and tired of being asked how many tickets are going to corporate hospitality,' indignant tournament organizer Ray Williams said in the *Guardian*. 'Tickets taken up by Keith Prowse represented only 0.68 per cent of all World Cup tickets.' RWC were also robust standing up for Callan against rival hospitality provider Mike Burton, who offered the most savage indictment of him (albeit, no doubt, prompted by his own commercial considerations) in the *Sunday Telegraph*. Pointing out Callan's links with Keith Prowse, the former British Lions prop forward accused RWC of putting the tournament in the hands of a man 'who advised them badly in almost every respect'. Keith Rowlands called the attack 'an amazing diatribe', and claimed he could refute 90 per cent of it. 'Alan Callan was part of the Keith Prowse Group but he bought himself out some two years ago,' Rowlands responded in the same report. 'Mr Callan has a contract with an option to renew the contracts he has created for this tournament. He has first option to bring sponsors to the next tournament.'

Rugby World Cup's defence of their 'commercial adviser' appears rather generous in the light of their losses, especially as others not a million miles away were much cannier. The RFU, for instance, did not release any tickets on credit to the troubled firm: 'We made it clear that we would not release any of the tickets for the World Cup tournament to Keith Prowse until they were paid for and until the cheque was cleared,' RFU secretary Dudley Wood said at the time. Heinz and the other commercial sponsors also declined to put in

Sir Nick Shehadie. Without his backroom and frontroom work, the inaugural 1987 World Cup would have foundered.

England training for the 1987 tournament. They suffered at the hands of the referee in their opening game against Australia, when David Campese was credited with a try which, on the evidence of the video replay, should certainly not have been allowed. Even so, England demonstrated in this tournament how far off the pace their game was.

OPPOSITE: John Kirwan was the dominant player of the 1987 tournament. He scored some outrageous tries and some important ones, too, none more so than this one in the final against France.

Wales v. Ireland, 1987. The Welsh success on the field was not matched off it. The WRU's administration was set in aspic in the late 1980s, and Wales were never again to reach such heights in a World Cup. Ireland were no better. Both committees considered success in the Five Nations Championship more important.

OPPOSITE: The 1991 semi-final between Australia and France was a classic. France beat favourites Australia by 30–24. It would have been a different story had Mark Ella, the Wallaby fly-half, not fallen out with coach Alan Jones, whose personal agenda disrupted the Australian camp.

David Kirk flanked by Albert Ferrasse, president of
the French Fédération de Rugby, and John Kendall-
Carpenter, chairman of RWC '87.

OPPOSITE: While successive Olympics had
demonstrated how important opening and closing
ceremonies were – Los Angeles in 1984 was
outstanding – it was clear that no one from the IRB
or RWC '87 had ever watched one.

No administrator did more for Rugby Union than Dudley Wood, CBE. His vision created modern Twickenham and stabilized a financial platform for the English game.

money up front. 'It is normal practice for the various sponsors of an event like this to keep in touch. We took each other's advice about the safety of depositing money with Keith Prowse,' a Heinz spokesman said in the *Independent*.

It was an ignominious demise for a company originally founded in 1800 by flute maker Robert Keith and music publisher and clarinet maker William Prowse. Less than a month after buying KPC, Wembley merged the company, together with Wembley Box Office, with Expedier's First Call in a fifty–fifty joint venture. In January 1993 it sold out completely, taking £2.6 million of troubled Expedier's shares.

Within three hours of the group going into receivership, Grant Thornton had sold the assets of the hotel reservations business to Jersey-based hotels and leisure firm Modern Group for some £3 million. Modern Group, owned by the Segal family, already ran the UK's second-largest hotel-booking operation. The deal raised eyebrows, however, as Devinder Singh remained as managing director. The sale of KPC and KP Hospitality to Wembley left just a few small travel agencies for the receivers to sell before they turned their attention to the task of tracking down any other remaining assets.

The group's losses for the year to end June 1991 had been put at £3 million, according to unaudited management accounts, but were understood to have been substantially greater. Among the many questions which remain unresolved is why a group that should have had positive cashflow should have collapsed in such a way. Where did all the £7 million plus of hospitality deposits, five weeks of theatre tickets and more all go?

On liquidation, Keith Prowse International BV, a Dutch-registered holding company owned by Burns and the Anands with operations in New York, was reported to have owed £5 million. 'We are looking into the background of these loans, which is really what killed Keith Prowse,' the administrating receivers said. 'Had someone given KP £5 million a month ago, they would not be in receivership today.' KPI BV, however, was quickly taken over by a consortium of investors, which included Paul Burns' brother John. According to legal adviser Nicholas Bitel of lawyers Max Bitel Greene, the group took possession as security for loans.

No further news has since emerged to shed light on these questions, nor news of Keith Prowse's connections with the crooked and collapsed Bank of Credit and Commerce International. The KP Group owed BCCI £1.5 million, raised in 1988, at its collapse. Mysteriously, it was not until 1 November 1989 that BCCI registered a lengthy (but worthless) charge for this – and then deemed it satisfied on the 15th of the same month.

Following the sale or closure of the operating businesses, most of the underlying companies have emerged from receivership and have since been wound up. The top company, KPH (renamed KP Realisations Limited), continues in the hands of Grant Thornton, however, and it is possible that further action may yet emerge later in 1995.

The IB members and RWC '91 directors delight in telling us that they were unpaid amateurs putting something back into the game. This attitude, coupled with an inadequately supported secretariat at Bristol, meant that the RWC '91 organizers were never in charge of the business of the World Cup. They were always going to be a reactive rather than a proactive administration, relying heavily on the 'expertise' of their commercial advisers. The 1991 World Cup was a brilliant success on the field. Off the field, it was not. It remained to be seen whether the controversial choice of South Africa as the venue for the third World Cup would create the perfect tournament. Perhaps it would be third time lucky.

PART 3: 1995

12

Welcome to South Africa

Fortune was on the side of the IB when they awarded the third World Cup to South Africa in the early part of 1992. There was little fuss about the decision then, yet the IB simply couldn't have anticipated the pace of change once Nelson Mandela had been sworn in as the new president in May 1994. Between 1992 and 1994, however, there was a catalogue of violence in South Africa, orchestrated by Chief Buthelezi's Inkatha Freedom Party in KwaZulu and the Nationalist government then in power against the ANC, especially in the townships. It threatened the very existence of RWC '95.

Indeed, contingency plans had been drawn up by the IB to return the tournament to the Five Nations in the northern hemisphere if South Africa looked too unstable to stage it. These were leaked to the press just as the England tour to the Republic was about to set off in May 1994. The major problem was that no insurance company would insure RWC '95, and the very existence of the structure created by the IB was endangered.

Before we begin the story of RWC '95, we ought to remind ourselves of the complex role South Africa has played in world rugby, a role which kept the country out of the 1987 and 1991 World Cups.

As a result of their abhorrent policy of apartheid, South Africa had been out of world affairs for the better part of half a century and their political isolation had cost them dear. Sporting links were severed when, to their enormous credit, the International Olympic Committee expelled South Africa from their movement in May 1970. South Africa had not participated in the 1964 Tokyo Olympics, but had gained re-admission to the Mexico Games in 1968. (Eventually, once the imprisoned African National Congress leader Nelson Mandela had been released in 1990, the country was welcomed back to the Olympic movement at the last gasp just before the Barcelona Games of 1992.)

Eventually, in 1977, rather late in the day, the Commonwealth Statement on Apartheid and Sport (known widely as the Gleneagles Agreement) was settled upon by the relevant heads of state. It said:

> Heads of government specifically welcomed the belief, unanimously expressed at their meeting, that in the light of their consultations and accord there were unlikely to be future sporting contacts of any significance between Commonwealth countries or their nationals and South Africa while that country continues to pursue the detestable policy of apartheid.

Rugby, meanwhile, followed its own agenda. Indeed, until RWC '87 had ended, the game's ruling bodies never saw that they had an obligation to any sporting authority or political organization other than themselves. The South African Rugby Board (SARB), even though it represented only a minority of the rugby-playing fraternity in South Africa – the whites – had for the past century been the only rugby body in that country ever to be officially recognized by the IB. This was a disgrace to international sport and a snub to the International Olympic Committee's charter. Between 1970 and 1992 only England, France and New Zealand of the senior nations ventured to South Africa. The USA, an odd choice, were invited to play a short Test series, and South America (Argentina by any other name) visited in 1980, 1982 and 1984.

New Zealand, despite its large Maori population and large contingent of Maori players, toured South Africa four times after the Second World War in 1949, 1960, 1970 and 1976. For the first two tours no Maori players were selected, a disgraceful situation. In 1976 the SARB, which had largely been infiltrated by the Afrikaner secret society, the Broderbond, relented and allowed the NZRFU to give honorary 'white citizenship' to their Maori players. To their shame, the Maori players agreed to this farce. Worse, the NZRFU accepted it too. Australia, too, made four post-war tours, in 1953, 1961, 1963 and 1969. England visited South Africa in 1972 and 1984 and the British Lions toured there five times, in 1955, 1962, 1968, 1974 and 1980.

To overcome the shortage of top-level international opposition, the SARB invited 'World XVs' to South Africa in 1977 and 1989, winning the so-called Tests by 45–24 in 1977 and 20–19 and 22–16 in 1989. In 1986, Andy Haden's New Zealand Cavaliers, another cloak-and-dagger act, played a four-'Test' series there, losing 21–15, 19–18, 33–18 and 24–10. South Africa did more to professionalize the game in this period than any other nation. Yet, despite the evidence, the IB did nothing. The country deserved its pariah status in the world at large. It was vital that the sports boycott gained acceptance within sporting committees themselves. 'No normal sport in an abnormal society' became our watchword.

South African rugby was dominated by the president of the SARB, Dr Danie Craven. In 1980 I asked him when he thought black players would make a significant contribution to rugby in South Africa. 'Black players?' he responded, in that famous gravel voice of his. 'Black players should stick to soccer, that's their game. We don't want black players in our game. It's our game.' Craven led the IB a merry dance during his presidency. He bullied and threatened, and then when it mattered, was sweetness and light. His carrot-and-stick approach was carefully orchestrated with the co-operation of some of the leading rugby correspondents in the world, such as John Reason of the *Sunday Telegraph*, which gave his views prominence.

In Britain in the 1970s and early 1980s, the rugby media, with some notable exceptions such as Clem Thomas, the *Observer*'s rugby correspondent, his sports editor, Geoffrey Nicholson, and Frank Keating of the *Guardian*, were, if not Nationalists in sheep's clothing, woolly liberals who believed that sport occupied a higher moral plane than politics. In the BBC, because of the views of Bill McLaren and Nigel Starmer-Smith from television and Ian Robertson and Chris Rea from radio, all of whom were sympathetic to the separation of sport from politics, there was little discussion of these issues. It was left to a former athletics coach and rugby player, the late Ron Pickering, to demonstrate the flaws of this argument in a brilliant television documentary (commissioned outside the aegis of the BBC's sports department). It took a new breed of younger and more aware writers – John Hopkins and Stephen Jones (*The Sunday Times*) and Steve Bale (the *Independent*) – in the early to middle 1980s to alter this perspective.

In the meantime it was left to the Anti-Apartheid Movement, Sam

Ramsamy's South African Non-Racial Olympic Committee (SAN-ROC) and groups such as the Campaign for Fair Play, which was set up in 1984 by British sporting figures including John Arlott, Mike Brearley and Ron Pickering, to raise the public consciousness on the question of sporting links with South Africa.

In New Zealand, meanwhile, where rugby was all-important, there was a growing realization within society that what was happening in South Africa was an affront to the dignity of its people and to the dignity of a substantial number of New Zealanders, too. As well as a strong anti-apartheid lobby in New Zealand there was also an organization called HART (Halt All Racial Tours). These groups were supported up and down the country by trades unions and their affiliates. There were street marches in every major city calling for the government to call off the invitation to the South Africans.

In 1966, the NZRFU had passed up an invitation to tour South Africa after the prime minister, Keith Holyoake, had suggested that the conditions of the tour were unsatisfactory. In 1973, Prime Minister Norman Kirk had flatly told the NZRFU to call off a Springbok tour of New Zealand that year. The Union had complied.

Prior to 1985, there had been two unsuccessful attempts by private individuals to use the courts to prevent the NZRFU from going on tour in South Africa or from receiving a Springbok touring party. The first, the case of Roy Parsons v NZRFU, was in 1970. Roy, a bookseller from Wellington, attempted to stop the NZRFU from selecting Blair Furlong, a Maori, for the tour to South Africa that year. The second case had a higher profile. It involved the Roman Catholic bishop of Auckland, Bishop Ashby. His case was not brought against the NZRFU, but against the minister of immigration. He asked the minister not to issue visas to the SARB's players and team members due to tour New Zealand in 1981.

Although Ashby's case failed, there were major protests everywhere the South Africans went on the 1981 tour, culminating in the third Test in Auckland being flour-bombed from a private Cessna 172. These protests went largely unnoticed by the Four Home Unions and by the UK press generally, but the tour caused deep divisions within New Zealand, a conservative country now led by a Conservative prime minister, Robert 'Spotty' Muldoon.

As a result, a third attempt to stop future tours through the courts was launched. This time it was successful in preventing the All Blacks' 1985 visit to South Africa, and Finnigan v NZRFU 1985 became a cause célèbre in the rugby world. The case was brought by a group of Auckland lawyers with a rugby player of their acquaintance, Paddy Finnigan, as their 'fall guy'. It was never plain sailing, but the case was finally won in the Court of Appeal, where it was decided that the tour contravened the constitution of the NZRFU in that it would not 'promote or foster and develop the game in this country'. There were cheers, shouts, jubilation – you name it – and the courtroom became a circus of happiness. The NZRFU had been defeated, and the judge's decision made its way out of the court like a wave and into the streets, where an enormous roar went up from the assembled crowd.

Of course, that was only the beginning of the end of the matter. There was an appeal by the NZRFU to the privy council, made up of law lords, in London, but owing to the time this took, it was academic. The tour was called off.

The case made little impression in the UK and was poorly and sometimes indifferently reported. I suppose all newspapers are 'nationalists' to some degree and that, as Rugby Union was not then a major UK sport, there were some sensible editorial reasons why this was so, in addition to the poverty of the thinking within the rugby pages generally.

The Finnigan judgement did not prevent other tours to South Africa, however. In 1986, Andy Haden was the focal point for the New Zealand Cavaliers tour, which was funded by a South African bank. The Cavaliers were precisely that – their tour gave new relevance to the word 'amateur'. The players were recruited carefully and the planning was thorough. Two current first-team players did not go: John Kirwan and David Kirk. Kirwan's father was ill, but this was not the sole reason for his absence from the party: he didn't want to go. Kirk was more indecisive. He was put under a lot of pressure to make the trip and initially he agreed to go. A week later, when he had thought the whole matter through, he knew it would have been wrong, and he pulled out. No one at that time could have anticipated that Kirk would become the captain of the 1987 World Cup-winning team. I suspect that the reason why the conservatives in New Zealand rugby – the Colin Meadses and Andy Hadens of this world – had trouble coming to terms with David Kirk was that Kirk had the courage of his convictions to stand with the New Zealand people.

The Cavaliers were no match for the South Africans, losing all four unofficial 'Tests' and giving greater credence to the SARB authorities' claim that their XV was the best in the world. The New Zealanders seriously besmirched the name of rugby. On their return, the NZRFU took the hardly courageous decision to ban the players for two Tests.

The Cavaliers demonstrated, or so they thought, that players were more important than the game. There was a new culture among the leading internationals: they wanted payment of some sort as compensation for their commitment to the game. With the first World Cup on the horizon, the Cavaliers were putting up another signpost to a possible professional circus. It is ironic that just about the only country in which a professional Rugby Union circus would never work is New Zealand.

If the IB had had any power at all, it would have suspended South Africa from their membership. The SARB wilfully encouraged the Cavaliers and spared them no expense. They were, in their own way, trying to break down the doors of the amateur ethic that had held the game in check for over 150 years. Of course, there was also Danie Craven barking in the background that if South Africa were banned or suspended from the IB they would create a professional circus anyway. He was, by some way, the most skilful of all rugby politicians. The IB could not ask the NZRFU to do anything about the tour because it was not under the union's jurisdiction. All they did was give tokenism a short revival.

It was apparent even to the slowest back-row forward in the game that 1986 showed the extent of the power gap between the IB, the nominal world governing body, and the players of international standing. The IB had RWC '87 on their mind and no interest whatsoever in the problems of South Africa: South Africa had already declined their invitation to the inaugural World Cup and in doing so had effectively unilaterally declared their independence on all rugby matters.

The success of RWC '87 hurt South African rugby. Here was the most successful rugby-playing country in the world denied a stage. The decision to award the 1991 tournament to the Four Home

Unions, and then – because French rugby president Albert Ferrasse kept complaining – to France as well, would bar the South Africans again. This was a further blow to the fragile ego of Dr Danie Craven.

To console themselves, the SARB tried to stage a repeat of the Cavaliers tour of 1986. This time Australia was the country they targeted. Alan Jones was keen to test his Wallabies side in South Africa, particularly after they won the Bledisloe Cup in 1986. The difference now was that the players wanted to be paid for going. There were allegedly some long and detailed talks on this score with Bruce Francis, the SARB's paid representative in Australia. The bans arising from a rebel tour would have decimated Australian rugby for years – they simply did not have the strength in depth that New Zealand had. Ross Turnbull, the ARU IB representative, who had argued successfully at IB level against the suspension of the South Africans from the board because of the Cavaliers tour, was not keen for the tour to go ahead without the full permission of the ARU.

Meanwhile, on the quiet, the Crawshay's Welsh, a team made up of past and present Welsh internationals, arrived in South Africa. Midway through their tour they threatened to cancel the remaining games and fly home unless they received more money. Turnbull met Danie Craven at an IB meeting in Hong Kong. They talked at length about an official tour after the World Cup, which they expected Australia to win. Subsequently, Turnbull briefed Sir Nick Shehadie, then president of the ARU. Shehadie, Norbert Byrne, Alan Jones, Ross Turnbull and Andrew Slack (representing the players) met Bill Hayden, the foreign minister, and John Brown, the sports minister, at Parliament House, Canberra. Further meetings were held with Hayden in Canberra and Brown in Sydney, but the result was disappointing for Jones and Turnbull. The Australian government refused to sanction a tour of any sort before or after the World Cup, and therefore so did the ARU.

This was not the end of the matter. The SARB officials tried at every level to circumvent the decision by offering large sums of money to both officials and players to tempt them to come. Turnbull himself was offered 'a lorryload of dosh'. After the World Cup Danie Craven tried to effect a rebel tour irrespective of the wishes of the Australian government or the ARU. He was supported by some of the players, who had heard how much money was available and had brought themselves up to speed by talking to the Cavaliers who had toured in 1986. The irony of all this was that at the IB meeting in Agen on 13 November 1987, the SARB's two representatives – Fritz Pickard and Jan Pickard (Danie Craven was unable to attend) – deliberately sought the sympathy of the IB, positioning themselves as the 'innocents of amateur rugby football'. The South Africans had corrupted themselves and had simply lost all notion of words such as 'values' or 'integrity'. However, they knew how to spell 'duplicitous' in twenty different languages. Had a rebel tour gone to South Africa from Australia in 1987, in the aftermath they would not have won RWC '91. Thankfully, the ARU stood firm.

These apparent kicks in the teeth from New Zealand and Australia deeply hurt the SARB, especially as it was still unclear why, out of the blue, the Lions management had backed down from the scheduled 1985 tour. The only solution was for them to invite players from all over the world on yet another pretext, this time to celebrate the centenary of the SARB in 1989. On this occasion South African Breweries were the house bankers. Rather than invite a national side to commemorate the occasion, the SARB tried, in a ham-fisted way, to put together an international side. To do this they needed the permission of the executive committees of every IB member.

Of course, they all caved in. No, they couldn't publicly sanction an invitation, but they couldn't stop individual players from going. Baloney. Of course they could. Every player has to ask his governing body's permission to play overseas. Yet still the South Africans could not raise a XV of any note. They started to up the going fee. The Welsh were targeted, and were told that if they agreed to make the trip they could expect to receive between £20,000 and £30,000 a player. Moreover, if the WRU committee members also agreed to accompany them, they too would be suitably recompensed. In another chapter from the cloak-and-dagger book of heroic failures, the players and administrators were spirited out of Wales to Heathrow.

For the record, two Tests were played and once again South Africa won them both, by 20–19 and 22–16 respectively, victories which maintained their hollow boast that they were still 'world champions'. Dr Danie Craven, with an open chequebook, had done it again. He had cocked a snook at the ethics and values of every rugby institution left in the game. Mind you, most of them seemed to share his aspirations.

You can guess the rest. The IB sat on their hands, South Africa remained a full voting member and none of the 'international XV' players were banned by their own unions. Except that something was stirring within the Welsh Rugby Union, something that was ultimately to result in the Pugh report. The Pugh report – or reports, there were three in all – was a profound indictment of the level of maladministration and corruption in rugby in Wales. These private documents assessed, among other things, the payments made to Welsh players and administrators on the South African tour. In the fall-out the Welsh IB representatives, Terry Vaux and Gwilym Treharne, were sacked and Rhys Williams, a WRU vice-president, was also fired. In England the RFU interviewed Jeff Probyn, Peter Winterbottom and Mike Teague as a result of the Pugh report, though no further action was taken. Thus was Vernon Pugh, in 1989 a QC tending the vegetables in his garden, by 1994 chairman of the WRU, catapulted on to the fast track of world rugby.

Dr Danie Craven died in 1992, just at the point when South African society was preparing itself for bigger things. On 11 February 1990, after serving twenty-eight years in prison on Robben Island, and later in Pollsmoor, near Cape Town, Nelson Mandela had been released by F. W. de Klerk's National government. Free democratic elections were promised for all the people of South Africa. They were eventually held over five days in the last week of April 1994.

As a consequence of this long-awaited move towards democracy, South Africa was awarded the World Cup. They did not have to tender for it. Normal relations were resumed with the SARB, which was in the process of merging with the South African Rugby Union (SARU), the governing body of the game among the non-white population, to create a new non-racial rugby authority to be known as the South African Rugby Football Union (SARFU). Ebrahim Patel, formerly the president of the SARU, was to become the president of the new body. I wish I could report that Patel immersed himself in his new position and started to see that the townships received such basic needs as rugby balls, tackle bags and shirts. But I deeply regret he did not bring about fundamental change to rugby in South Africa.

His tenure was brief, and he was very quickly replaced by Dr Louis Luyt of the Transvaal Rugby Union.

The SARFU, keen to be back in world rugby, quickly – too quickly – invited world champions Australia, and in their minds the real world champions, New Zealand, to play back-to-back Tests on 15 and 22 August 1992. The visits were very nearly an operational and public-relations disaster. But for the intervention of Steve Tshwete, then the ANC minister for sport, and the good sense of Bob Dwyer and Nick Farr-Jones of the ARU, South Africa – or rather Louis Luyt – would have blown it. It was agreed that the old national anthem, 'Die Stem', with its reminders of the old regime, would not be played before the New Zealand match at Ellis Park. But Dr Luyt owned the stadium, and no one was going to tell him what he could or couldn't do on his home patch, whatever had been decided earlier. The rugby world was outraged and took it as a sign that South Africa's change in attitude was only skin-deep. While Johannesburg wasn't exactly the heart of liberalism, it wasn't the home of the dullards of the extreme right wing like Eugene Terre Blanche, either. There was hell to pay, and only Tshwete's intervention prevented the cancellation of the Australian game the following week.

Those two Tests, both of which were lost, by 27–24 and 26–3 respectively, had a devastating impact on rugby thinking in South Africa – especially the comprehensive defeat by Australia. In their isolation, the South Africans had clung to the conviction that as they held the best Test record against all countries and had won all six of the mercenary Tests of 1986 and 1989, they were the best in the world. But the rest of the world had moved on. Worse was to follow. A few months later, South Africa played a one-off Test at Twickenham against 1991 World Cup finalists England who had recently added back-to-back Grand Slams to their list of achievements. They lost 33–16. Before the teams came out, Sir Peter Yarranton, chairman of the UK Sports Council, and a past president of the RFU, called over the microphone for a standing ovation for the man who had made this game possible and who was now about to take his seat in the RFU's committee box, one F. W. de Klerk.

The sheer effrontery of it took one's breath away. Needless to say, the occupants of the West Stand complied with alacrity. Was there no shame in the innermost circle of the RFU about what De Klerk's government represented? Apparently not.

In 1994 South Africa, captained by François Pienaar, a man who was soon to become a household name, toured Wales, Scotland and Ireland. They won the Tests, against Scotland (34–10) and Wales (20–12), but there were indications that perhaps, at long last, some of the old arrogance was beginning to fade. At least, on the PR front, never a strength of the Springboks, they appeared to have been taking a few lessons. By the end of the tour, the countdown to the 1995 World Cup, now only five months away, had started in earnest for both South Africa and their international rivals.

13

The Rainbow Nation: One Team, One Country

This was my third visit to Cape Town in four years. When the sky is fiercely blue and Table Mountain is free of that old grey beard about itself, this has to be where God first put man and woman on this bounteous earth. This morning Table Mountain is clear and the omens are set for the greatest rugby match so far this century – the opening game of the 1995 World Cup.

But that's tomorrow. Today, the squads trained in private. President Nelson Mandela had asked to see the Springbok team and does so in private at their practice ground at Silvermine, a naval base. Private meant only a few thousand were let in on the secret. At one of three press conferences I attended, François Pienaar, the Springbok captain, said: 'There is an aura of excitement. We might have feared failure three years ago when we re-entered the international scene, but not this time round. It is more that we are nervous.' Morné du Plessis, the former Springbok captain and now the new manager of the team, put it differently: 'There's been a huge wave of interest. Stemming it has been difficult. I've cut the phones off for three days and the hotel is quiet and I hope it will stay that way.'

Press conference number two for the day, but number ten so far in just under a week in Cape Town, was with Chester Williams, the talented Springbok wing threequarter whose hamstring injury had caused him to pull out of the squad for the World Cup. Chester is a likeable Western Province boy whose father and family played for the Proteas, the national black and coloured rugby team, back in the old days. Mick Cleary of the *Observer* asked him a double-edged question: 'If your injury clears up will you be back in the squad?'

'Only if there is an injury to a squad player,' he replied.

'You mean you'd be happy to play second row?'

It was clear to everyone present that Chester would be back. As the only non-white in the side it was important from all sorts of perspectives that he returned to the squad, and to hell with the rules. I asked him why it was that the Ithuba (meaning 'chance') seven-a-side team, which had made it to the Middlesex Sevens final two weeks earlier, hadn't received any press back home. 'I'm afraid I didn't know anything about this team. What were they called again?' was Williams' response, and yet, in the next breath, he was applauding the work the SARFU was doing in the townships.

After this press conference, I was bearded by Edward Griffiths, chief executive of the SARFU, who is head cook and bottle-washer in the Cape Town operations. He was rattled. 'You know, sevens is such a small sport here in South Africa that it hardly ever gets any press here anyway,' he grumbled, as though that somehow made it right. He pointed to his article in the South African media guide. I hadn't yet read it. It said, among many things, that more than 30 per cent of all SARFU income went to development; that 40 per cent of their World Cup profits would fund development; that SARFU employed development offices in all twenty-three provinces; and that they had built or renovated seventy-two fields since 1992. Later in the tournament Edward confirmed that he saw as his main objective the development programme for the townships, and to this end he hoped that the 1996 All Blacks tour to South Africa would begin with a game in one. Rugby has a massive potential in South Africa which now needs to be realized among the urban black and coloured populations.

The third press conference of the morning was held a few miles from the Newlands Stadium at the Baxter Theatre. Fronting it was Sir Ewart Bell, supported by Marcel Martin, Leo Williams, Keith Rowlands, Nick Labuschagne, Riaan Obelhauzer and Craig Jamieson. Aside from the ticket issue – only 1 million of the allotted 1,350,000 had been sold (42,000 had gone to the townships) – there really wasn't much to report. Journalists wanted to know how the 1999 tournament was going to pan out and how the rucking laws were going to be interpreted by the referees. On the subject of the laws, Marcel Martin responded: 'You know, in 1991 we only met the teams two days before the tournament began. This time round we have been holding conferences and seminars throughout the northern and southern hemispheres for the past four years, so the message ought to be getting home.' I asked him: 'What would happen to the 1999 World Cup contracts if we woke up to a headline tomorrow morning that Rupert Murdoch had bought the International Management Group?' Martin treated the whole exercise as though he was chief executive of the IB, if not RWC '95. 'IMG–CPMA have the contract for 1995 and have fulfilled all their obligations, raising over £30 million already. Three years ago, when we did this deal, we put in place an option clause for ourselves in which we would renegotiate the contract for 1999 with them. If we didn't like their terms, then we could put the contract out to the marketplace. Of course, even then IMG–CPMA have a topping right.'

Watch this space. Leo Williams who wears many hats, some of them incongruous, was silent about the whole issue. Williams had been a supporter of IMG, so I found it mildly amusing that his own union had been to see Rupert Murdoch's Newscorp in London a week earlier.

I flagged down a combie, a black taxi, to take me home. The fare was a mere 30p. My hosts told me I was barking mad to have travelled in one, let alone hail one. I retorted that all over the world there were these cheap and efficient taxi systems; I'd used them before and would use them again. On the trip, the Cape coloured driver told me that the most important thing was economic empowerment for his people. I said that might take five to ten years, and was he prepared to wait?

'No,' he said. 'We must have it now.'

All over town the atmosphere for the game was building. Bunting was everywhere. The radio and television news highlights led with rugby first. In the local pubs in the evening, South Africans were debating whether their team could win. Few thought they could. I had bet on them winning by 23–17. President Mandela, who had been helicoptered into Silvermine, said, 'We have adopted these young men as our own boys, as our own children, as our own stars. The country is fully behind them. I have never been so proud of my boys as I am now, and I hope that it's a pride we all share.' Later, over tea, he was reported to have said to Pienaar: 'If you want to keep the Springbok emblem on your jerseys, you'd better win.' Otherwise, presumably, he would change their name to the Proteas. 'It's true that when there was a visiting team I wished they would beat the Springboks,' the President continued, 'but now our loyalties have completely changed. I am confident about South Africa pulling off a sensational victory. I am really excited. We will all be there cheering them to victory.'

The day of the game was a virtual replay of the day before. Still blue skies looked down on Table Mountain, which glistened in the sunlight. The railway stations were already overflowing by eight o'clock as the city visitors came out to Newlands early to make a day of it. Newlands' and Claremont's cafés and bars were already awash with slashes of singing and bonhomie. Helicopters and private planes were busy overhead. Everyone who was anyone was making a last-ditch attempt to make it to the match.

The ground was wonderful. Workmen were still finishing off the last bits and pieces that morning. Newlands had much that was new but a fair amount of the ringside was standing room only, and standing tickets were still available at noon the day before. If Western Province Rugby Union, who own the ground, want to attract all of the population it might be no bad idea to keep a standing section available over the next few years and to resist yet more hospitality suites. The PA system was working, which even in these days is unusual. It was playing Bruce Springsteen and Chris Rea. Twickenham suffers by comparison. The press box had been especially extended – there were about 800 print journalists there as well as 1,600 television personnel and over 250 photographers. This accommodation, along with a first-class media centre, cost RWC '95 £2 million.

Almost the first person I met was Edward Griffiths, who told me, further to our conversation the previous day, that I had a point and the next day I would read in the newspapers that the Springbok Under-21 side to tour in Argentina would have seven black or coloured players in the squad. He said that when he saw the first, seventy-strong list a few days before it had contained seventy white players. He had insisted that the selectors rethought and selected ten non-whites for the final squad of twenty-six. Seven was the compromise. 'You know,' he said, 'we've a massive amount of work to do but we are starting from the bottom.' Griffiths had been made chief executive only two months before and he knows the task ahead. Still, it cannot be too bad to have a rugby World Cup at home within eight weeks of taking office.

Derek Bevan, today's referee, who had recently eclipsed Clive Norling's world record of officiating in twenty-five Tests, was walking around the ground trying to capture some of the atmosphere. It was available in buckets. In the Aussie section a banner was unfurled which claimed 'O. J. Simpson is an Aussie', to much merriment. Then some of the Australian players and coaches, including Bob Dwyer and Bob Templeton, Michael Lynagh and Willie Ofahengaue, strolled out in their striking green-and-white-striped blazers. But all this was ignored when the Springboks walked out to a tumultuous reception. Not bad when you consider there were seventy-five minutes still to go before the start of the tournament.

And then the opening ceremony was upon us. Brilliantly conceived and wonderfully orchestrated, here, finally, after the damp squibs of 1987 and 1991, was an opening ceremony of celebration of which to be proud. The rainbow country, as South Africa was calling itself, came alive for the very first time. Later on in the tournament, I spent a couple of hours with Merle McKenna, the genius behind the opening ceremony, in Johannesburg. She ran a small company called Pro Touch Promotions. With Natalie Webster and Janet Lindsey, she dreamed up the whole wonderful show. On the day after the ceremony, Nelson Mandela's office was full of praise and admiration for what he had seen; Louis Luyt, while congratulating her, also said that he hoped her closing show would be better. Later, Chris Liebenberg, the minister of finance, had also called to tell her how powerful and moving he had found it and how he thought it had given the nation back its dignity.

'We were asked to pitch in August 1994, to Craig Jamieson and John Gainsford,' Merle told me.

They liked what we had to offer and so we then went to Bristol to the IB headquarters to pitch to the RWC '95. We won the contract, I think against four other companies, on 20 October. We had forty-five minutes to give to the world a vision of the diversity of our culture and to make a statement about the uniqueness of our people.

The planning and preparation were formidable tasks. All the

performers had to live in Cape Town. As there were thirteen hundred children drawn from throughout the Cape, there simply couldn't be too many dress rehearsals. In fact, there was only one, on 19 May at Newlands, six days before the real thing. We began the rehearsals in the middle of March this year. We rehearsed the groups separately and at different venues in Cape Town, including the University of Cape Town's playing fields and the Good Hope Centre. On the day, the children had to get to UCT, then they had to be made up and changed before boarding twenty-four buses. The police had to make sure we could get to the ground in time.

McKenna had assembled a brilliant, innovative team. The musical director was Alistair Coakley; the choreography was the responsibility of Neil McKay, who had danced on Broadway and in *Ipi Tombi* in London's West End. He was ably assisted by Neil Lessick and Erna Ackerman. Gavin Joubert, the production manager, kept the show on the road. The fantastic costumes were the responsibility of Janet Lindsey and Sally Prior; Diana Celliers, the owner of the Theatre and Film Costume Workshop, did the wardrobe and the ever-creative Louise Knepscheld found the props. Much later I learned of the 'near catastrophe of the opening tournament'. At twelve noon on the opening day, 1,300 children were assembled at the campus of the University of Cape Town. A representative of the groups of children expressed his dismay that all they were promised was a certificate of attendance. He wanted them to be paid, and told the organizers that unless they were, they wouldn't go through with the ceremony. Can you imagine the scenario? Eventually, a certificate and a T-shirt – but no money – was the compromise, and the band played on. After they had finished, the 1,300 children were ushered to Villagers Rugby Club. Despite their efforts they were not able to see the game live. What a shame.

The only downside to the opening ceremony itself was the coverage by the host broadcaster, SABC. First, the stadium had been prepared for the game, not the opening ceremony, so the camera positions were hostile and much of the beauty and simplicity of the display was missed. Secondly, there was a row between the light entertainment department and the sports department at SABC as to who should direct the show. The sports department claimed it was their day, but they couldn't direct their way out of a paper bag.

Even this, the show we had all hoped for, but dared not believe would happen, was but a prelude to what was to come. When President Mandela arrived, he was rapturously received by the 50,000-strong crowd, many of whom broke into a spontaneous chant of 'Nelson, Nelson.' He went through the motions of giving a speech – written by his staff, but that didn't matter. The great man of the twentieth century was here, and the almost all-white crowd rose to salute him. The new South Africa had a chance.

Interestingly, when Louis Luyt was introduced there was silence from the crowd. This was a marginal improvement on the reception he was given last time he was at Newlands, a few weeks before, when he had been booed. But then, this was Western Province. Another jarring note was struck by four of the Australian team, who chose to ignore all the officials and came out to have a run-around during the opening ceremony, which was bad manners by any standards.

Finally, the show was on the road, and Michael Lynagh, the Aussie skipper, kicked the 1995 World Cup into life. The early exchanges, as you would expect, were nervous. From the first scrum, Joost van der Westhuizen was blatantly offside and Australia went three points ahead. Within three minutes, Joel Stransky had levelled the score, also following an offside decision. The adrenaline was reaching places it had never been before. Lynagh then had a chance to pot an easy penalty but, uncharacteristically, he missed. A minute later he was back in the groove, succeeding with his third penalty attempt. There then followed a ten-minute passage of play with Joubert as the instigator, in which South Africa threw caution to the winds and attacked from deep within their own half. To Australia's great credit their defence held out, and all there was to show for the Springboks' pressure was a further penalty goal, which took the score to 6–6.

Thereafter the game picked up in pace. South Africa couldn't win a line-out – they lost the first four, and it looked as though this would count against them. A further Stransky penalty goal, which gave the Springboks the lead for the first time, was swiftly followed, almost inevitably, by a wonderful Australian movement, stemming from a line-out, begun by Eales and taken on by Willie Ofahengaue into South Africa's 22. The ball moved from left to right and back on six occasions, and once Australia were guilty of missing an overlap. It looked as if they had missed their opportunity when suddenly Lynagh sliced through. He converted the try himself to restore the Wallabies' advantage.

It wasn't over quite yet, however. South Africa continued to press. Their first efforts to move the ball wide had been too frenetic but at last they were able to claim a try when Hendriks went round Campese. The crowd could hardly contain themselves. Two minutes from half-time the hosts were 14–13 ahead.

The second half passed so quickly that it is hard to remember the sequence of events, but the upshot of it all is well known by now: South Africa whipped Australia by 27–18. It just wasn't Australia's day. They were let down most by the ineffectiveness of their front and back rows and particularly by their midfield attack. Stransky dropped a goal and kicked a penalty, and for good measure he scored a performance try and converted it. The Springboks' line-out improved marginally, but, for once under the new laws, scrums mattered more. Here South Africa were, to use Will Carling's overworked expression, awesome. Ten minutes from time, Australia finally worked another try through Kearns, the hooker, who was loitering on the wing, but Lynagh missed again with the conversion to prove that even the best can be affected by pressure. It was not enough for them to catch up with South Africa. The crowd could hardly have expected a win, let alone a substantial win; indeed, most television and radio news bulletins around the world featured the result as their lead or second lead story of the day. It would be of little import in terms of the World Cup as a whole, except that it meant Australia would now probably meet England in the quarter-finals while South Africa had the easier route: barring upsets, either Western Samoa or Argentina in the quarter-finals and Scotland or France in the semis. There was no evidence of any over-aggressive play, Derek Bevan refereed well, and the game was the best possible start to the third World Cup. Rugby was on a roll. For many South Africans present, it was the greatest day of their lives.

Yet the after-match press conferences were subdued. Of course, television, being the most important medium, was given first bite and so most of our conferences took place thirty to forty minutes after the final whistle. The losing side batted first. Michael Lynagh thought the Aussie ball retention was poor and that 'maybe the pressure got to us today'. He hardly had a game of which he would be proud, but he's old enough to know that that can be put right next time. Was this team too long in the tooth? I thought of IMG's bid of AUS$52 million for the home rights to Australian rugby for the following three years and wondered, had they been on the stockmarket, whether their stock would have fallen ten points. Bob Dwyer was philosophical, reminding us that England had lost their opening game in 1991 but made it to the final. He did admit it was 'a real big blow' and that they must 'play much better' which, of course, they would.

The South African press conference was altogether more upbeat, as you would expect of the winners. Edward Griffiths had added Joel Stransky to his usual panel of Morné du Plessis, François Pienaar and Kitch Christie. Pienaar was a PR dream. Blond, good-looking and comfortable with the media, he would make a great spin doctor in politics.

Back in the bars of Claremont and Newlands, which extended their hours of opening on the hour, every hour, there was real wonderment at what had been witnessed. One South African said: 'It was just an amazing day for us as a nation.' Another opined: 'Unbelievable. Unbelievable. Unbelievable.' And another: 'First the ceremony, then Mandela, then the game and we won, we won, we won . . .' Three hours after the event, and still sober, it seemed to me that on this great day for rugby, God had leased himself to the new rainbow nation of South Africa. I would probably feel differently tomorrow. Cape Town partied throughout the night as, I suspect, did most of the country. It transpired that Nelson Mandela was due to have left the game early but insisted on staying right to the end, which endeared him to everyone. He sensibly did not order a public holiday for the next day, though I had a feeling that most of the white male population of the country wouldn't make it to work anyway.

On day two I was moving on from Cape Town to Durban, where England were based. Still the buzz everywhere was the game, the spirit in which it had been played and the way it had touched the nation. I had a sense that as the importance of this match sank in, the number of South Africans who said they were there would rise to half a million. The Springbok squad, meanwhile, were being brought down to earth. Morné du Plessis had organized a day out for them at Robben

Island. I somehow doubt that this would have been top of their travel plans had Morné not been the manager, but the idea was inspirational; it must have concentrated their minds on the suffering that had gone into laying the foundations of the new rainbow nation they represented, and especially that of their president.

Durban was, as Tommy Bedford, the former Oxford University and Springbok captain, once said, 'the last outpost of the British Empire'. It was altogether more English, and therefore, in a South African context, more liberal than any other city in the Republic. This was the home of KwaZulu, the tribal homeland of the Zulus, and therefore a strong Inkatha area. It was the only province where the ANC had only a small following, and that concentrated in the cities. The local press were as caught up in the happenings of the previous day as everyone in Cape Town. Even the black township papers had caught the fever. The headline in the *Sowetan*, a black paper whose sports pages are normally reserved for soccer, proclaimed 'AmaBoko-boko' (The Bokboks), adding: 'South Africa re-established themselves as a rugby force to be reckoned with as serious contenders for the World Cup.' The Afrikaans *Beeld* ran a headline 'Ongelooflik!' (Unbelievable). A leader in *Business Day* put it thus:

> The apartheid legacy is still with us. In its player composition and following, rugby is and will for many years be a predominantly white sport. But it is fair to say that it is no longer a specifically Afrikaner nationalist project, and that it is beginning to play a role in forging a new national identity. A new professionalism and global perspective have entered South African rugby. Personifying this approach is South Africa's diplomatic and sophisticated captain, François Pienaar.

It was a struggle to want to watch more rugby, but I finished day two by watching on television, with idiosyncratic commentary in a mixture of English, Afrikaans and Xhosa, Scotland's comprehensive victory over Ivory Coast by 89–0, France's cumbersome 38–10 win against Tonga and Canada's adventurous 34–3 defeat of Romania.

Saturday 27 May was England's day. The local press had all pounced on a Carling quote intimating that perhaps England would have to throw a game to ensure that they had the easiest passage to the final. This was the subject of much comment, all of it futile. The continuing talk about the South Africa–Australia game and what it meant to the Republic was suspended briefly as we turned on the television to watch the Western Samoans dismantle a disappointing Italian side by 42–18 in Pool B, England's group. At half-time the score stood at 12–11, but the Italians couldn't take the free-ranging, free-thinking attacking movements of the Western Samoan threequarters. By the time we had made it to King's Park for the England game, Wales had swatted the poor Japanese by 57–10 in the Pool C match in Bloemfontein.

King's Park was reminiscent of London on a bad day. Pouring rain was bad enough; worse, the spectacularly revamped ground had no cover, and we endured a drenching before the two teams came out to play. Rob Andrew soon put three points on the board. A dropped goal was disallowed because under the new laws you may not drop a goal directly from a free kick. It didn't matter much, since the next foray into Argentina's 22 gave him a simple penalty. The ground was immaculate, the grass short and the turf ideal for fast, open rugby. Under the lights it was quite magnificent, especially as the swallows overhead were making almost as much noise as the crowd.

The first quarter was, frankly, pretty dull. England, aside from the front row, which looked under great pressure – Victor Ubogu was later to admit that Argentina's was the toughest front row he had played against – were hardly bothered. They were playing at a canter. By half-time Andrew had kicked four out of four to take England into a 12–0 lead. It was hardly earth-shattering. And that's how it stayed, except for six more points by Andrew and a penalty for Argentina from Lisandro Arbizu, until fifteen minutes into the second half, when Argentina forced their way over the try-line with a wedge from a five-metre penalty and converted to bring the score to 18–10. This pleased the crowd of 35,000 no end, and although most of them had been supporting the English, they suddenly turned on them to cheer on the underdogs. Who could blame them? England's canter had become complacency and then the players seemed to turn in on themselves. They were simply dreadful, and the crowd justifiably gave them the bird. On this form, they would go out in the quarter-finals. Andrew dropped another goal and kicked a final penalty, and just as we were all packing up our bags to go to the press conference, the plucky

Arbizu touched down close to the posts. He failed to convert the try – indeed, all told the Argentinians missed six kicks at goal – and England were home by 24–18. What was that about Carling wanting to throw a match?

The England captain missed the post-match press conference. He had come off injured a couple of minutes from time. In fact he had called for Phil de Glanville to come on for him barely fifteen minutes into the second half, but in view of England's degenerating performance, he decided to stay on after all. He had bruising on the back of his ankle and leg and would not play for a week. Instead, Jack Rowell brought Rob Andrew and Mike Catt to face the music. Rowell pulled no punches, readily admitting to the assembled hacks that England's display had been downright wretched. 'We couldn't put two passes together. The team was very disappointing. We will have to play better or we'll be on an early plane home.' I asked him if the weight of expectancy on the side had increased since Thursday's Springboks result. 'I don't know about that, but if there was an assumption that we were already in the quarter-finals, I'd be very disappointed,' he said. Rob Andrew opined: 'Our minds were elsewhere, and we know we have to improve if we are to go further.'

The win showed signs of all the angst of the old England of ten years ago. Rowell would no doubt explore his options, but against Italy he could not afford to rest his best players as the Springboks and the Wallabies were to do for their second games.

For most of the night I took a fair amount of ribbing from my South African friends. 'What was that about fifty points, then?' they asked. What indeed. We took supper in Kloof, a village in the hills some twenty miles west of Durban, at the Station Tavern – not solely, unfortunately, for its food and wine list, but because we could see New Zealand v Ireland on the large television screens. There was a danger of becoming punch-drunk from the sheer number of games in the opening rounds, but at last we had a contest. Ireland, as only they know how, tore into the All Blacks and established an early lead of 7–0. Eventually, however, they became ragged and tired and short of ideas, and were seen off by 43–19. New Zealand were not their old selves. They made a legion of errors under fierce pressure from the Irish, but they looked to have the two best, as well as two youngest, players of the tournament in fly-half Andrew Mehrtens (aged twenty-two) and Jonah Lomu (twenty), the left wing, who makes up for his lack of grace with immense strength. I was also taken by Josh Kronfeld in the back row.

All the opening games of the first-round pool matches had now been completed. Three teams had emerged as the favourites – South Africa, New Zealand and Australia. South Africa couldn't really believe their luck in securing a pretty easy route to the final. England now needed to beat Australia in the quarters and New Zealand in the semis to set up the dream final. It was a tall order for a team not playing at its best, but England had beaten France away in Paris in the 1991 quarters and Scotland, also away, in the semis, so they had been along this path before. Scotland and France were harder to call. In 1987 their pool match against each other had been drawn 20–20. France had gone on to the final and Scotland to meet New Zealand in the quarters. To progress to the semis in two consecutive World Cups, then, they needed to beat France. The opening game between Australia and South Africa had been such a perfect start that I think it had seriously affected some of the other sides. Everyone had anticipated an Australian win, and now the favourites in each pool were left to consider the possibility of a different route through the competition as a result of the upset. The whole occasion, too, had been unexpectedly overwhelming. The teams would need to play a couple more games to rid themselves of its influence. The South Africans themselves now had to play to a new standard in their remaining pool games. The wonderful fascination with the 1995 World Cup that was to overtake the Republic was already developing within the country.

Sunday 28 May was a rest day for everyone. The England team attended the first-ever Sunday raceday at the local course, which attracted a crowd of 8,000 plus the odd camera crew. Betting was not high on England's chances of progressing further than the quarter-finals. Meanwhile, I flicked through the newspapers. A piece in the Johannesburg *Sunday Times* business section by Don Robertson caught my attention. Corporate spending on RWC '95 for entertainment would touch £14 million; spending by major sponsors and tourist packages would top £70 million. Megapro, a hospitality services company, would provide 34,000 meals in marquees around the grounds and a further 8,000 nearby, in the many tented villages which had sprung up, at a cost of £400,000. The profit for RWC was, according to Brian Levine, a project co-ordinator with IMG, likely to be in the order of £20 million. This was the first time I could remember the word profit being mentioned anywhere since the RWC Sevens in Edinburgh in 1993.

The nine corporate sponsors – Toyota, Coca-Cola, Xerox, VISA, Heineken, SAA, Famous Grouse, Flemings and Iscor – had contributed £1 million each. Eleven smaller South African companies, including Avis, Agfa, Vodacom and Telkom, paid £80,000 for further benefits. Leon Els, the public relations manager for SAA, estimated that 55,000 overseas visitors would make the trip for the World Cup, which was not that many. The pricing policy must have been putting off a lot of supporters, which is probably why so many tickets were returned unsold. All told, SAA would be providing 220 internal flights.

All night long I was waking up, putting on the light and checking my watch. I had foolishly agreed to take a 6.20 a.m. flight down to East London for Western Samoa's game against Argentina. I dragged myself up at 5 a.m and sleepwalked to the airport. The flight, in a twin-propellered aircraft, was uneventful, though as dawn broke the view of East London and its hinterland was impressive. The airport there is something out of *Casablanca*. Three derelict cars cover as taxis; one of them, a Datsun of twenty years' standing, spluttered and coughed its way into town for me. Its driver bore an uncanny resemblance to his car. Not knowing what one is expected to do at 7.30 a.m. in a town that is barely awake, I asked him to give me a guided tour. 'I don't talk politics,' he told me, speaking out of the corner of his mouth. 'I'm from Jo'burg but I been here twenty year. I like the small-town atmosphere. I wouldn't go back, not now. You gotta be careful about these blacks and them coloureds. Ain't right they've taken over just like that. I mean, they get drunk and kick up a fuss and hotels lose their liquor licences and the discos are a riot . . .' I cut short the tour. We made for the Holiday Inn on the front of the wild seashore, where, as it turned out, the Western Samoans were staying.

As I made my way to the Basil Kenyon Stadium, home of Border rugby, the temperature was moving up past 20 degrees Celsius. 'Jeeze, if this is winter,' I muttered to myself, 'what the hell is summer like here?' The streets were paved with men, boys and young men sitting

125

listlessly a few paces down from people who might be their dads. These are the 50 to 60 per cent of the urban population out of work. Their day has already passed its peak. The stadium was a delight. The local people had done their very best to make everyone welcome. It was their big day. The two long stands were fullish and the two grass ends were packed with children from the local black and coloured schools. This might have been the first game of rugby some of them had ever watched. A cooling wind blew down the middle of the pitch as the anthems were played. Both must qualify for some kind of award or record as they stretched into second and then third verses. Still, the spectators respected them – indeed, there had been a new admiration for anthems since the opening ceremony. The game was a thriller: part Chinese firecracker, part a redefinition of the word risk, part a battle between the intuitive skills of the Samoans and the instructive skills of Argentina and part a combination of poetry and magic. From the time that fly-half Darren Kellett kicked a penalty for Western Samoa to take the score to 26–16 midway through the second half, the black sections of this gregarious and animated crowd had begun to dance and cheer in their own version of a Mexican wave. They had adopted the Samoans and desperately wanted them to win. The dancing was taken up at both ends of the ground. You could sense that we were watching something very special unfold in front of us. I was exhausted by the end of it, as were the soulful Argentinians, who, with fifteen minutes to go, had been leading 26–13. They trooped slowly off their field of no dreams, having lost by 26–32.

Worse, having conceded two tries in the space of two minutes in the last five minutes of normal time, they had found the reserves from somewhere deep within their collective psyche to pitch up in front of the Samoans' posts with a penalty in injury time. A converted try could have won them the match. All game they had outscrummaged their opponents, as they had England the previous Saturday – indeed, the game had begun with a penalty try when the Samoans, in desperation, collapsed a scrum on their line for the third time. Against England, Argentina had scored from a short penalty by creating a wedge and forcing their men over the line. It was obvious what they were going to do again. The crowd drew in a collective breath. Were the Samoans, after all their heroics, now going to blow it? Amazingly, the Argentinians went for a pushover try, the higher-risk policy. It

126

meant they had to achieve it in one go, for if the scrum wheeled, or mysteriously collapsed, or whatever, there would not be time for a second scrum before David Bishop, the referee, signalled the end of the match. As Western Samoa prayed that they wouldn't give away another penalty try, the scrum started to go forward. It was moving in the direction of the posts. It looked to be all over. And then the ball got stuck and the Argentinian pack wheeled. The referee called for another scrum, and just as Argentina broke up to prepare to go down for one more last push for victory, Bishop blew his whistle.

For a millisecond, the Samoans could not quite believe it. Argentina, to a man, were utterly overcome by the tragedy they had just enacted. They stood there, looking up to God and down at themselves. How could they have lost this game when the statistics would show that they had won the line-outs and scrums with ease? It was a question which was going to haunt them for a long time to come. This was their third World Cup, and the third time they had failed to progress to the quarter-finals, yet by common consent they had a front row the equal of any, if not the best, in the world and skilful backs. The side found it hard to leave the field, even if it was to a standing ovation.

And the Samoans? First there was the obligatory team photograph and then they moved up to the top end of the field to thank the children for their support. The kids were ecstatic. Next the side went to the far side of the pitch and thanked the crowd there, and then, and most memorably, to the bottom, where they gave a spontaneous demonstration of their version of the *haka*. The children gave them a massive cheer. The game of rugby in South Africa was on take-off. Harness the enthusiasm of these kids and the national side would have tremendous strength in depth. Finally, it was back to the main stand, where even the press stood and applauded them off. We had, to re-emphasize the point, just seen one of the great games.

At the press conference afterwards, the Argentinians failed, understandably, to appear. After an interminable delay, it was the victorious Western Samoans in the persons of Pat Lam, the captain, manager B. G. Williams, the former All Black wing, and Peter Schuster, the coach, who turned up. I asked B. G. where this victory put Western Samoan rugby, given that it was South Africa, Australia and New Zealand who were calling the shots in the southern hemisphere. 'Our players will go and have already to some extent gone to the green fields of New Zealand, Australia and even South Africa. Players will walk. I hope Western Samoa won't be forgotten,' he said, adding later: 'This was the worst game I have had to watch in terms of the heart; it was hair-raising and heart-stopping. It's the most excited I've ever been.'

As I entered the airport departure lounge for my flight back to Durban you could hear a pin drop. No one was moving. All faces were fixed on a point I could not immediately see. And then the penny dropped: of course, South Africa were playing rugby and the country had ground to a halt for the second time in five days. This time they were making a real meal of Romania, and eventually won the game by only 21–8.

Back in Durban I dropped into the media centre and picked up a press release: 'It is with regret that Rugby World Cup, after consultation with the broadcast members of the RWC media consultative committee and with Rushmans, has been forced to withdraw accreditation of Sky Television personnel for the Rugby World Cup 1995 Tournament.' Both Sky and the BBC had been transgressing the rules on news access. The BBC had received a written request to desist; Sky a verbal warning. ITV had been incensed by the presence of cameras in the England dressing room prior to the match against Argentina. Jeremy Thompson, the former ITN correspondent, and now bureau chief of Sky News Africa, said, 'They've been gunning for us from the start. We will continue to cover the World Cup even if we have to report from a car park. Losing accreditation is no big deal. All it means is that we have to buy tickets to the matches. We will now operate as a loose cannon.' Sky's accreditation was reinstated before the quarter-finals after the intervention of Dr Louis Luyt, a rare sensible move. But another agenda was being tabled here, as we were to discover at the end of the tournament.

In the England team hotel some of the players appeared to be involved in making some kind of television show. For the next day's game against Italy, Victor Ubogu had been dropped, Jason Leonard moved across and Graham Rowntree selected for his first full game. Steve Ojomoh, who played for himself against Argentina, made way for Neil Back. Dean Richards had yet to play – indeed, he had yet to finish a full training session, although there was nothing unusual about

Australia were the team of the 1991 tournament and in Nick Farr-Jones and Michael Lynagh they had the two best decision-makers in the game. Here Eduardo Laborde of Argentina attempts to tackle Lynagh.

(*Above*) In 1991 England started badly, losing to New Zealand, but grew in strength with famous victories away to France and Scotland in the quarter- and semi-finals. They could and should have won the World Cup, but crucially they lost their confidence at the last.

(*Left*) They think it's all over…it is now. Australia know they have beaten England by 12–6 – and deservedly so.

David Campese and Nick Farr-Jones. Campese charmed us with his captivating play. Farr-Jones was so overcome by the whole thing that after the game he went home to his wife and baby, leaving Michael Lynagh to do the honours at the official dinner.

And afterwards – champagne in the Cup in the baths at Twickenham.

'I've started so I'll finish.' Rob Andrew's dropped goal cruelly landed Australia in the mire and RWC '95 had its third semi-finalists.

In the third World Cup yet another wing threequarter took the headlines. Jonah Lomu was like a rhinoceros in ballet shoes.

The French deserved a place in the final and should have had it, but their semi-final pitch was more suited to water polo than to rugby. In Marc Cecillon they had the best back-row player of the tournament.

Josh Kronfield just didn't get going in the final. In every other game he played he was Mr Perpetual Motion, scoring some superlative tries and forming a great double-act with Jonah Lomu.

South Africa threw up a number of remarkable players – André Joubert, François Pienaar, Chester Williams, Mark Andrews and Joel Stransky – but one player was irresistible: Joost van der Westhuizen. He had the lowest centre of gravity and the best sense of humour of any player in the tournament.

OPPOSITE: South Africa celebrate after defeating New Zealand 15–12 in the final.

OVERLEAF: The man of the tournament.

that since he is well known for his aversion to training. But serious doubts were being raised about his fitness and the perceived wisdom was that he would be risked in the quarter-finals but might only last a half. England lost the second World Cup because of Richards' absence; without him it was likely that they'd lose the third, too.

The other games on 30 May were France against the Ivory Coast (or Côte d'Ivoire, as they preferred to be called), and Scotland versus Tonga. The Ivorians played well in their 54–18 loss to France, scoring two tries, but the match took a heavy toll on their players and at the end their front row consisted of a substitute prop, a hooker and a substitute hooker as the other prop. France played well below themselves; they seemed, like England, to be waiting for the quarter-finals before they switched up a gear. Scotland, who could do no wrong – especially captain Gavin Hastings, who was playing like his old self – devoured poor Tonga by 41–5 in front of a crowd of 21,000 at Loftus Versfeld, Pretoria. Hastings, who scored a record forty-four points the previous week, claimed a further thirty-one in this game.

On the morning of the England–Italy game I received a cutting from *Business Age*, a remarkably sharp article by Peter Kirwan about RWC '91, RWC '95 and our old friend Alan Callan. It dealt with the widespread unease over the 1991 World Cup finances, which we have already examined. The main sources for the piece appeared to be John Reason, Dudley Wood, Mike Colley and Cliff Morgan. Soon, all the RWC '95 directors, Louis Luyt and Vernon Pugh would be poring over the article too.

Later in the afternoon, surprise, surprise, the heavens opened up yet again to welcome the large crowd to King's Park for the Italian game. The press box, which is in the open, was drenched. The television sets became dangerous and their signal disappeared; our notebooks were useless and our computer screens wouldn't work. Soon the phones were out of action too. All we had to cheer us up was the hope of a vintage performance from England. Some hope.

Unlike South Africa and Australia, Jack Rowell had resisted giving a game to the members of the squad who had not yet played and had selected what he thought was his best side on the day. During a World Cup, a team has to find a rhythm, and playing the whole squad denies the best players that chance. South Africa had demonstrated this the day before in their disappointing match against Romania, and Australia, playing earlier today against a game Canada, followed suit by struggling to win by 27–11.

England beat Italy by 27–20. The Italians had many more ideas outside the scrum but didn't quite have the back row needed these days to support them. Certainly their fly-half, the former Argentinian international Diego Dominguez, was easily the most creative player on view. While England had still to move up a gear, they were beginning to show their old form, although some of us wished they had shown it earlier. I suspected that, providing Western Samoa didn't have too many injuries from their game the day before, they would just beat England. I was to be proved wrong.

At the break, England were leading 16–10, but seven of those points had come right on half-time as a result of a charged-down kick of Mike Catt's. With fifteen minutes to go, they were ahead by 27–10, but they fell asleep in the last quarter, which is unlike England. The changes in the front row proved nothing, and Neil Back didn't have one of his better performances. Bayfield was the pick of the forwards. Still, the win meant that England had made it through to the quarter-finals. Italy, like Argentina, had nothing to show for their two games, but they had won a large number of friends around the world for their endeavour and attitude. At least they seemed to be gaining a foothold towards competing in the International Championship back in Europe for 1996 and beyond, even if it was not in the form they would like: plans were under discussion for each of the Five Nations to play Italy on the odd day each would not be competing in the tournament.

Immediately after the game, those English players on the bench – or at least, Steve Ojomoh and Jon Callard – went through the motions of a training session. It's incredibly difficult being on the bench and knowing that you are unlikely to play. Damian Hopley and Graham Dawe looked to be in this category. Rowell could have boxed clever by playing Callard and moving Catt to fly-half for Saturday's decider against Western Samoa, knowing that they had lost Kellett, their talented fly-half, for the rest of the tournament, but he wouldn't. He'd stick to Andrew and Catt. He had problems in the back row, but Rodber and Clarke were likely to pick up their form at any time. The problem was Neil Back, and whether, after three full internationals, he had found the pace to his liking. The jury was out for the time being.

Before England's game I watched Ireland against Japan on television in the well-equipped and smoothly run media centre by the side of King's Park. The spectators in Pretoria, probably the most knowledgeable rugby crowd in the world, took the Japanese to their hearts. And at one stage the underdogs were giving the overdogs a run for their money. At half-time the score was only 19–14 to Ireland. The best try of the match came in the second half and was scored by the beautifully balanced Japanese fly-half, Seiji Hirao, who had one season playing for Richmond in the mid-1980s. However, it was not enough to eventually prevent the Irish from running up a score of 50–28.

Strangely, although Ireland's and England's matches were live on SABC, the station had chosen to offer a delayed feed for the game of the day between New Zealand and Wales. New Zealand had followed England's example, merely fine-tuning the team rather than going for the wholesale changes South Africa and Australia had embarked upon. The All Blacks had slunk into this tournament by the back door and were delighted not to be considered hot favourites, the tag they had carried through the two previous World Cups.

Laurie Mains, their coach, might not have been everyone's cup of tea in New Zealand, but he had assembled a formidable side if their one showing earlier in the week against Ireland was anything to go by. In his second game, while Alex Evans, the Aussie coach of the Welsh side, had foolishly gone public about his team being able to walk on water, Mains had kept the press at bay. Zinzan Brooke was still unable to play – he and Dean Richards should form a club – but with Andrew Mehrtens, the Durban-born fly-half, Josh Kronfeld, the all-embracing back-row forward who reminded me of a younger Budge Rogers, and Jonah Lomu playing, the omens did not look good for Wales. I listened on the radio, which shared with its television counterparts the tendency to move between Afrikaans and English.

The drift, if I understood the excitement of the Afrikaner commentator correctly, was that the All Blacks were creaming Wales. Later still I caught the highlights on television. The radio boyos were absolutely right. All three of my favourite players performed well, though Mehrtens needed to be more accurate with his place-kicking. Otherwise, he was a joy to watch. Kronfeld looked as though he had a twin

– he was all over the park, tackling and supporting play, and his reward for backing up another of Lomu's barnstorming runs was a try. Lomu seemed to pick up more travellers as his engine moved up a couple of gears on his way to the try-line than any wing threequarter I could recall. Perhaps the only way to contain him would be to nationalize his talents.

New Zealand had begun to look the likely winners of the tournament. The other favourites, South Africa, Australia, England and France, had not found their form in two consecutive matches. Scotland had been untroubled, but their game against France would be their first real trial of the tournament. As we all anticipated, Ireland's game against Wales had become the decider for the other quarter-final spot from Pool C. With one round of matches still to be played at the weekend, only Western Samoa and England from Pool B and Scotland and France from Pool D had definitely qualified for the quarters at this stage. South Africa would surely account for Canada the next Saturday, and Australia likewise for Romania, in Pool A. And so it was to prove.

14

The End of the Pool Matches

I was glad to be back in Jo'burg. I was about to witness two very important games. In Pretoria, Scotland were taking on France and then on Sunday, at Ellis Park, Wales were to play Ireland. Jo'burg, which billed itself as the murder city of the world, had its detractors. Certainly, there were too many no-go areas, but sadly, these days those are a fact of life in most capital cities. Despite a stupid boast from Louis Luyt that visitors to RWC '95 would be safe, Bob Howitt, a journalist from New Zealand, was held up at gunpoint, duffed up and relieved of all his possessions – and this within a so-called safe area inside an apartment block. Two other local rugby journalists were also mugged. Later, David Miller was mugged in Durban, Mick Cleary lost his portable computer and Graeme Thorne, a former All Black, was held up at gunpoint and had his BMW stolen. There were complaints, too, about hotels. As the tournament wore on, there were signs of some residual anger at South Africa having been awarded the event.

Both Johannesburg and Pretoria, especially Pretoria, were home to the more conservative elements of South African life, and the natural language is that of the Afrikaners. But this was also the home of the ANC and the area where, in the national elections in 1994, they gained their highest polls. The South-West Township (Soweto) and Alexandria had yet to appear on a published map of South Africa: as far as the Afrikaner had been concerned, the constituency and its people did not exist. Thankfully, all this was changing.

Pretoria, one of the two South African capitals, hosted the first of the two really important remaining games of the first-round pool, France versus Scotland in Pool D. Earlier in the day, Tonga had beaten the Ivory Coast by 29–11, also in Pool D. Tonga had led 24–0 at half-time, so the Ivorians gained some credit for their second-half display. Sadly, Max Brito, the Ivorian wing, was carried off the field after two minutes following a tackle. The prognosis was bleak. The worst fears were later to be realized. Brito was to end up a quadriplegic. It was the tragedy of the tournament. Nothing could have been done to help him which wasn't. He was whisked by helicopter to the Clinic Holdings Unitas Hospital trauma unit in Pretoria. 'Thankfully,' Sir Ewart Bell said later, 'professional paramedics and air transport were pitchside at all matches to cater for such injuries as these.'

Meanwhile, Australia, after another hesitant start, had accounted for Romania by 42–3 in Pool A. They had rested Lynagh, Campese, Willie Ofahengaue and Little. John Eales surprised us all with some first-class place-kicking, finishing with four conversions. The game was held in the magical arena at Stellenbosch, now called the Danie Craven Stadium, and a crowd of 15,000 turned out to watch in the bright sunshine. The second-half performance of the Aussies showed glimpses of their old form. They might have been coming late to the dance floor, but they could not yet be written off.

The ground at Pretoria was named after Loftus Versfeld, a local administrator and founder of Pretoria RFC in 1899. He was a former Springbok and played against the 1891 British Isles team. The stadium was built to house the Northern Transvaal RFU when they broke away from the Transvaal Union in 1938. The ground has changed much over the past twenty years and today looked quite resplendent, and even though a game between France and Scotland held no real interest for the local population, a crowd of 39,000, just 10,000 short of the capacity, was recorded. It illustrated the extent to which this World Cup had caught the imagination of the South African public.

As the anthems were played, it was quite apparent that support for the Scots was four or five times that for the French. The referee, Wayne Erickson, had a bad game last time out officiating when New Zealand played Ireland. This match was like the curate's egg, good in parts. Well, actually, good in the last ten minutes. In the first half, France simply couldn't get into their stride because of the strength and power plays of the Scottish forwards, who were simply outstanding. 'Del Boy' Cronin was taking all the ball at two in the line and in the back row Rob Wainwright, Iain Morrison and Eric Peters were everywhere. The French simply couldn't settle into any sort of rhythm.

However, a minute before half-time, Scotland were ahead by only 6–3, as a result of the customary exchange of penalties between Hastings and Lacroix. Emile Ntamack, the black winger from Toulouse, had displayed the first glimpse of his talent when he glided effortlessly out from his try-line, going right, and then, just as suddenly, doubling back across his 22, he changed gear and surged past several Scottish players. He reminded me of Guscott at his best in 1989 and 1990. The move petered out 15 metres from the Scottish line, but we had not heard the last of Ntamack, who was revelling in the hard grounds.

For Scotland, Craig Chalmers was having a fine game, mixing high balls with runs close to his back row. On half-time he put a lovely ball up on the blind side for Jean-Luc Sadourny to catch. He did so with ease, swivelled round and aimed the kick towards touch with his left foot. It didn't quite carry. Bryan Redpath intelligently called for the ball and, running parallel to the touchline, set off straight. Suddenly there was no French cover and a try was on, for coming up like a steam train was Gavin Hastings. He cut in and was caught, but Rob Wainwright was there to take the final pass. Hastings converted, the whistle went for half-time.

For the first thirty minutes of the second half, the game had still to catch fire. My notebook recorded two missed penalties from Hastings before Lacroix narrowed the gap to 13–6 in the fifty-fifth minute, and to 13–9 in the fifty-eighth. Hastings responded for 16–9 in the sixty-second minute; Lacroix, sixty-fifth minute, 16–12; Hastings, seventieth minute, 19–12. Then Lacroix, with a monster of a kick from just inside the Scottish half, made it 19–15 with five minutes to go. Lacroix had potted five out of five, Hastings four from seven. But statistics do not tell the picture of how the French tried to play themselves back into the game by using their expansive backs. Time and time again they tried to run indifferent ball; time and time again they were thwarted by the brilliant Scottish defence. Could the Scots hold out? Would the French give away another soft penalty? Christophe Deylaud made two desperate attempts to drop for goal to try to ease French worries. Both failed.

Still the French came again. In their opponents' 22, the ball went from right to left and was held; it went left to right, Ntamack to the fore, and was held. The Scots had done it. The referee signalled that there were two minutes left at a line-out. France won it and spun it yet again; play was held up in midfield. The referee awarded France an indirect free kick for a reason that was unclear. Quickly, they spun the ball back to where it had just come from. The French backs had an overlap, Ntamack appeared from nowhere, dummied, and was over the line. Lacroix converted. The referee blew for full time. The French were through by 22–19. The crowd were stunned; the Scots were shellshocked. Ten minutes earlier they had led by 19–12 and were dreaming of Wales or Ireland in the quarter-finals and a semi-final place; now they faced the All Blacks, a side they had never beaten and everyone's favourites to win the tournament.

France lost two players – Philippe Benetton at number 8 with a fractured right arm and Guy Accoceberry, their scrum-half, with a fractured left arm. Both players were X-rayed on site and their hands were in plaster within twenty minutes of their injuries occurring. First-class rugby players need the medical support currently given to Formula 1 drivers. On this score, the South African authorities couldn't be faulted. Their facilities were simply the best in the world.

After the match, Gavin Hastings said: 'We're still shellshocked. The boys in the dressing room can't believe we've lost. We're feeling the same as the French did in Paris in the Five Nations. Dougie Morgan came in and told us we'd lost a game, not the World Cup, and that we've another game next week.' Pierre Berbizier, the French coach, who admitted to being mightily relieved, commented: 'It was a very emotional moment at the end. It will keep us going now for the rest of the tournament.' Technically, the French backs, though the best on view from the northern hemisphere, were taking the wrong line in attack. They were a metre slower than their All Black counterparts. The Scots, without Gregor Townsend, had no options outside Chalmers. The impartial observer would always, I hope, reward ambition which was why, in the end, I was pleased for France.

Somehow, in the dark without a map, I negotiated my way out of Pretoria. I wanted to get back to catch the Springboks' game against Canada on television. I calculated that I should make it by half-time. When I turned on the set I saw that the score was 3–0 to South Africa. More perplexing, that the game was only a few minutes old.

It was not until I read the next day's papers that I gleaned that the floodlights failed and the kick-off, scheduled for 8 p.m., had been delayed. Not once during the match did SABC bother to put a strap-line across the screen to inform their viewers about what had gone on. 'Just after the anthems, the power to the floodlights went down,' a Canadian told me later. 'There was power in the press box and in the hospitality suites. The spectators, especially those on the far side, became restless and started climbing over people. It looked very dangerous. It was not clear why there wasn't a back-up source for the floodlights.' The delay enabled me to witness the first controversy of the tournament when three players were sent off by referee David McHugh, who was handling his first World Cup game. Shown the door were James Dalton, the Springbok hooker, and from Canada Gareth Rees, the captain, and Rod Snow, a prop.

The game had gone off the boil once South Africa had established a 17–0 lead at half-time; a score which included two pushover tries. Only three more points, for the Springboks, were to be added to the board. Canada could only stay in the game by avoiding both line-outs and scrums. They tried to puncture their opponents' gain-line but time and again they found a robust and organized defence. South Africa's only further chance came when Joubert tried to field a pass meant for Hendriks, but he knocked on. And then it happened. Pieter Hendriks, the Springboks' left wing, was tackled into touch by Winston Stanley. Stanley wanted the ball quickly because the Canadian tactics were to try to keep the ball going to upset South Africa's flow. Hendriks played hard to get and prevented Stanley from grasping the ball. It was a minor fracas. The score was 20–0, and there were only ten minutes to go. It had been a hard but fair contest, and there had been no off-the-ball incidents that I could see.

As Hendriks and Stanley fussed over the ball, Scott Stewart, the Canadian full-back, challenged the world 100-metres record to join the fray and fling himself at Hendriks. Then Dalton arrived. Suddenly, the teams were at war. Whatever had been festering underneath erupted into mayhem. It was unpleasant to watch and for a few moments the referee lost control as there were two separate fights going on. Fortunately, one of the touch-judges was the experienced Stephen Hilditch, who had watched events carefully. Had he had a whistle and been empowered to intercede, he could have stopped the proceedings earlier. Perhaps this might happen in the future.

After a five-minute delay, Dalton, Rees and Snow were sent off. Frankly, he could have dispatched more. I thought the referee should have abandoned the game, but I was unsure of what the repercussions of such a decision might be. It certainly wouldn't have made the game too popular, nor South Africa, but the fact remained that the incident had spoiled the tremendous atmosphere that was building for the final. Immediately afterwards, before he had had time to discuss the matter with his management, François Pienaar, captain turned spin doctor, was being interviewed on live television and already launching into a Free James Dalton campaign. 'We'll definitely appeal,' he declared. Later this became 'Dalton went in as a peacemaker and never threw a punch.'

At the ludicrous hour of 1 a.m., the disciplinary 'committee', which consisted solely of Ray Williams, was held. There were three separate hearings.

The ruling was:

Following the sendings-off of Canadian players number 10 Gareth Rees and number 3 Rod Snow, and South African number 2 James Dalton, three separate disciplinary hearings, chaired by RWC match commissioner Ray Williams, have been held at Boet Erasmus Stadium this evening.

The results of these hearings are as follows:

James Dalton
James Dalton was sent off for fighting. The hearing supported the referee's report, and Dalton has been suspended. He is banned from playing Rugby Union football for a period of thirty days, beginning Sunday 4 June 1995.

Gareth Rees
Gareth Rees was sent off for fighting. The hearing supported the referee's report, and Rees has been suspended. He is banned from playing Rugby Union football for a period of thirty days, beginning Sunday 4 June 1995.

Rod Snow
Rod Snow was sent off for eye-gouging. He has been exonerated

of the eye-gouging charge, but on his own admission, and the evidence submitted by a fellow Canadian player, he has been found guilty of punching, and has been suspended. He is banned from playing Rugby Union football for a period of thirty days, beginning Sunday 4 June 1995.

Any appeal against these suspensions must be made within four hours of 0100hrs on Sunday 4 June 1995.

This was silly. As Canada had been eliminated from the event the suspensions carried different weights. Snow played only eighteen to twenty first-class games in a year, most of which this season would take place immediately after the tournament. Rees wouldn't be playing again until August at the earliest. Dalton, on the other hand, was South Africa's best hooker and his side were favourites to reach the final, so the implications of his suspension were far more serious. Worse, it appeared that Ray Williams had not taken the video evidence into consideration along with the reports from the referee and the respective players and their managements. The requirement for appeals to be lodged within four hours of the hearings – that is, by 5 a.m. – was equally daft.

The full might of the SARFU was brought into operation. They needed to obtain a reprieve for Dalton. Good though Chester Williams was, even he couldn't double as a hooker. Edward Griffiths started to marshal support. I was told by a Canadian source that Canada had received phone calls asking them to change their story. Money was said to have been mentioned, though I found that hard to believe. In due course they made their appeal, which was to be heard on the Monday afternoon. The Canadians, however, caved in. I checked the video of the fight. Gareth Rees did not hit anyone. So why was he dismissed?

From left of field, the RWC directors issued a further press release: 'The Rugby World Cup directors believe that the violence at Boet Erasmus Stadium brought the game into disrepute, and in view of the gravity of the incidents, and after viewing the videotape of the game, they decided to cite Stewart and Hendriks.' It was clear from my own memory that Pieter Hendriks had kicked Gareth Rees on the floor, yet Louis Luyt was incensed that the directors had decided, as they could lawfully do, to ban another South African player.

The last minute of the France–Scotland game and the punch-up at Port Elizabeth dominated the newspapers, the radio and the television coverage on the morning of the Wales–Ireland match at Ellis Park in Johannesburg. But forgotten quickly when we witnessed one of the truly amazing games in the history of rugby as New Zealand's second team beat Japan by 145–17. It was awesome, and I mean awesome. It installed New Zealand, if they weren't already the hot favourites, as the side to beat. The record book was rewritten throughout the game. The previous record victory in a World Cup finals game was Scotland's 89–0 against the Ivory Coast, which was just a week old; the record for any World Cup match had been established by Hong Kong when they defeated Singapore by 164–13 in the qualifying stages for 1995.

The All Blacks' play was quite exhilarating. Marc Ellis scored six tries, another record, which would put pressure on Frank Bunce and Walter Little, the other two centres, for their quarter-final against Scotland. The second-string fly-half, the Southlander Simon Culhane, kicked a prodigious twenty from a possible twenty-one conversions from all over the paddock and his only try gave him a total of forty-five points, one more than Gavin Hastings' tally in the Ivorian match. Poor Japan were simply overwhelmed by the power rugby of the New Zealanders. They could have tackled with greater enthusiasm, but they never gave up and the crowd cheered hugely for their two tries, scored by flanker Hiroyuki Kajihara. Zinzan Brooke couldn't have wished for an easier debut match for his third World Cup. This was a perfect game for him to settle his injuries and wipe the cobwebs from his mind.

Earlier in the afternoon, Italy had achieved the most important result in their history. In Pool B they had beaten Argentina by 31–25, another last-minute upset. This had not been Argentina's tournament. Three close games – indeed, three matches in which the difference was no more than six points – and they had nothing to show for it. For Italy, especially for the Durban-born Cuttitta brothers, the tournament had been a huge success. Had the team tackled in the first half against Western Samoa, they would have qualified for the quarter-finals. Next time, in 1999, they must do so or the game will not grow there. At no stage did the game stand still. Italy led until midway through the first half, but by the interval Argentina had caught up to 12–12. With seven minutes to go, the talented José Luís Cilley scored a try to put Argentina into the lead for the second time, by 25–24. But three minutes later, the little Italian fly-half Diego Dominguez (himself a former Argentinian international), sneaked an interception (mind you, he was a metre offside at the time, at a critical breakdown on his opponents' 22) and before the Argentinians could believe it, he had scored. It served only to disprove the remark, attributed to Gary Player, that the harder he trained the luckier he got. The ball had not run for Argentina in this World Cup and, as in 1987 and 1991, they took an early plane home. If only Cilley had had his kicking boots on. Against Italy he missed two penalties and three conversions, whereas his opposite number, Dominguez, missed just one conversion and two drop-goal attempts right at the end.

For 1999, Wales have borrowed an idea from the Australians' tender document and have agreed to run a plate competition for those eliminated after the pool rounds. Such a bridesmaids' tournament would have provided Argentina with some crumbs of consolation in 1995. They had improved beyond belief in the forwards, but their back play was sterile. Now, they must rethink their domestic and international rugby calendar. Much the same could be said about Italy. The game has taken root in Milan and in and around Venice, but the clubs need to be part of a European league. At least the national side now has the chance to pit itself as a potential 'sixth' nation in the Five Nations Championship.

Meanwhile, in Johannesburg, we prepared for the last match in Pool C, in which Ireland and Wales were to battle it out at Ellis Park for the remaining quarter-final place. The stadium is situated in downtown Jo'burg in one of the worst parts of the city. There was no car parking close to the ground and public transport was indifferent. At the Whitney Houston concert earlier in the year, there had been muggings both inside and outside the ground. The ensuing public outcry led to a noticeable improvement in security for the Phil Collins and Rolling Stones concerts. For the World Cup, the last thing Louis Luyt could afford on his home patch was an outbreak of serious crime, and so a number of secure park-and-ride bases had been organized a mile or so away.

For Ireland and Wales, as for France and Scotland yesterday, a meeting outside the Five Nations Championship was both unfamiliar and important. This encounter would be on a world stage as opposed to a local one. Ireland had beaten Wales at the Arms Park in the last game of the 1995 Five Nations to record their only win of the tournament. Wales thus finished bottom with four losses out of four. They then fired their coaches and brought in an Australian, Alex Evans, who had done wonders with Cardiff. In choosing his squad for South Africa, Evans in effect deselected the Llanelli players and reselected the Cardiff players, swapping the captaincy from Ieuan Evans to Mike Hall. It hurt Ieuan Evans and his form, probably already on the wane, may never recover. The Welsh pack lacked the bulk and the technique up front to trouble anyone. In the backs, even though Jenkins had at last been moved to inside centre, without David Evans, the Treorchy fly-half, the team still lacked anyone who could take on and beat a man, though Skipper Mike Hall at centre gave himself plenty of practice.

All the Irish had going for them was passion. Moreover, it had been a notable element of their play that they had rarely learned from one game to the next. Their matches against New Zealand and Japan had been played at a furious rate but without a cool head to guide them in the backs. Simon Geoghegan, after a disappointing season in 1994, was now back with a vengeance and was their one truly world-class player.

The ground was two-thirds full. There seemed to be some discrepancy as to what the exact capacity of Ellis Park was for the World Cup. One source said 62,000; another 70,000. Whatever it was, the stadium was magnificent and again the turf was short, springy and welcoming, faster than anything I had experienced back in the UK.

Eric Elwood kicked off, and for once the height of his kick allowed his forwards to reach the ball. From the maul, Ireland were very nearly over and had Hogan, at scrum-half, not dummied and been caught, Ireland would have scored in the corner. A penalty was awarded, but uncharacteristically, Elwood missed. What a start, though. Then a lovely penalty from out of the hand by Elwood was caught by Clement, but his footprints just fell on the line. Ireland had the throw 5 metres out. Gabriel Fulcher caught it at the line-out, and after a diving wedge, Nick Popplewell was over. Elwood converted and six minutes into the game Ireland were 7–0 ahead. Wales had hardly been visible.

Soon afterwards, Elwood tried to increase the lead with a 55-metre penalty, but it fell just under the posts. Elwood, for some reason, was not half the player he had been. Although his up-and-unders generally had more snow on them than anyone else's in the tournament, his penalties, drop attempts and line-kicking were no longer out of the top drawer. Within the first three minutes he had missed a penalty kick he could have normally taken with his eyes closed and then he fluffed a drop kick. Maybe the tension was getting to him. The Ireland team, though, were looking sharp, taking quick throw-ins and working the ball faster through the hands than they had done in their game against the All Blacks. An innocuous line-out ball landed in the hands of a surprised Denis McBride. He charged to the Welsh 22 to set up a maul, but found it was unnecessary: he escaped with the ball intact to race to the posts for Elwood to convert. With fourteen minutes gone it was 14–0.

Wales must have wondered if their game had a second verse to it, but much was at stake here. A penalty in the twenty-seventh minute from Neil Jenkins gave the Welsh more confidence and a beautifully stroked kick by fly-half Adrian Davies rolled into touch and offered the Welsh a chance on the Irish line. The line-out went against the Welsh and a scrum ensued. The Welsh tried twice to push the Irish over their own line, but they were having none of it. When the ball went wide Hall gave a high half-chance to Evans on the wing, but he was held in the tackle by Geoghegan and although the ball was released to Jenkins, Bell tackled him out of sight. It was great defence.

And that was it in the first half, aside from a Mexican wave which went three times round the ground – a comment, perhaps, on the entertainment value of events on the field. Thankfully, it was punctuated at the last by an Adrian Davies dropped goal which seemed to take an age to go over. Curiously, the Ellis Park PA system also played music whenever there was a stoppage to the game, including a reprise of the national anthems. Perhaps the DJ was at the wrong party – or perhaps, like the Mexican wave, it was an attempt to provide an alternative diversion. The crowd certainly needed one.

The second half at one stage resembled a game of aerial ping-pong, the Irish apparently content to kick the ball over the Welsh dead-ball area and then wait for the resultant long drop-out from Adrian Davies. Wales, finally becoming aware that this was getting them nowhere, changed tactics and Neil Jenkins took the long drops instead. David Evans would not have stood for this. Still, the inevitable penalty arrived from Jenkins' boot, and with twenty-five minutes to go the score was 14–9.

Ireland mounted one last attack. Elwood collected a loose kick from Ieuan Evans, not noticing that Clement was inside him. Elwood had a rush of blood to the head and started to run. It didn't last long, but he rolled a kick into touch 10 metres from the Welsh line. At the line Gareth Llewellyn knocked on and from the scrum Ireland brought Geoghegan twisting in from the left. He went through three tackles and set up a maul which led to Eddie Halvey, on as a blood replacement, crashing over. Elwood converted for 21–9.

But Wales had not quite given up yet. A piece of quick thinking by Ieuan Evans led ultimately to Clements, easily the best Welsh back on view, going through some poor tackling to put hooker Jonathan Humphreys in under the posts. Jenkins' goal made it 21–16. Once again, a game of mind-numbing badness had raised itself and the crowd to the edge of their seats. Another match was going to the wire. Elwood then killed it dead with his first penalty goal and we all began to mentally pack our bags. And that, in a sense, was the wonder of this tournament, for no sooner had we 'left' the game and begun to think about our opening paragraphs than Wales scored at the last gasp, Hemi Taylor going over and Jenkins converting. But it was just too late. Ireland had scraped through by 24–23.

What of Wales now? Vernon Pugh had had the IB on his mind for the previous year and although he hoped to be made the long-term first chairman of the IB in 1996, for a period of three years, he still had to mastermind the 1999 World Cup and the renaissance of Welsh rugby. He is used to working long hours, but this demanding schedule was too much for any one man to shoulder.

On the team's return to Wales, Mike Hall, the captain, gave an interview in which he chastised the current thinking in the Principality, concluding with a statement that he was considering going to Rugby League. A lot of Welsh players would be considering their future. The real problem was a dearth of creative thinkers in club coaching. Wales needed to plunder the best from New Zealand and Australia before others did.

There was one last pool game to go: England against Western Samoa in Durban that evening. It appeared as though England had, at last, found second gear and sometimes third, but that a lack of concentration caused the scoring to lapse from 21–0 at half-time to 21–17 after twelve minutes of the second half. Nevertheless, whereas before they would have folded and hung on, this time England responded more like their old selves, in the main because Richards was playing, which also meant that Dewi Morris at scrum-half had his best game to date. Without Richards this team would not win the World Cup.

15

No Quarter Asked; None Given

The quarter-finals, then, were to be largely as everyone had predicted: France–Ireland in Durban; South Africa–Western Samoa in Johannesburg; England–Australia in Cape Town and New Zealand–Scotland in Pretoria.

The week between the pool matches and the quarter-finals was the toughest for the media, who were reduced to writing gripping articles about Back's hamstring or Bracken's heels. All the sports editors of radio, television and newspapers had to try, however difficult it was, to engineer enough stories to keep our appetites whetted. It was pretty obvious, then, that in Monday's and Tuesday's newspapers Welsh rugby would be in for some unwelcome attention, and so it proved. 'Wales sink to new depths of ineptitude' was the headline in the *Independent*. 'Wales back to basics' announced the *Guardian*. England, meanwhile, received half a fanfare for their steely performance against Western Samoa. Thereafter, everyone was struggling. Stories about hotels, dangerous downtown Jo'burg, Scotland's pettiness about having to move hotels (they'd known about it for nine months), and player 'inside story' columns predominated. There was no news.

The South African Free James Dalton campaign failed on Monday afternoon. Pieter Hendriks was suspended for ninety days and Scott Stewart for sixty. The rules permitted South Africa to replace their two players. Chester Williams, who was spared from having to try his hand at hooker by the call-up of Naka Drotské, was given the wing place that had originally been his before his hamstring tweak. Morné du Plessis admitted that he was a little surprised that the regulations allowed him to bring in a player as good as Williams. Most of us were pleased that one of the world's great players had at last been able to join the rugby circus. The Springboks had packed every high and every low normally experienced in an eight-week overseas tour into eleven days. It had taken more out of them than they had realized, and this meant they could come unstuck against the French in the semi-finals. Only time would tell. The week off was good for everyone. Only the English and the Western Samoans did not go on safari or to Sun City for a day. Instead they trained.

There were three stories that made an impression during the inter-regnum between the pool games and the quarter-finals. Martin Bay-field's discussion about the nature of cheating in the line-out (now there's a surprise) became major news; David Campese came out of hibernation to sledge England and James Dalton's solicitor went public about her intention to sue RWC but then changed her mind.

Despite viewing figures of 7.9 million for Wales versus New Zealand and 8 million for England–Italy and Ireland–Japan, back in Britain ITV's press coverage of the tournament was taking a bit of a pounding. Giles Smith commented in the *Independent*:

> ITV's Rugby World Cup symbol, which flashes at us before and after the commercial breaks, is a flaming oval ball. There have been times this week when it's been possible to assume the fire was started by angered viewers and likely to spread to the studio at any moment. We're not through the preliminary rounds, but the channel has already come in for some vigorous mauling and many now wonder whether it might not have to come home injured before the later stages . . . ITV's main problem at the moment is, it seems to me, neither lateness nor replays, but a lack of focus. There are too many faces out there – Alastair Hignell, Mark Austin, Mary Nightingale, a posse of Chrises, one or two Steves, various Clives and the occasional Gareth. And none of them dominates or anchors the coverage. We're talking about a tragic lack of Lynam. But what is odd is that, while the new boys Austin and Hignell smile and try not to look as if the water has just reached their chins, the amplified Jim Rosenthal is out there, mysteriously consigned to the interview beat.

Essentially, the programmes between the pool matches and the quarter-finals suffered, like the print reportage, from the lack of news.

The coverage was fronted by Alastair Hignell, a former England full-back and Gloucestershire cricketer, who lacked gravitas. Editorially, the programme I saw couldn't make up its mind whether it was a Hello-style magazine show or a proper preview of the quarter-finals. In fact it was neither, and the worse for that. There was far too much cutting in from other presenter journalists, and consequently the pieces lacked depth.

The advertising and communications industries – don't ask me what the difference is – took the closest interest in the rugby World Cup. In both South Africa and Britain it was easily the biggest event of the year and therefore created enormous media activity; in South Africa it was overwhelming. In South Africa there were some very funny advertisements, which pleasantly surprised me, and again demonstrated the social changes that were being wished for. Generally, in the commercial breaks in the SABC coverage, via TopSport, five of the six or seven ads had a rugby theme. Shell had a Morné du Plessis ad, Standard Bank an over-long spoof of the All Black *haka*, which on first showing was extremely amusing, although by the thirty-first time it had become a shade tedious. A restaurant chain did a rip-off of the *When Harry Met Sally* orgasm scene with François Pienaar playing Harry. Unfortunately, as well as the conventional commercials, there were also 'spot' advertisements during the programmes. These were decidedly intrusive and, combined with the three different language commentaries, made you want to switch channels. I'm not sure it was possible for the viewer to accept the very poor production values of the coverage of the matches on top of all the messages flying about on the screen.

In Britain the messages were more subtle, it being, apparently, a more sophisticated audience. The agency S.P. Lintas launched a series of thirty print ads to promote Radio 5 Live's coverage. Before the first England game, against Argentina, they used Carling's 'farts' comment to good effect. A picture of Carling bore the strapline 'Silent But Deadly', followed by 'Will Carling Lets Rip on Radio 5 Live'. Nike, who provided boots for the England squad and who have won a series of awards through their agency, Simons Palmer Denton Clemmow and Johnson, for their poster campaigns, featuring, among others, the England front row, returned with a TV commercial using an extract from the Rupert Brooke poem 'The Soldier' – 'think only this of me: That there's some corner of a foreign field That is for ever England'. It included fabulously shot footage from the Five Nations and Hong Kong Sevens tournament. Indeed, it was often better than the rugby itself.

The team news for the weekend matches attracted most attention. Four sides were announced. England had reverted to form. Although Jack Rowell described Kyran Bracken's game against Italy as 'easily his best game in an England shirt', he was the only change in the XV that took the Five Nations Championship, losing out to Dewi Morris. Bracken was injured, which might have affected the choice. Dean Richards was back, but we still did not know for how long. Victor Ubogu was retained in the front row, Tony Underwood just survived the challenge of Ian Hunter on the right wing and Jeremy Guscott kept his place in the centre, where Phil de Glanville had deserved his chance.

Australia, their quarter-final opponents, brought back the centre partnership of Tim Horan and Jason Little. Matt Burke was preferred to Matthew Pini at full-back and Tony Daly failed to win back his spot at loose-head prop. George Gregan was lucky to survive at scrum-half.

For South Africa, James Small and Joel Stransky were unavailable through injury at right wing and fly-half respectively and Hennie le Roux and Gavin Johnson were selected in their places. Chester Williams and Chris Rossouw replaced Pieter Hendriks and James Dalton respectively. In the back row, where South Africa had an incredible number of outstanding players, Rudolf Straeuli and Ruben Kruger got the nod alongside François Pienaar.

France were, of course, decimated by the injury count from the previous Saturday's game against Scotland. Aubin Hueber and Abdelatif Benazzi replaced Guy Accoceberry and Philippe Benetton with 32-year-old veteran Louis Armary being recalled at loose-head prop for Laurent Benezech. France could just go all the way to the final.

Scotland kept the side which started against France; Ireland selected newcomer Darragh O'Mahony on the wing instead of Richard Wallace and New Zealand were spared having to make any difficult decisions about the full-back spot when Gary Osborne pulled out. Jeff Wilson was moved from wing to replace Osborne, which allowed Marc Ellis to remain on the right wing with Bunce and Little staying in the centre and Jonah Lomu coming in from left field. Mike Brewer was preferred on the flank and Richard Loe was picked ahead of Craig Dowd at loose-head prop.

Driving into Jo'burg for South Africa's quarter-final against Western Samoa, the city looked more welcoming than of late; the crisp air was matched by the steely blue skies, and only the odd puff of smog spoiled the skyline. The local paper, the Saturday *Star*, was still wallowing in the Dalton Affair. One whole page of a broadsheet was given over to it in the main part of the paper. The drift in all the articles was that he was basically innocent. The media centre was packed. We had clearly all had the same idea, which was to make it to the ground before France versus Ireland kicked off on television from Durban. In 1991 the bill for media accreditation was close to £3 million; for RWC '95 it was reduced to £2 million. The television and, to a much lesser extent, radio companies, whose global presence underwrites the profitability of each rugby World Cup, pay a considerable amount of money to ensure that they have exclusive access to it. The print journalists do not pay a penny. Soon, an issue that will be fiercely contested by the print journalists, their sports editors and newspaper owners has to be confronted. They cannot expect to receive such outstanding facilities free. Moreover, photographers take pictures of players and then sell them on without the player or his union receiving a fee.

The players, too, had excellent facilities at Ellis Park. Throughout the tournament the Springboks, like all the other teams, naturally spent hours dissecting their own play and that of the opposition, and to help them Rudy Joubert, director of coaching at Transvaal, on loan to the South African side, had installed a digital editing suite at the stadium. A player no longer had to rewind or refind information – the technology did it for him. He had the facility to type in, say, the word 'line-out', and within minutes all the line-outs in a game would appear on one piece of film which could then be dumped on to a video. The player could then take the tape home or to his hotel room for further study. The system was de rigueur in American football, but as far as I was aware only the Australian Rugby Union so far used such advanced equipment. For RWC '95, the ARU brought a six-man video unit to assist Bob Dwyer and his coaches.

The first quarter-final was not difficult to predict. France were likely to win it with something to spare. The second one here at Ellis

Park between South Africa and Western Samoa would go the hosts' way. Australia versus England was harder to call. England, said my heart; Australia, though, had the greater potential. I plumped for England. New Zealand would account for Scotland.

France's game against Ireland kicked off ten minutes late owing to some kind of technical difficulty. The first half was patchy. These were two nervous sides unable to impose any kind of order on their respective games, a problem which was compounded by the fact that neither set of forwards seemed able to exert their authority over the other. In the early exchanges, France were the edgier. It was always going to be a question of whether or not Irish fervour coupled with Eric Elwood's boot would suffice for eighty minutes. Ireland put the first points on the board with a penalty goal, and by half-time four penalties to Elwood matched by four from Lacroix took the score to 12–12. But France had shown in flashes of play that their game plan had a little more flexibility to it. Deylaud missed a brace of drop-kicks, but otherwise it was an eminently forgettable first half.

Going into the last quarter of the game, France led by 18–12 – yes, two more penalties by Lacroix was all the French had to show for their overall dominance. Ireland's line was not exactly under siege, but it was certainly under intense pressure. Twice the French scrum tried for a pushover try: twice Ireland refused to budge. With fifteen minutes to the end, the Irish finally found the markers to take them into the French 22 for the first time in the second half. The inevitable penalty followed, but instead of going for a flying wedge or its equivalent, Elwood was asked to go for goal. Crucially, he missed, and with his failure went the end of the Irish challenge. It was left to the trusty boot of Lacroix to kill the game with his seventh penalty goal from eight kicks. There was time enough for the eighth, and Ireland finished desperately trying to attack. However, you cannot suddenly attack at the end of a game and expect results.

At the last, or so we thought, Philippe Saint-André, the French captain, scored by the posts and Lacroix added the extra points. Ireland, though, had by then lost the game. They valiantly tried to attack again, but on his own 22, Emile Ntamack intercepted and scorched the turf to score on full-time. The 36–12 result fairly reflected the difference in ability between the two sides. France had been notoriously slow starters, but I felt there was still much to come from them.

So we had our first semi-finalists and, more importantly, France had given themselves a chance to pre-qualify for RWC '99, because even if they progressed no further, they would play off for third place – for 1999, only the two finalists, the third-placed team and the hosts, Wales, would qualify automatically. Ireland had done well to reach the quarters, but this was the limit of their ambition.

Ellis Park was nearly full for the second of the four quarter-finals. Quite why it wasn't completely full was difficult to fathom. The ticketing operation had been out of kilter for the whole tournament. The crowd waved the new South African flag in large numbers. One of the many handmade posters read: 'Your Verdict Stinks. You Old Farts. Dalton is Innocent.' The ground had some new sponsors not previously announced. Gauloises Blondes had crept in, as had Welcome to Wales 1999. The latter was understandable; the former a disgrace.

The spectators struggled with the new 'Nkosi Sikelel'iAfrika' anthem, but were desperate to show their enthusiasm for it; the old anthem, 'Die Stem', was sung with gusto and you could almost hear the jackboots marching. The Western Samoan anthem started with the words 'Oh Flower of Scotland'. I could imagine a phone call from Louis Luyt's private suite firing the controller of music at the ground. After about six or seven bars the tune was changed, but the damage had been done. Pat Lam, the Western Samoan captain, had of course realized that a mistake had been made and had drawn his side into a circle to save further embarrassment.

Western Samoa kicked off, intelligently going blind, but the kick went into touch. From the scrum, Joost van der Westhuizen was off galloping like a gazelle through the Western Samoan defence. The ball was kicked desperately out of defence but on first bounce it landed in André Joubert's hands. A nanosecond later, his neck was nearly deposited in the third row of the stand by a high tackle from George Harder. There seemed to be twenty Springboks on the field during the opening exchanges. They were everywhere. The score in the previous encounter between the two countries, 61–8, sprang to mind. Gavin Johnson completely missed his first kick at goal – it narrowly avoided the corner flag – but calmed down for his second to give South Africa the lead. The Samoans looked bewilderingly out of their depth, which was not how I remembered them from their previous game, in East

152

London against Argentina. Twice, fly-half Fata Sini kicked the ball; twice it went into touch. It simply wasn't their style. They'd been watching too much rugby from Wales and Ireland.

Western Samoa seemed to realize the error of their ways, for the first real chance they had to run the ball left and then right seriously threatened the South African defensive record that had stood up so well against the Canadians. It led to a penalty from Tupo Fa'amasino, but kicking with his left foot, and from the 'wrong' side, he too missed. The supporters wanted more, and soon a wonderfully flowing movement ended with Chester Williams scoring from the first pass he received – but not before André Joubert had been brutally felled by Mike Umaga, the Samoan full-back. The referee missed it, as did most of the spectators, but on the large replay screens it was difficult to avoid noticing it a second time. Joubert was off and Brendan Venter replaced him. The advantage the screens gave the crowd in identifying illegal hits not spotted by the referee set some of them against him. Nothing less than a thrashing would satisfy the crowd now.

Fa'amasino missed a kick in front of the post from 40 metres. Then Van der Westhuizen made another major indentation in Western Samoa's defence and, with two players outside, kicked ahead. At the same time he was felled with such ferocity that the culprit, Mike Umaga, should unquestionably have been sent off. But as the referee, Jim Fleming, missed this incident, as he had the attack on Joubert, all South Africa had to show for it was three points from a penalty by Gavin Johnson. It was 11–0. For ten minutes the Springboks were sucked in by the indiscipline of their opponents and their approach was ragged and not worthy of potential finalists. Still, their second try, also scored by Chester Williams, was a beauty, coming from sustained pressure in which the back row featured strongly. But the 16–0 lead had a price: Joubert had been led from the field holding his left hand. An X-ray later revealed a broken bone and Joubert was out, a serious blow for the South Africans.

What was becoming obvious was the brilliant form of Joost van der Westhuizen. His sniping runs from the base of the scrum and loose play created huge holes in the Samoan defence, but rather than stop and look for support, he preferred to kick through, almost as if he had decided to do so before using his peripheral vision to check who was up in support. From another of these many runs, in which he was again felled, South Africa were awarded a penalty, and Chris Rossouw, the new hooker, scored with ease. Johnson converted for a 23–0 lead at half-time.

The waiting was definitely over for Chester Williams, in more ways than one. Seven minutes into the half, he had scored a hat-trick. Johnson converted all three tries. From then on it was really a question of how many the Springboks could score without resting on their laurels. Mark Andrews was well supported when he took a two-handed catch at a line-out on the Western Samoan line and was thrust over.

Yet the expected avalanche of points never arrived. The crowd, impatient with the game, which had nowhere to go, started their customary Mexican wave. It went on and on and on. Somewhere amid all this, after many attempts and near-misses, Tu Nu'uali'itia, the jack-in-the-box Western Samoan scrum-half, scored a try, which was converted by Fa'amasino. This was the last sight of any purposeful rugby, for the South Africans, now devoid of any discipline, then let Shem Tatupu in under the posts. Fa'amasino added the extra points for 35–14.

At least Chester Williams could claim he had tested his hamstring to the full, even if his fourth try was a result of his pack carrying him over the line and, by the look of it, failing to ground it anyway. But the try was awarded, and Johnson, now getting the hang of things, nonchalantly converted to bring the final score to 42–14.

It was a game too far for the effervescent Western Samoans. One aspect of the South African play which had so far been overlooked was their robust and organized defence. As for Jim Fleming, he had had better games as a referee. He thought he ought to be awarded the final, but on this showing it was unlikely. He had missed too much both at the line-out and off the ball. The referees were beginning to hope that they would be the lucky one to be awarded the final. There were mixed feelings about their own countries doing well – if a referee's home nation reached the final, it would of course put him out of the reckoning. The two best referees to date had been Derek Bevan of Wales and Ed Morrison of England. Bevan, it was felt, was clearly the best in the world at that moment.

After the match it was suggested that Pat Lam, the Western Samoan captain, had been bitten either on the ear or the leg and that racist comments had been made to him as he left the pitch. It was all a storm in a teacup. Most people were still wincing at the ferocity of Western Samoa's tackling. The next day, Sir Ewart Bell announced that the Rugby World Cup directors were again citing a player, this time the Western Samoan full-back, Mike Umaga, and that there would be a meeting on the Monday to decide his fate. Umaga was to be suspended for ninety days, reduced to sixty on appeal.

On Sunday I made my way to Loftus Versfeld for the New Zealand–Scotland quarter-final. I had come to the ground early because the RWC directors had organized a press conference for Max Brito's mother. Max, the player caught at the bottom of ruck during the Ivory Coast versus Tonga game, had now been diagnosed as quadriplegic. Marcel Martin had in fact been at the match at which this tragic incident had occurred. He addressed the gathering with a degree of sensitivity frequently lacking in rugby circles.

'We all have mothers,' he said, 'and we must have some idea of how Madame Brito feels at this time. The RWC directors have flown her and her son, Fabrice, here so that she can be with Max. Understand what she is going through too.' He asked Madame Brito if she would like to say something to the assembled press. Gently, he put his arm round her and spoke softly to her in French. It was clear she was not ready to say anything. Her other son, who had accompanied her, seeing her distress, bravely stepped in. Fabrice was only nineteen years of age. He too played rugby in France, for Tiros, and but for a knee injury he would have been playing alongside his elder brother. 'My brother has been very well looked after. I hope the injury will never be allowed to happen again. Thank you,' he said. Eventually, Madame Yolande Brito responded, but it was all she could do to stem the tears: 'Thank you for your support. Max has been well looked after. Thank you. Thank you.'

There were no questions from the press. The Britos left, but Sir Ewart Bell and Marcel Martin remained to take further questions. 'I've had some experience of dealing with these types of injuries and I know that the injured need somewhere between £300,000 and £500,000 to have a secure future,' I told them. 'In twenty years' time they will need their bungalow to be completely refitted and will have got through a couple of specially designed cars. How much will Max receive?'

'That is a matter between the medical insurance company and Max,' replied Martin. He would not be drawn on the exact amount that would be available for Max and his family. He expressed his own thanks: 'I would like to thank everyone who has helped in this tragic case, especially for the feelings of sympathy that have come in from all round the world; the Northern Transvaal RFU and their liaison officers, who have been quite wonderful, and finally the hospital and its staff, who have been outstanding.'

The directors were asked their views on mismatches. There had been some in this tournament, and for Rugby World Cup '99 the tournament was due to be extended to twenty countries, which could lead to more and increase the chance of this type of injury occurring again. Sir Ewart Bell replied: 'Off the top of my head, let's see who those four additional countries might be. From Africa probably Namibia; from the Americas, the USA; from the Pacific, Fiji; and from Europe, maybe Spain is the emerging nation. They would run a number of countries currently here pretty close. I watched the Ireland–Japan encounter; you know, twice Japan came within five points of Ireland's total. They have said that they would rather be here than not, and I think that would be the view of all the countries, even the Ivory Coast, who improved in every game. I grant you we must look at how the tournament for 1999 should be run, and we will, and you're right to ask us how we should do this but we haven't made up our minds.'

Marcel Martin chipped in: 'You must remember that it wasn't so long ago that a [Five Nations] country lost to New Zealand by forty points.'

'And that was under the old try-scoring laws, too,' prompted Bell.

As none of us could recall which game this was, Martin put us out of our misery by reminding us that it was New Zealand against Scotland in 1981 (40–15), but he could just as easily have mentioned 1994, when Scotland lost by 51–15.

On the question of whether the large replay screens at Ellis Park should be allowed inside a stadium, or whether, as happens in cricket with a third umpire, the technology should be used to help with difficult decisions, Sir Ewart said: 'I can see and understand the use of them in cricket when there is a run-out and the decision is close. There really are not the same kind of decisions in rugby. We will have to address the point about screens in the stadium, but I wouldn't be in favour of using television during a game: I think it would hold it up.' Marcel Martin added: 'You must remember that American football did use [the screens in making decisions] for some years, but have now discontinued it.'

Sunday 11 June 1995 was a big day for the global game of rugby. One of the two fancied seeds for the final had to go out. South Africa, by beating Australia in the opening game, had affected the progression of the tournament (which, remember, had been recast in 1993 in favour of the southern hemisphere countries) in two ways: they had virtually ensured their own place in the final by avoiding England in the quarters, and in the process they had dealt everyone else a harder route.

England would be playing Australia at Newlands exactly one year to the day after they were humiliated by South Africa in the Second Test of their last tour there by 27–9. There was more than rugby honour at stake: at home, England's soccer team had been comprehensively carpeted by the bejewelled Brazilians, 3–1; the cricket team was experiencing similar pain against the West Indies attack in the opening Test and the first Derby to be run on a Saturday had gone to a complete outsider, Lammtarra. So the whole sporting reputation of England rested on the shoulders of Jack Rowell's side. If there was an omen, it was that a horse named Carling was to win a French Classic run during the England–Australia game.

By the time I got to a television set Dean Richards was already off the field. Michael Lynagh and Rob Andrew had soon exchanged greetings cards before Andrew took England into a 6–3 lead with a difficult penalty on the right-hand side of the 22. Great pressure close to the Aussie line led to Andrew missing a crucial dropped goal when he had spare men outside. The Wallabies always looked on the drop-out from the 22 or the kick from the centre as an offensive tactic, and over the years they had devised a number of ruses to ensure that they gained from the situation rather than their opponents. This time Campese kicked very, very deep, thus relieving the pressure at one end and creating it at the other. From this scenario Lynagh moved the ball wide on what backs call a run-round – that is, he passed to Horan and then he ran round to collect the ball again. But this time he dropped it. Carling picked up and passed down the line to Tony Underwood, and all of a sudden a try was on, just like the one England scored against Italy. It only remained for Underwood to fend off Damian Smith, 3 metres out. Fortunately Smith went high and Underwood was in close to the posts for a breathtaking try. Andrew's conversion made it 13–3.

Lynagh then missed a relatively easy kick at goal, and you felt that he wasn't enjoying the day. Campo, as he so often is, was the defensive inspirational force; some of his line-kicking was excellent. England had the measure of the Aussies in the line-out, there was nothing in the scrums yet and the ruck and maul ball was going England's way. Lynagh, though, had another chance, and this time he did not disappoint, taking his Test record to over 900 points. You hoped England were not going to defend for the next forty minutes, but the half-time score of 13–6 did not represent the true superiority of their performance.

In the second half Australia kicked off and the England forwards failed to gather correctly. From the scrum, Lynagh chipped a high kick into the box. Both Tony Underwood and Mike Catt uncharacteristically chose to be out to lunch and Damian Smith, the left winger, took the opportunity to sup at the high table. Lynagh converted from touch. Game on. All that effort in the first half had come to nothing – the scores were now level at 13–13.

It was then a question of who would wilt first. It was evident that the match would be decided by either Lynagh or Andrew, as both defences preferred to give away penalties rather than score tries. Andrew was first to respond, with a goal from a forward maul which the Aussies had deliberately collapsed. England should have run the penalty using a wedge-style tactic, or even asked for the scrum again. But, six minutes into the second half, it was another goal from Andrew and 16–13. Two minutes later, Lynagh returned the compliment for 16–16.

England's tactics were predictable and effective. The forwards won the ball, Andrew kicked it up in the air; the Australians caught it or shielded it, won the maul and/or scrum and tried to run it or kick for touch. This was not their game plan, but under pressure they had forgotten their script. True, John Eales was having an immense game in the line-out, but all too often Australia's kicks weren't even reaching touch. In the fifty-ninth minute, Lynagh popped over another penalty after Morris was found guilty, wrongly, of being offside at scrum, and Australia took the lead for the first time, 16–19. Sure enough, Andrew returned the honours barely two minutes later to level matters again. Neither side were able to establish dominance. The game moved fractionally in favour of Australia when, in the sixty-fifth minute, Lynagh made it 19–22.

The tension was unbearable. I couldn't watch; I went for a walk and found myself in front of someone else's television set. England could not afford to blow this one. If I was having trouble watching, the Newlands crowd and the players must have really felt this game going to the wire. Andrew missed a penalty from 55 metres. Who was going to break the deadlock? Finally, with four minutes of play to go, Andrew brought England back to 22–22. The relief was felt around the world (Australia excepted). Two poor Wallaby touch-kicks kept the ball in play and England in the game.

As the seconds ticked away, extra time seemed a certainty. Then Mike Catt stroked a penalty from the England 22 to the 10-metre line. Dean Richards asked Andrew what he wanted. Space for a drop, came the reply. Bayfield won the line-out; the England forwards drove on to the 22; Morris released the ball – Andrew dropped the goal. We were two minutes thirty-six seconds into injury time. The ball went through the posts ('and on round the world', wrote Frank Keating in the *Guardian* the next day). For an instant no one could quite believe what had happened (with the possible exception of those Bath supporters who had seen Stuart Barnes perform the same feat to demolish Harlequins in the 1993 Cup final). At last the whistle went for full time. The players went bananas. Very soon the whole stadium was awash with emotion – for both the winners and for the gallant Australians. England were through by 25–22 and the world champions were beaten and out of the tournament. The rugby World Cup had finally come alive. You had to pinch yourself to check that you weren't dreaming. 'Perhaps,' said John Reason to me, 'they'll give Dave Alred a knighthood.' Kicking coach Alred had honed Andrew's technique in rather the same way as David Leadbetter had restyled Nick Faldo's swing.

By making it to the semis, England now stood a chance of pre-qualifying for the 1999 tournament. Better still, the northern hemisphere had secured two of the four berths in the penultimate stage of this one. Yet I wasn't so sure that the England win was necessarily good for rugby in the long term. The team, particularly the forwards, were bearing more and more of a resemblance to a basketball team of 7ft wonders. They would go to one end and score (or their penalty-taker would) and then retreat and wait for the opposition (or their penalty-taker) to score. Was this end game what the new laws intended? It seemed more like a cross between American football – especially the hits – and rollerball – especially the hits.

I pictured the nation mopping up floods of tears at home. Watching such an emotionally charged game on television, even if you are in the country where it is taking place, cannot be the same as being there or at home viewing with friends and sharing a beer or two.

The fixture between New Zealand and Scotland could hardly be considered a game of no importance, whatever had happened in the Cape. Scotland had never beaten New Zealand. Gavin Hastings was playing his last game and no doubt a number of others would be thinking that this might be their swansong, too. This World Cup had taken its mental and physical toll of a large number of northern hemisphere players. For the All Blacks, Sean Fitzpatrick, their captain, was playing his hundredth game in a New Zealand jersey (his sixty-sixth cap). Only 2,500 New Zealanders had decided to come to South Africa. One theory for this modest showing was that it was just too expensive, another was that they didn't think they were going to win. Now, however, the All Blacks were installed as firm favourites.

Scotland needed to begin the game with exactly the right mental attitude. They had to unsettle the Blacks, rather as the Canadians had done the South Africans and the Welsh should have done the Irish. They did just that. They kicked off with a short kick which trickled over the All Blacks' 10-metre line in the centre of the field. They even won the race to the ball, though they could not secure it. This move was the first evidence that the Scots were in a different ball game from the one they took part in a week previously against France.

For the whole eighty minutes the Scots tried to make a match of it, and as the final score suggested, the traffic wasn't all one way, for they managed to score three tries in their 48–30 defeat. But in truth, they were never in it. They had a chance to seriously influence the game when, at 7–6, Redpath chose to run a short penalty close to the

New Zealand line. His upper-body strength was insufficient and his challenge was repelled. So Scotland, instead of being 9–7 up, remained a point down. By half-time the game was lost. New Zealand were leading 17–9, and had Mehrtens been on full kicking duty (he was for the conversions, but not for the penalties) their score ought to have been closer to thirty points. Jonah Lomu had twice sliced his way through the fickle Scottish defence, scoring once and making another try. His speed off the mark made Martin Offiah look slow. His size – he was 19st of hard muscle and 6ft 4ins tall – and his fast forward gears gave him a locomotion to frighten the bravest. To make matters worse, Craig Chalmers, the Scotland fly-half, had to be substituted when he suffered a crack on the head.

In the second half, Ian Jones tipped back with his left arm from Mehrtens' high kick-off. The ball came back to Mehrtens. He gave it some air. Hastings chose to misread the situation and Little waltzed in under the posts unimpeded. Game over. New Zealand had stretched their lead to 24–9. In the fourth minute of the half, Mehrtens ran in from 65 metres without a hand on him, showing that he was the best-balanced player of the tournament. This took the score to 31–9 and thereafter the Blacks lost their control of, enthusiasm for and concentration on the game. It was just too easy.

The final score was 48–30. Much was made of the Scottish revival, and it was suggested that if Scotland could do this, then England had a chance. The reality was very different. Scotland never threw in the towel – they were competitive to the end, despite a further injury to Cronin. They were simply outclassed. Some of the delights of the game were Bachop's passing through the hand (often his passes reached inside centre), Lomu's running, Wilson's all-round ability, Bunce's and Little's power in the centre, Zinzan Brooke's close control and Fitzpatrick's speed on the wing. Scotland had improved during their Cup run but were now mentally and physically drained. They would have to renew their effort to stay in the big time.

As for Gavin Hastings, of course he will be missed. After a wretched few seasons (in fact, since he captained the Lions his form had suffered), in 1995 he had been much more like his old self. But he'd lost a metre of pace and his play had become more cautious. Under pressure, too, his place-kicking had deteriorated. He was, though, often all Scotland had, and he bore their crosses and led them out of the wilderness. He will enjoy his well-earned rest. After the game, the Scots sensibly came back out to thank their loyal supporters. The fans then had their own fifteen minutes of fame.

All four games were under-supported. The gate at Pretoria was 28,000, some 20,000 short of its capacity. Large sections of both Newlands and Ellis Park were empty. It was obvious that the ticketing had been a disaster. Returning 350,000 tickets only a week or so before the opening ceremony was too little and too late to maximize the interest within South Africa. Indeed, the selling of these tickets in general and the manning of the booths at the grounds in particular left a lot to be desired.

In England, meanwhile, the reaction to the victory of Carling's men was spectacular. ITV dined out as the overnight ratings, 8.3 million, gave them the best ever lunchtime viewing figures in the history of television sport. The newspapers colourfully overdosed, Rob Andrew's dropped goal claiming universal front- and back-page headlines. The *Sun* gave us 'Arise, Sir Rob' and 'He's a Boot of All Right'; the *Mirror* 'Rob Joy'; the *Star* 'Robsmacked!' and 'You Booty!' The broadsheets were equally effusive. Later in the week Andrew was awarded the MBE. England, it seemed, had hit the crest of the wave at last, but the glory was to be short-lived.

16

The Semi-Finals: So Near and Yet So Far

Back in Durban, it was raining, to put it mildly. There was a plague of the proverbial cats and dogs. At least the place was consistent – this was my third visit in as many weeks and the third time I had found it raining on match day. This afternoon South Africa were to meet France in the first semi-final.

South Africa had gambled again with selection. Mark Andrews had been preferred to Straeuli at number 8. Andrews had been the best South African front-five forward throughout the tournament, but it was a bit late in the day for Kitch Christie to start experimenting. In his place at number 4 was Hannes Strydom. Otherwise, the side was unchanged from the team that had played against Australia what seemed like years ago.

André Joubert had made an astonishing recovery from the broken bone in his left hand. Immediately after the match in Johannesburg, he had been taken to hospital, where Dr Mark Ferguson had performed an operation under a local anaesthetic so that there would be no bruising or swelling. Ferguson, using a device similar to the one orthopaedic surgeons use for keyhole surgery in knees, placed four small pins in Joubert's broken finger. He had had a special casing couriered from Ireland, where such injuries are commonplace in hurling, so that Joubert could play. To speed up the healing process the doctor had Joubert spend a considerable amount of time in a decompression chamber. In the end he was the only player suited to the conditions at King's Park.

South Africa's opponents, France, still had not settled on a satisfactory half-back partnership. The difficulty was not only the injury in the Scotland game to Hueber at scrum-half. The real problem was

Christophe Deylaud at fly-half. But Pierre Berbizier kept us guessing by selecting a new scrum-half, Fabien Galthié, who had last played against England in March 1994. Berbizier explained that Deylaud couldn't go on playing as badly as he had. That was confidence for you – or kidology. Otherwise, the side was the same as the one which defeated Ireland.

The rain would make the game more even. Losing in a semi-final is the absolute pits. No one remembers you for the achievement of reaching the last four, only for the fact that, having got there, you lost. It's a killer for the players. Over the following twenty-four hours thirty players would know that feeling. Durban, despite the rain, was in a festive mood. The country had come to see their side win through to the finals. President Mandela had even sported a Springbok cap the previous day at a children's event at a township and the photographers and their editors made sure it featured on every front page. SABC showed game after game after game throughout the morning. First England's match with Argentina, then the Springboks against Romania. What was really needed was some cleverly crafted editing to bring the best tries together along with an extensive analysis of how each side was going to play.

The rain had become what I could only describe as a tropical storm arguing with a monsoon. The very brave and slightly better attired journalists, some with dustbin lids acting as head cover, made their way over from the media centre to the stadium. Quite how anyone was going to be able to write about the game was not the issue. The issue was to be able to say, 'I was there,' rather than 'I was there in the media centre.' The pitch was flooded. A decision was made to postpone the kick-off for an hour, but even an hour would probably not be enough to clear the pitch. To delay the game by twenty-four hours was not a decision anyone wanted to take. Marcel Martin, Bernard Lapasset, the French rugby president, and Louis Luyt, his South African counterpart, went out to centre field to examine the state of the pitch. It was still being swept by a coterie of black women.

The delay caused pandemonium with timetables. Most journalists had agreed to go down to Cape Town after the semi-final rather than wait until the next day. There were few flights to Cape Town and those that existed were jammed full. Some were going to have to make tricky decisions. Certainly those who worked for a daily newspaper could safely miss the game, for it was the England match that would make their headlines on the Monday morning. When the kick-off was delayed again, this time for half an hour, it seemed inevitable that the game would be postponed for a day. But many South Africans had come to Durban just for the day and they wanted to see their team play. Even those who could change their flights would have a real problem finding accommodation. The only thing to do was to go for a 1 p.m. kick-off on the Sunday at Newlands. But the police, the stewards – all the officials involved in the staging of any major game – would have to be consulted. Meanwhile, the good-natured crowd waited patiently for a decision, any decision.

There was a chink in the dark clouds and the rain stopped. An announcement over the PA system told us that the game would start at 4.30 p.m. What a farce. Thirty players had trained their hearts out to win a place in the third rugby World Cup final and it had come down to what amounted to a lottery. It was most unfair. It seemed doubly unfair to me, because all I had for cover was a black plastic bin bag. The players would have warmed up for the 3 p.m. kick-off; warmed down; warmed up again for the 4 p.m. and then cooled their heels again. Finally, they had to try to get their minds together for a third time, and to really believe that they *were* going out to play now, albeit at Durban Lido rather than King's Park.

The pitch itself had been specially laid to new turf for the World Cup. No one could be quite sure how it would stand up to the torrential rain that had fallen and was continuing to fall from the sky like one-inch pellets. There was no machine like the one they have at Edgbaston for cricket to squeeze the water from the pitch. Still the women busied themselves pushing the surface water to the ends of the ground. There were no duckboards for the cameramen or photographers – one cameraman finished up barefoot in the park, while the photographers struggled to keep the water off their lenses. Upon their great skill and endeavours would rest the images of today's game.

The noisy but tolerant capacity crowd of 52,000 wanted the game to go on. They did not know that, if the game commenced and was then abandoned in the first half by Derek Bevan, the referee, without a try being scored, France would go through – in those circumstances the finalists would be decided by the number of sendings-off each team had had during the tournament. If the match went into the second half before being called off, the score as it was then would stand. What sort of pressure was Bevan under? Abandonment would only arise if there was lightning and/or further rain that made play difficult. Still, such a decision would probably have caused the first lynching of this World Cup.

At last, at 4.35 p.m., slightly later than expected, the teams appeared for the national anthems. There was a good number of Frenchmen and women in the crowd, but their singing was drowned out when it came to the South African anthems, particularly by 'Die Stem', which was, for no obviously sinister reason, shouted from the rafters. All the waving flags were those of the new South Africa. The state of the pitch was such that many players, as well as the match officials, would have liked to have changed their studs for wellington boots or flippers. Wayne Erickson, one of the two touch-judges, looked as if his boots had rubber studs on them. You could but hope that he wouldn't be called upon to referee if Derek Bevan needed the attention of the Baywatch team.

At the first line-out on the French 22, South Africa called a four-man. They were bunched in a group of three at the front, with a space of 6 or 7 metres before Andrews took up the slack at the back. It was a very interesting opening gambit. The ball was thrown to Andrews, who tapped it down to Joost van der Westhuizen. He then made off with his low-flying gait, ready to surf to the French line. It was a tremendous first wave. The French decided to try to run the ball whatever the weather, and they did so with their customary elan. Running was their best option because Deylaud was struggling; he appeared to be the only French back not to have webbed feet.

It was a cracking game in spite of the conditions. In the end South Africa won an incredibly close match, the result remaining in doubt, as had those of so many of the important games in RWC '95, right until the end. By half-time penalties were the order of the day – no surprises there – and Stransky and Lacroix traded two each. The difference was a pushover try, credited to Ruben Kruger, and the conversion by Stransky.

The second half could not have been more tense. After six minutes Stransky had kicked two more goals and Lacroix had responded with one. At 19–9, South Africa looked to have it wrapped up. Then Van der Westhuizen went off and the game changed. Johan le Roux was simply not in the same league, and gradually it dawned on the French water-polo team that they could sneak a win. With ten minutes to go, the score stood at 19–12 to South Africa, Lacroix having kicked another penalty goal, yet France exerted the greatest pressure and it was rare for the Springboks to venture out of their own 22, let alone their own half. France had done this before, against Scotland, and they knew the rules. A try on full time would suffice. And many of us thought they had indeed scored a try when Benazzi, who had a colossal game, forced his way over – and if he didn't, wasn't Cecillon over the line anyway? There were maybe as many as six scrums 5 metres or so from the South African line in the last few minutes of the game. The French tried to push the South Africans over the line but not only did the Springboks repel the threat, but they also refused to succumb to French attempts to get them to drop the scrum and give away a penalty. This showed great strength of character. When France finally realized that a pushover wasn't on, they tried to run it, but Christophe Deylaud had had such a poor game that he hadn't a clue what to do, except give a hospital pass to Lacroix. He was tackled and the game was saved.

Three minutes into injury time, with the crowd yet again on the edge of their seats, Derek Bevan blew his whistle. François Pienaar, with a huge smile and a whip of his right hand, acknowledged the victory and its importance. The French weren't quite sure what to do. Eventually, Philippe Saint-André gathered them together in a huddle. After thirty seconds or so it broke up, by which time Olivier Roumat and Christian Califano, still hugging one another tightly, had broken down. Tears were pouring down their faces. Tears poured down mine. There is much more to this most beautiful of games than money or even winning.

Afterwards, Pierre Berbizier found nothing to say about the referee, the pitch, the conditions or the 'nearly' try. The only point he conceded was that, tactically, his team's kicking had been poor. This was an indirect criticism of Christophe Deylaud, who managed to kick every ball to André Joubert's left foot (I hope Joubert sent him a thank-you note). His one consolation was that Lacroix had established a new record for penalty goals in the World Cup. Not surprisingly, the South Africans were more upbeat. Pienaar was ecstatic, and he deserved to be. Kitch Christie now had a record of played ten, won ten. Some statistic for a coach. Du Plessis was just Du Plessis, quiet and thoughtful. André Joubert appeared with his hand wrapped in a couple of telephone directories. He said that the lessons of touring Scotland and Wales 'hadn't been for nothing', a reference to the rain that had affected them in two of their matches there. 'It was a bun fight and we won the last bun,' concluded Christie.

Marcel Martin explained the decision-making process that had led to the game being delayed and then played. He had done everything by the book, but the last on his list of concerns had been the players.

Entering Durban International Airport, it didn't take a brain surgeon to appreciate that it was under severe pressure. The queues stretched almost out of the doors; the baggage-loader was jammed and luggage was piled high. It was chaos, yet it was a good-humoured crowd anxious to make it to Cape Town on time for the New Zealand–England semi-final.

Flying into Cape Town was surprisingly enjoyable. Perhaps the acres of sunshine on offer had something to do with it. For the first time, I saw Robben Island. As we arrived the Cape Town musicians known locally as the 'coons', who had been in the opening ceremony, were playing to welcome us. There was a festive spirit abroad.

Newlands was crawling with English supporters. The South Africans wanted England to win, though it must be said that this was because they thought their team could beat England in the final. Jack Rowell had resisted making any changes to the line-up. He had decided not to bring in Ian Hunter to mark Jonah Lomu and still preferred Morris to Bracken. Among the 50,000 capacity crowd, the England supporters appeared to outnumber the Kiwis by five to one. Though I'm no royalist, there was a huge lump in my throat as I watched the England team belt out 'God Save the Queen'.

Mehrtens lined up to kick right for the first time in the tournament (people usually kick left because it is easier for them). Everyone was taken in. As Scotland had done in their opening gambit against the Kiwis in the quarter-final, Mehrtens changed tack and kicked high and short for Lomu – that is, he kicked left. It was a great starting ploy. Tony Underwood and Catt then collided, and the All Blacks were suddenly very threatening. Indeed, they had half-chances on both sides of the field within the first two minutes and there was

Lomu walking over Tony Underwood and through Catt to score. Three minutes gone and the score was 5–0. England weren't in the game.

From the kick-off the All Blacks rucked the ball. Bachop's pass missed Mehrtens, but Bunce picked it up on the first bounce, and instead of kicking, broke Guscott's tackle to put Osborne clear with 60 metres to go. He wasn't to score, but Josh Kronfeld, who must have covered 85 metres, took a return pass from Bunce to touch down in the corner. Mehrtens added two points and it was 12–0 after only five minutes. This was going to be a firecracker of a game. When Rob Andrew MBE did get a penalty he missed the kick in front of the posts. Eleven minutes into the game there still hadn't been a line-out. A penalty goal from Mehrtens made it 15–0 – more than a point a minute. Suddenly, every All Black looked a metre faster to the ball and they were hitting the rucks at real pace and with an overwhelmingly superior technique.

The kickers hoofed the ball up and down the field to each other. From one such exchange, Zinzan Brooke lazily dropped a goal from all of 45 metres. With Zinzan, these drop-kicks can sometimes clear the stands, but this one was the last straw for England. They had no plan B. They were completely overawed. They had to run ball they had not run before and they simply hadn't the strength in the close-quarter play to break through the third and fourth layers of defence the All Blacks had in place. Moreover, it seemed it would be only a matter of time before Lomu featured again, though Tony Underwood had managed to tackle him once. Sure enough, there was another lovely floated pass from Mehrtens and Lomu was striding under the posts. Rob Andrew finally put some points on the board for England when he kicked his first penalty from three attempts almost on half-time. The score was 25–3.

During the interval Laurie Mains, the New Zealand coach, looked a bundle of nerves, though his face remained unmoved. A minute later, even he was jumping up and down. Bachop had a number of options from a maul. He went left and chipped the ball over the England backs for, need I say it, Mr Lomu. He just failed to take it, but the usual blanket of All Black attackers were ready and Lomu popped up again to take the final pass to score in the corner for 30–3. The New Zealand bench were ecstatic. England had no answers to the fast switch play of the All Blacks. All Andrew and Catt could do was to kick the ball aimlessly up in the air. This was futile. It was as if they had never practised counter-attacking. The All Blacks scored again. Bachop ran flat and right, sold a dummy pass, and gave a wonderful ball to Wilson, who got outside a lacklustre Rory Underwood. Very quickly, Bachop, backing up, crossed the line.

Eventually, three-quarters of the way through the game, Rory Underwood scored in the corner after Ben Clarke had led an almost solo charge at the Blacks. None the less, the New Zealand defence was as robust as it would have been had they been losing. The English were now trying to make a game of it, but through the efforts of individuals rather than as a team. It was an attempt by some players to salvage their own personal pride, and Morris, Johnson and Clarke succeeded.

The cleanest break, one of all of 65 metres, was by a streaker. This sparked a small England revival and Will Carling reacquainted himself with the try-line when he chipped over Lomu and, catching a deflection, scored in the right-hand corner to reduce the margin to 35–15. And then it was Lomu again. From the kick-off, England fumbled, and in a trice Mehrtens went left and the ball was in Lomu's hands. He pushed off Tony Underwood, glided inside Catt and was over for his fourth try which Mehrtens converted. Lomu was in danger of being arrested on hit-and-run charges. With ten minutes left the scoreboard read 42–15.

England were not quite all spent. The effervescent Morris was in the thick of things and finally Will Carling, making a break, scored his second try in as many minutes. Andrew provided two more points for 42–22. All that was left was a last sight of a vintage Guscott break. Alas, instead of finishing with a try, it resulted in a forward pass which prevented England from making up some of the shortfall. Boredom then crept into the All Black ranks. Mehrtens casually dropped a goal to take it to 45–22 and at the very last Rory Underwood stepped inside Jeff Wilson for his second try, which took him past David Campese's record for tries in World Cups. Andrew converted and the final score was 45–29. Thankfully for England, the game, beautifully handled by referee Steve Hilditch, was over.

Jack Rowell, Will Carling and Rory Underwood emerged afterwards to face the music. Jack said that the New Zealand forwards played as their forwards had always done whereas now their backs played like Western Samoa. I thought by that he meant he was not happy at the ease with which players switch countries down under and that he wanted the IB to close the loop.

'We had the worst possible start,' said Carling. 'We were shocked by the awesome attack.' And on the subject of Lomu, he expanded on his views that the giant wing's was a freak talent. 'The sooner he goes away, the better,' he declared with feeling. Rowell was at a loss to explain the extra pace of the All Blacks. He did say that the quality of competitive rugby was stronger Down Under and that for England to maintain their position for 1999, they would have to get among the southern hemisphere nations more frequently than was the case at the moment. This would effectively mean England taking a different route from their Five Nations colleagues, and possibly telling players that they could no longer go on Lions tours. It would also require a re-examination of the Five Nations competition.

New Zealand captain Sean Fitzpatrick said: 'I remember going down to Cardiff in '91 to play in the play-off and I wasn't looking forward to repeating that exercise. The England win in '93 was on our minds a little, but we were focused and knew how to beat them.' And on Lomu: 'It's good to see Lomu running out there. We kept his efficiency hidden.' The man himself was notably absent from the post-mortem. Lomu had so excited the world's press that before the semis he had given over a hundred interviews. He was hounded by the UK tabloid hacks. He fielded calls between two and three in the morning and some of the more insensitive hacks were following him back to his hotel and even into the lift and on to his room. All this had led him to call a halt to giving interviews. Brian Lochore, New Zealand's senior manager, said: 'Lomu right now prefers to keep his own counsel. He does not want the furore of the press.'

Lomu struck me as an essentially quiet and shy person who preferred to let his deeds on the field speak for themselves. He was brought up in Mangere, in south Auckland on what might be described as the wrong side of town. He played Rugby League at his junior school and it was only after a move to Wesley College, a Methodist boarding school, that he switched codes. He played in most positions, and indeed until two seasons earlier had been known as a flanker rather than a wing. He toured Australia, England and Ireland with

New Zealand Secondary Schools in 1992 and 1993. He was capped aged eighteen against France in 1994, the youngest player ever to be selected for the All Blacks. He was 6ft 4ins tall and weighed in at 19st, but it was his speed off the mark which made him such an outstanding athlete. He was timed at 10.8 for the 100 metres. He took size 15 boots, both of which have crosses on the back to remind him of his Christian faith, and he has had the number 11 shaved into an eyebrow. Peter FitzSimons described him in the *Sydney Morning Herald* as a rhinoceros in ballet shoes.

Laurie Mains, the coach, said: 'He nearly wasn't selected for RWC '95 because we needed to get inside his head and he needed to understand the demands of a team game. But this was achieved during the rugby camps held prior to the final squad being announced.' Lomu was a regular guy with a penchant for scoring tries, and South Africa would have to stop him if they wanted the World Cup. England had failed to do so; they had had no plans to deal with him. They should have selected either Ojomoh or Hunter to play on the right wing in defence and opted for Rory Underwood to play openside wing in attack. Earlier in the week, the London *Evening Standard* had offered several tips on how to cope with Jonah Lomu. They included bear traps along the touchline and carrying a baseball bat in your rugby shorts.

For many England players this was the end of the road. Richards had played his last game for England; Morris, too, was already retiring. Andrew ought to follow suit. Carling might remain, but not as captain; Guscott was history, and there were question-marks against both Underwoods. I thought Moore and Ubogu in the front row would also be put out to grass shortly. We missed Paul Hull's speed at full-back and we needed Catt to have played more games at fly-half before this World Cup. Would Jack Rowell recast the side and set it the goals of total rugby? We had to hope so. Meanwhile, England had to pick themselves up for the play-off and share an evening plane back to Johannesburg with the All Blacks.

On the flight from Cape Town to Johannesburg were two players representing the Old Farts and the New Farts. For the OFs was Tom Kiernan, now the Irish representative on the IB, and for the YFs was Mark Ella, the finest fly-half of the century. Mark now worked for the ARU. There was a body of opinion which felt he ought to succeed Bob Dwyer as coach, but he didn't have enough coaching pins in his lapel. Ella had been coach to Milano, David Campese's close-season team, for three years, and for two of them they finished up as club champions of Italy. Dwyer would no doubt be replaced by John Connolly, the Queensland coach who had done so well with his team in the Super-10 series, but on reflection it seemed to me that if a country was to harness its coaching strength, it might be better if the Aussies pushed Dwyer upstairs but retained his knowledge and input for 1999, and brought in Ella as well as Connolly. After all, had Alan Jones not precipitated Ella's early retirement, Australia would have won the World Cup in 1987.

The team news for both the play-off and the final was, in the end, no news. France had finally located their collective intelligence and dropped Christophe Deylaud for Franck Mesnel, two matches too late. England had 'rested' Tony Underwood for Ian Hunter and Steve Ojomoh came in for Dean Richards, who had carried a bruised shoulder during the semi-final. Both South Africa and New Zealand had kept the same teams for the final, which meant that Mark Andrews retained his number 8 position. Kitch Christie sure loved a challenge, and playing Andrews there again was certainly that. The only change was on the bench, Jamie Joseph coming in for Blair Larsen.

The play-off between England and France took place at Loftus Versfeld with a kick-off at 5 p.m., which was rather mystifying. A later start, perfectly possible considering the excellent floodlights, would have brought out a larger local crowd and at the same time satisfied the television audiences back home in both countries, an hour behind.

At the ground I fell into conversation with Billy Miles (aged twenty) and Lee le Roux (twenty-two). They ran a tray service to one section of the ground, selling cigarettes and confectionery. They were paid not by the hour, but by what they could sell, and received 10 per cent of their takings. On a good day they made R50 (£9) each, but they often earned more from tips than they did from commission. Billy and Lee had arrived at Loftus at 8 a.m., having left their township, Eersterlist, 20 kilometres to the north of Pretoria, an hour earlier. They had travelled by train. By the time they had started queuing a hundred boys had beaten them to it and by the time they found employment, another two hundred hopers had arrived. I asked them about the impact of RWC '95 on their township. 'We're a coloured township, so soccer is our game, but there has been much, much more interest in this World Cup than at any time before. Children are out in the streets playing with a rugby ball. This is new for us.'

The ground was ringed by men in yellow bibs bearing in orange the legend 'DS Security'. I had already been into the police station at the stadium to inquire about the sort of thefts and drunks they had to deal with only to be met with a gruff 'We have no problems here.' James, one of the security men, came from a mixed area called Springs. He had travelled in that morning in a truck cabriolet. There had been eighteen of them when they left and by the time they'd arrived at Loftus, their numbers had grown to thirty-three as they had picked up a few more along the way. He was paid a set fee of R50 for the day, which was much more than he earned at the factory where he usually worked. It was his boss who had organized the employment at Loftus and the transport.

Behind the goalposts, Gilly Hansford of Rushman's was sorting out the photographers' positions. Pinned to the ground, occupying a metre of space, were numbers, one for each photographer. For today's game, the English and French daily newspaper photographers had the positions behind the goals. Along the side, twenty or so agency photographers were allowed free rein, but this meant that they had to lug their massive cameras as they chased up and down the touchline. Today ninety-five photographers had been granted accreditation.

The England–France game was refereed by David Bishop of New Zealand, whose last international it was to be. There was a goodish crowd of 44,000. The essential question was, would this be a game too far for England? They had never really had the full weight of Dean Richards' experience, and without him they had suffered. Rowell should have given the team he selected for Western Samoa a run-out, but he didn't. I was beginning to wonder whether he wasn't too conservative a figure to be the national coach. France hadn't beaten England since 1988, Carling's debut game, but they had been only centimetres away from winning in their semi-final and would therefore be in a better frame of mind. The match, such as it was, was of the lowest possible standard. England, playing their first game at altitude, were lucky not to be on the receiving end of a second thrashing. They were simply awful.

The match bore all the hallmarks of an encounter between two northern hemisphere teams. It was cold and calculating, and characterized by the mediocrity of European fail-safe game plans. The French had a greater sense of urgency, but they needed to be more flexible and less open to intimidation. Nevertheless they made mincemeat of England in the scrums and line-outs. In the first half Andrew managed one penalty goal from three attempts. Lacroix replied with three points from what was almost the last kick before the break for a less than thrilling half-time score of 3–3.

Within a minute of the restart Lacroix put France ahead after Ben Clarke was penalized for stamping. Andrew's boot brought England back on level terms after seven minutes, but Lacroix soon regained the advantage with another penalty goal. Midway through the half the crowd struck up a 'boring, boring' chant, but thankfully we were spared a Mexican wave as they were diverted by a try from France. A move involving Galthié, Ntamack and Cabannes took the French to within a few metres of the England line, where it was halted by Hunter. But Merle won the line-out and Roumat was propelled over. Lacroix's conversion attempt hit the posts, but England were now two scores down at 14–6.

Andrew clawed them back to 14–9 almost immediately, but Carling's men were clearly mentally exhausted and it was only a matter of time before the French ran away with the game. A minute from the final whistle, Ntamack waltzed through a dozy England defence to round off a 19–9 victory for France. Lacroix's missed conversion was academic. So England lost, and they deserved to, too – they were just going through the motions. Their forward control had gone to pieces and without it they struggled; they looked second rate, and they were.

17

The Road to the Final

In the week between the semi-finals and the final, I was meeting Keith Rowlands for breakfast at the Cape Sun Hotel, the epicentre for all things Rugby World Cup in Cape Town. As chief executive of the IB in all but name, Rowlands had seen two World Cups at close quarters, the last one and the current one. He soon admitted: 'I wouldn't want to go through 1991 ever again. It was a nightmare.' A French source had told me that one of the RWC '91 meetings had ended with the lights off and everybody locked in the room. I assumed Rowlands meant that he did not enjoy the pressure brought by the Four Home Unions and France upon the structures then in place within the IB and RWC '91.

'There was and is too much ignorance within the Four Home Unions, and even their IB representatives, as to how the RWC functions, both as a business and as an organization,' Rowlands said. I asked him to clarify the claim made to me by one senior Four Home Unions official that there was, if not a Customs and Excise investigation into the 1991 accounts, at least some kind of investigation. 'It's lavatory talk that there is an investigation by any tax authority into the way in which IB Services and RWC '91 was organized,' he replied. 'Eddie Tonks [then chairman of the NZRFU] basically guided us through the kind of offshore financial package that is now in place. He was familiar with this territory. We were not.' I asked him about the article in *Business Age* concerning Callan and the alleged missing millions, which the RWC directors had all read. He was decidedly unsympathetic.

'Look, that article was basically written by John Reason. We've had the accounts audited by two separate firms of accountants and checked by a third, and there is no money missing. CPMA delivered. The problem is that people do not get on with Alan Callan. It's a personal thing. We've distributed, through the Isle of Man trust, £6 million pounds or so to forty-odd rugby unions throughout the world.' I had asked at the opening press conference three weeks earlier who had applied for the money and who had received it. Now Rowlands told me: 'It's up to the individual unions to announce what they have received, not us. I do know that the American rugby union were given sufficient money – and very grateful they were, too – to establish the hardware and software for a national register.'

We moved on. Given that South Africa did not have to tender to win the rights to the 1995 World Cup, was he happy at how things had gone, particularly with the television coverage? I had expressed my deep dissatisfaction with the technical and editorial quality of SABC's efforts. 'Some might think that's a very arrogant attitude to take,' he responded. 'You are exposed to a different television culture.' I asked him whether he knew that the IOC had decided to create Olympic Television as an entity, and that Adrian Metcalfe, previously head of sport at Channel 4 and Eurosport, was one of the directors. I had written to Vernon Pugh to suggest this route for future rugby World Cups but had never had a reply. 'Maybe that's where we should be going, especially if we want to see the World Cup in countries such as Argentina and Italy,' Rowlands conceded. 'But that will be a matter for my successor. I retire at the end of the year and I suspect that my job will be carved up between three new people.'

'But, still in Bristol, not Dublin or Monte Carlo?'

'I can see no reason why the IB needs to relocate. RWC BV and RWCL are registered in Holland and the Isle of Man. It therefore is irrelevant where the IB headquarters are. They may as well be in Bristol.'

In spite of the fact that the sole recommendation from both RWC '87 and RWC '91 had been that the World Cup should be staged in one country, the 1999 tournament had again been awarded all over the place. True, in theory Wales were the hosts, but in practice, Ireland, Scotland, France and England would share it. Another disaster was on the horizon. Moreover, for 1999 the seedings had been changed. I couldn't quite work out what the benefits were for the seeds, particularly as there would be twenty teams.

'Well, we might review the twenty,' said Rowlands. 'We might reduce it. We've already spent a full day during this competition trying to establish how 1999 would work. We've looked at five pools of four and four pools of five.' I could not see that either of those options would work. We did not want scores of 80–5 or for that matter 2,001–3. We wanted a fair and sensible competition. There needed to be a preliminary competition between the twelve lesser nations, who would then qualify to play the eight seeds – New Zealand, South Africa, England, France, Western Samoa, Ireland, Scotland and Australia. It's absurd that Wales should start the 1999 competition by losing by fifty points or more to New Zealand. The soccer World Cup doesn't start this way, why should the rugby tournament do so?

'It's important that the rugby World Cup has a focus and that on the opening day the whole of the world concentrates on one match,' argued Rowlands. 'Last time it was England versus New Zealand; this time it was South Africa against Australia, and the impact around the world was terrific. You've got to remember we're still in the business of establishing the World Cup as a world competition. We need maximum exposure.'

I could see the essential faith in the desire to extend the next World Cup to twenty countries, especially as there appeared to be some enthusiasm for a plate competition, but my suggestion to Keith Rowlands was that there should be an opening tournament comprising first seeds nine to twenty. From each of these four pools of four would come one qualifier to join the final eight, who would be divided up into four pools of two, and would thus finally become four pools of three. One winner from each would go into a semi-final. (I hope you're still with me.) This would make a special opening game irrelevant, and it should therefore be axed. Instead, the Welsh Rugby Union should offer a proper floodlit opening ceremony on a par with that, say, of the Barcelona Olympics to kick-start the whole bonanza. The 1995 opening ceremony cost £250,000 and united a country. The 1999 opening ceremony could offer a laser show supported with fireworks and accompanied by choirs from the twenty teams from the hills of Wales. Music is, after all, the hidden agenda of every rugby tour. We could but hope.

I did not favour an opening game and I did not see any advantages in allowing countries to pre-qualify. Before Murdoch announced his 'new deal', which we shall come to, there was so little meaningful international rugby, aside from the Five Nations each year, and the lesson from 1995 was that there needed to be much much more. Pre-qualifying would kill this idea at birth. Moreover, it might well have contributed to the downfall of Australia and England in 1995.

Leaving the Cape Sun Hotel, I made my way to the Ministry of Finance. I had not visited the parliamentary buildings before. The whole area was very tranquil, which I supposed acted as some kind of counterpoint to what was going on inside the white Victorian buildings. I was hoping to discover what kind of research was in place to measure the impact of RWC '95 on the South African economy. I had first contacted Dr Dawie de Villiers, the minister of tourism, but he had refused to see me, even though I had sent a list of questions to him in advance. Mr Cyrus Rustomjee at the Ministry of Finance, however, could not have been more helpful. He called endless government ministries and quangos and soon the fax was churning with bits of the information I was seeking. 'You see, the main problem the government is facing at the moment is threefold,' said Mr Rustomjee. 'The inheritance of apartheid, the transition from that situation to a mixed economy and the long-term vision of establishing a South Korean or Taiwanese model here. We have had to convince the civil service of these arguments and bring in new blood to provoke them into more creative thinking.'

Meanwhile, at a more mundane level, it was difficult for me to understand how the government had gone about collecting its data on how much money had come into the country during the previous five weeks. For instance, when we came into South Africa, we had to fill in a registration form, the details from which were put on to a computer at passport control at every airport. Nowhere on the form did it ask us if we were here for the World Cup.

A fax from David Hall, the managing director of Gullinjet, the official tour operators, supplied the following information. They had sold 3,400 packages for the pool matches, 5,100 for the quarter-finals, 8,800 for the semis and almost 11,000 for the final. They had also catered for 6,800 media personnel, sponsors, officials and team packages. The packages were broken down further. There were 2,600 from England, 2,200 from New Zealand, 1,800 from Australia, 1,100 from

179

France, 700 from Japan, 600 from Wales, 300 from Ireland and 1,500 from the rest of the world (Scotland seemed to have been overlooked).

SATour, the government travel quango, had tried to anticipate numbers and problems earlier in the year. James Seymour of SATour had written two documents in March and April about tourist flows. In the April investigation he commented: 'The impression created in the media is that there will be an unmanageable number of international tourists entering South Africa for the duration of the RWC tournament ... Accommodation is adequate, except for three- to five-star hotels in Gauteng [Johannesburg] and surrounds, specifically during the semi-finals and the final ... The concern over the availability of luxury coaches does indeed seem founded.' In the March document Seymour stated: 'If one considers the assumption that every thirty foreign tourists create one direct job year and two indirect years, then the 1995 tournament will create at least 866 direct job years and 1,666 indirect job years.' Then there were the stadia themselves, which had undergone major refits to the tune of R117 million (about £19 million).

Most rugby visitors had bought two-week packages or, if they had come under their own steam, could only afford to stay for a similar length of time. The average spend of a tourist was estimated to be R200 per day (£35), which comprised mainly food and drink, though not necessarily in that order. Fortunately, South Africa's restaurants were relatively cheap by European standards.

The Ministry of Finance was housed in a seventeen-storey block to the side of Parliament. As I was leaving I noticed that the Ministry of Tourism was in the same building. I searched for an open door and found Luise Nicholson, the minister's speechwriter and general factotum. Although she was busy she put aside her work and tried to help me, and after a further hour, we had tracked down a number of fruitful sources. The interesting thing Luise told me was the major reason why I was being chased from pillar to post: in the interim constitution, tourism had been devolved from national government to regional government, and so, after fourteen months, it still had no infrastructure in place. Consequently, it was bleeding. Nothing was being achieved. And it didn't sound to me as if Dr Dawie de Villiers really had a grip on this. Tourism is the world's fourth largest business, South Africa desperately needs foreign currency, and one way to attract this would be to capitalize on its phenomenal potential as a tourist haven. Some hope, I thought.

Through Luise's contacts I was able to gather some information on the ticketing operation for RWC '95, with which there had obviously been problems. Even when stadia posted sold-out notices all over town, as they did for the two semi-finals, there had been large numbers of empty seats at matches. Clearly all was not well. I discovered that a firm called Computicket was the only company in South Africa which had a mainframe computer ticketing operation with three hundred outlets across the country. Why, then, was it impossible to buy a World Cup ticket from them?

The tickets for RWC '95 had been aimed primarily at the corporate market, both in South Africa and from abroad. The packages sold in the Republic cost R14,000 each (about £2,500). For this you received a bundle of tickets covering the pool games as well as the more important quarters, semis and final. Those companies which bought the packages did not necessarily have to turn up to the minor games or, for that matter, if they decided they couldn't run to accommodation, even the more serious matches later on in the competition. But there was no way of knowing if the tickets were not going to be used, and no system to allow a central ticketing agency to resell them. In May, just before the tournament began, the RWC '95 organization returned 350,000 tickets. These were distributed to the individual unions – Western Province for Newlands, Natal for King's Park, Northern Transvaal for Loftus Versfeld and Transvaal for Ellis Park. The four grounds were not connected by a mainframe computer and it was evident from watching the booths trying to sell these tickets that the rugby unions simply did not have the appropriate staff or software systems – for either computers or credit cards – to cope. The fact that there wasn't a foolproof system for the secondary ticketing market was the major headache of the whole tournament. Bernard Jay of Computicket in Johannesburg told me:

We did apply to be the official ticketing agency. We had twenty-three meetings with Craig Jamieson and the RWC '95 officials between July 1994, when we were first approached, and October 1994. We must be the only organization to be able to sell single tickets. There was an accusation that because of the nature of the design of our cinema-style tickets, we couldn't deliver a sophisticated version such as that required for RWC '95. This was quite untrue. We knew right from the off that RWC '95 wanted a different operation and we told them we could deliver it.

Another company, PSM Group, was appointed to handle the ticketing, allegedly by Craig Jamieson, but in fact the decision went higher up the South African RWC organizational tree. In the end PSM added a flat 10 per cent charge on top of the R14,000 packages, which was 2 or 3 per cent more than Computicket had quoted in their original document. Nevertheless, all of the corporate hospitality packages were sold out in South Africa. Where the whole thing went wrong was back in Bristol, where 600,000 hospitality tickets were returned in April and May. There was something decidedly fishy about the whole thing. One of the stories that did the rounds was that someone within the SARFU had been out buying black-market tickets and had managed to obtain a thousand at a cost of R1400 (£280) each.

Edward Griffiths, chief executive of the SARFU, explained: 'When RWC '95 in the UK wildly overestimated how many packages they could sell and then dumped nearly 600,000 tickets on us in April and May, we had sold out our corporate packages and it was too late in the day to create more.' The return of such a large number of tickets came far too late for such a fundamental system to be put in place. They could have come from anywhere. I felt it was the rumour mill on overtime again. Conspiracy theories ran deep in this rugby World Cup.

One day to go before the final, and rugby fever had hit town. There was a real belief among the South African media that South Africa could win. Meanwhile, New Zealand's secret weapon, Jonah Lomu, had now had a new Tongan volcanic island named after him.

At 9 a.m. Louis Luyt was due to address a press conference, hastily arranged by SARFU chief executive Edward Griffiths. Luyt does not find talking to the press easy, so this was a rare event and perhaps as many as fifty journalists turned up. Griffiths waited until all the television cameras were properly lit before signalling for Luyt to enter the room. There was a delay of thirty seconds or so during which we half expected a drum roll to usher in the new power in world rugby.

When Luyt finally arrived he was flanked by David Moffatt of the New South Wales RFU, Leo Williams, president of the ARU and a Rugby World Cup director, and Richard Guy, the chairman of the NZRFU. This was not going to be just any old conference.

Three statements were read out. Moffatt's explained that he was to be the CEO of the working body of a new triple alliance between the three rugby unions of South Africa, New Zealand and Australia, to be known by the acronym Sanza. Dr Luyt revealed the juicy bits, which consisted of the announcement that Newscorp, Rupert Murdoch's media company, had acquired for over US$550 million all television rights for ten years to the three rugby unions. Edward Griffiths read out a statement from Rupert Murdoch.

The face of Rugby Union had changed forever. The confirmation of the new triple entente, which most of us had been briefed on beforehand by members of the IB or Four Home Unions or friends thereof, took none of us by surprise. However, the amount, US$550 million, was unexpected. A quick piece of arithmetic valued each game at about US$400,000 (£250,000), which was not unreasonable at 1995 prices – and it would have been deemed extremely generous of any sporting rights-holder to have committed their property for a period of ten years. It looked on the surface a win-win for both sides, but the reality was that it was a much bigger win for Newscorp.

There were dozens of questions. Was this the death knell of amateurism? How soon would it be before Jonah Lomu was employed by Newscorp? Had they conceded pay-per-view in the contract? They had. Hadn't IMG a five-year contract with the ARU? 'The contract had been agreed but not signed,' said Leo Williams. Writs might fly, but Newscorp would probably pick up the tab. Loitering casually in the audience was the RFU's new secretary-elect, Tony Hallett. He was the only secretary or committee man present from the whole of the Five Nations. He too was pestered about the new arrangements. Didn't this mean the end of the World Cup as we knew it? How would England be able to join it? Wouldn't this lead to a world league within three years? How could England maintain their competitive edge without being a party to it? Didn't this mean paying the players? Even England players? Given this was his first 'formal' appearance at the World Cup, he did well not to overreact. On payments or trust funds, or whatever you want to call them, he was unequivocal: 'The game has gone open and we must ensure that our England players are fairly rewarded financially.' Dudley Wood must have been eating his heart out.

I asked him: 'How can England compete in the new world of rugby if they remain in the cosy cartel of the Four Home Unions and the Five Nations Championship? Surely they must extricate themselves from both?'

'Well,' said Hallett, 'there is a good deal of tradition behind the Four Home Unions and a great deal of loyalty about the Five Nations. I don't see us moving from either just yet.'

It was my belief that if England stayed in the cartel they would be doomed forever. The third World Cup would be won, yet again, by a southern hemisphere country. Only France had stayed the course over the previous eight years, and only England had joined the course in the last six. Neither of them could afford to stay in the Five Nations as they stood. A new entente cordiale was necessary: England needed to play France on a home-and-away basis every year.

18

The Final

At 2 p.m., one hour before lift-off, the South African supporters were still practising their newly adopted anthem, 'Shosholoza', an old migrant song, with the help of Radio 702 DJ Dan Moyane. His mini-CD of the song was the fastest-selling recording of the week. Before coming to the stadium he had done a signing session at a store in Rosebank and the queues had stretched throughout the mall. Moyane was a rare example of a true overnight success story – he hadn't spent a lifetime getting there. One day he sang 'Shosholoza' on his show and the next day he had a hit. His backing group was the Soweto College of Education choir. However heart-warming all this was, as Ellis Park was supposed to be a 'neutral' venue for the final, I thought it was a bit rich that the crowd were being whipped up by the officials. There was enthusiastic applause for the announcement of the arrival of President Mandela, Thabo Mbeki and F. W. de Klerk in the royal box. Mandela, outrageously, was wearing a Springbok jersey and cap. I could see only two old-style South African flags amid the 20,000 or so copies of the new version.

The pre-match festivities were jolted by the arrival, bang on 2.30, of four planes which passed, all too briefly, overhead. There were two forty-year-old Dakotas, a DC4 and a DC3, accompanied by a Harvard and a 1937 Junkers. While our gaze had been turned upwards, hundreds of children, dressed in green, white, yellow, red, blue and black leotards and carrying dozens of similar-coloured balloons, appeared on the pitch. And then, just as suddenly, no more than 500 metres above us, loomed a Jumbo with the words 'Good Luck Bokke' written on its undercarriage. It must have broken every civil aviation law in the book, but it was a stunning and audacious ploy that took our breath away. It passed over the stadium and then, for good measure, it came at us from the opposite direction. You felt as though you could almost reach up and touch it. 'So this is the Lomu factor,' somebody remarked. South African Airways had, it transpired, spent R200,000 (£33,000) on the Boeing 747 Classic's three-minute flight.

Next a posse of Zulu warriors appeared in front of us, wearing giraffe and zebra costumes. A pulsating drum beat ushered in sixteen bearers carrying a false leopard which clearly had something or somebody inside it. 'It's Winnie Mandela,' commented another wag, to much laughter. It was, actually. More elfin children stretched white, black, red, blue, green and yellow bunting across the ground. Interspersed with it were the sixteen flags of each competing country. At the appropriate moment, each group was called upon to dance and sing a typical song from the nation they were representing. For Australia, there was a detachment of Aborigines; for Romania, a band; native dancing for the Ivory Coast; drummer boys for Japan; more native dancers and a band too for Tonga; black hats for Argentina; Indians for Canada; busbied guardsmen for England (big cheer); Venetian dress for the Italians; native dancers again for the Western Samoans; the gendarmerie for France (another big cheer); national costume for the Welsh; pipers for the Scots (huge cheer); Maoris for the Kiwis (major applause); Zulus for South Africa (bedlam).

Five army helicopters, one bearing an RWC flag and the other four the sixteen flags of the competing countries, circled the stadium; from somewhere, planes dropped two parachutists who skied through the blue sky, one with the flag of New Zealand, the other the South African flag. Janie Jones repeated her adopted anthem, 'The World in Union', and when we least expected it the two teams came out. As a mere appetizer it was almost too much.

Then Mandela was out on the field. His Springbok shirt had the number 6 on it – it had been a gift from Pienaar. 'The Queen missed a trick in 1991,' somebody said. 'She should have worn Carling's shirt. That's why we didn't win.' Behind Mandela came the RWC team – Steve Tshwete, Bernard Lapasset, Richard Guy, Marcel Martin and Louis Luyt. Luyt rather than the respective captains introduced the teams, and when this was complete, the anthems were beautifully sung by the Ladysmith Black Mambazo, wearing costumes that depicted the new and fabulous South African flag. And just when we thought that was that, there was another perfectly timed flypast. What a day.

The All Blacks started their *haka* and the South Africans watched from the halfway line, as had become the tradition since Willie Anderson introduced it for Ireland at Lansdowne Road. One or two of the Springboks broke rank and so a couple of the Kiwis charged them. This was intimidating stuff. One of the aggressors was a fired-up Jonah Lomu. After the *haka* Sean Fitzpatrick touched him on the arm as if to remind him that he needed to focus on the game.

The home ground had been wound up by the public announcer. South African songs, mainly 'Shosholoza', were belted out. South Africa simply had to win. At not quite 3 p.m., Ed Morrison blew his whistle to start the third World Cup in front of a capacity crowd.

The opening moments were more nervous than we could believe. Mehrtens kicked off short, towards the 10-metre line almost in front of him, but the ball failed to travel the requisite 10 metres and the South Africans won a scrum. Mehrtens, nervous? Were the All Black youngsters affected by the occasion? We would see. Stransky then missed touch with a simple penalty. Both fly-halves needed to settle. And then, just as in the England game, in the second minute Osborne broke out of defence and made it to the South African 22. The ball out was thrown wide, but it bounced badly for Lomu and this time he had to stop to collect it and was caught. In any other situation he would have scored in the corner. Was this an omen? It was all New Zealand; South Africa appeared to be in shock.

In the fourth minute, Mehrtens kicked his first penalty from the right-hand side for 3–0. The All Blacks were buzzing; the ball was being flung around just as it had been in the England match. But Mehrtens missed with a drop-goal attempt, and finally the Springboks got themselves into the match. Stransky kicked sweetly into the New Zealand 22. The crowd buzzed; their team picked up the tempo. They knew they had to return the pressure with a score. It was New Zealand's turn to look fragile in defence, particularly in the back row. Stransky dummied to drop a goal but cleverly went for the line instead. The attack was held, but South Africa were back in the game. A minute later, Stransky had levelled the scores with a penalty.

Back came Lomu with a wonderful run down the middle. He took out three men, but their presence prevented him from gathering full speed. Mehrtens then kicked his second penalty in front of the posts to put New Zealand back in front by 6–3. The pace was furious, but South Africa no longer seemed intimidated. Then, Mehrtens dropped out from his own 22 and the ball bounced 2 metres from the South African line. It was an astonishing kick, one of a number he was to display throughout the match. There simply wasn't a better kicker in the game.

The line-outs, thought to be the crucial area of the game, were keenly fought over. Both sides used four- and two-man line-outs from the start, South Africa having the edge. Joost van der Westhuizen, who was being closely patrolled by Michael Brewer and Graeme Bachop, then announced his arrival on the scene. It hadn't taken him as long in previous games. He almost squirmed his way over the line but was held. Then Kruger was over the line but he was twisted as he fell and may not have grounded the ball. The referee couldn't see, despite being on the scene, and ordered a 5-metre scrum.

Each time the South Africans arrived in their opponents' 22, they exerted tremendous pressure. They were unlucky not to get a try, but in due course, Stransky obliged with a penalty, which levelled matters again after twenty minutes. It was at this stage that it became noticeable that the Kiwis couldn't find their rhythm. The South African back row was dominating play and Zinzan Brooke could not get into the game. The match was turning.

Joost was back again. This time he hoisted a beautiful kick, which fell between Wilson and Osborne, and as they waited for the bounce, always a dangerous game in defence, Wilson was turned over in the tackle by Van der Westhuizen and New Zealand were forced to concede a penalty, which Stransky, uncharacteristically, missed. Ed Morrison was a bit too quick with the whistle – on many occasions he refused to allow advantage, which spoiled the flow of the game, especially for the All Blacks.

The public-address announcer then shamefully intruded into the game when, during a stoppage in play, he jocularly asked whether there were any New Zealand spectators present, and then whether there were any South Africans. Such interference was totally offside – it was merely a cue for another verse of 'Shosholoza'. But the crowd's hysteria was quickly brought to a shuddering halt as Lomu took off on a magnificent charging run. A try beckoned, but Josh Kronfeld, up in support, chose to take the tackle rather than give a scoring pass.

New Zealand badly needed to settle into the game and five points then would have done the trick. Once again, South Africa entered the All Blacks' 22 and once again they came away with the points. This time Stransky dropped a goal to give South Africa the lead for the first time, by 6–9. The Blacks brought pressure on themselves: Osborne and Lomu mysteriously fell over or slipped at critical times. Did they have the right studs in?

Like Van der Westhuizen, André Joubert had a quiet start. Mehrtens had managed to pin him down by kicking at his right foot so that he could not make those raking long touches. We also had to remember that it was only two weeks earlier that he had broken his hand. It was still sheathed in a green cover, a different one from the one he wore in the semis. Ian Jones had a towering game in the second row, but the All Blacks could not capitalize on his talents to score points, and sometimes they became frustrated at this and conceded silly penalties. The game was ebbing away from them. As half-time arrived, the 'Boks led 9–6.

South Africa were gradually suffocating the All Blacks' game. They had known since the opening match that line-out possession would be a problem. They had partially solved this in attack by getting Andrews to jump at 2, and in defence by moving him to the back of the line. This was an admirable ploy, and although it was a major gamble, it proved to be one of Christie's best decisions. Pienaar and Kruger in the back row and Mulder and Le Roux in the centre constantly hassled New Zealand, ensuring that Lomu was always under pressure when he received the ball so that even when he had space, Van der Westhuizen and Joubert – once with an ankle tap of the finest judgement – brought him down.

Eleven minutes into the second half the only surprise had been a stab at a dropped goal from halfway by Joubert, which had the distance but not the accuracy and drifted to the right. Yet it seemed to unnerve the Kiwis, for when Mehrtens had the chance to kick a long touch from the halfway line he chose instead to go for goal. His left foot slipped as he approached the kick and the ball bobbled away in embarrassment. To his great credit, Mehrtens did not lose his courage or his confidence, and a few minutes later he atoned for the error with a lovely dropped goal, which brought New Zealand back to 9–9. Marc Ellis came on for Jeff Wilson, who looked sick and out of sorts, and

Mehrtens almost immediately missed another drop. It had desperation written all over it, but maybe he was acting on instructions.

As we entered the final quarter of the game there were chances at both ends. Lomu looked clear and destined for the try-line when the referee, wrongly, called play back for a forward pass. Almost immediately, James Small was held up on the line at the other end. If anything the game seemed to be going back New Zealand's way, but the fact remained that neither set of forwards had achieved domination. At this critical juncture, the wretched public-address system was switched on to encourage the now quiet crowd. They were quiet because they were absorbed in an intense game. It might not have been a classic, but because it was so close, it was becoming evident that one mistake might win or lose the World Cup. No player wanted to be the one to commit such a heinous crime.

For the final twenty minutes, the All Blacks had more of the game but they couldn't quite hold that final pass or sew up periods of strong pressure. The South African defence was quite outstanding. One score would do it. With three minutes to go, Ian Jones won another line-out for New Zealand and Mehrtens went for fame and glory and tried for a dropped goal. It was high enough, but veered to the side. The South African nation heaved a collective sigh of relief. On full time, Joubert took a brilliant line-kick which found touch 15 metres out from the New Zealand line. Stransky was poised for the drop from the line-out. It was Sean Fitzpatrick's most crucial throw-in ever – or so we thought then. Up soared Ian Jones again. New Zealand were safe for now: the game was going into overtime.

During the five-minute break, Morné du Plessis came on to talk quietly to his players. Laurie Mains did the same for New Zealand. There were twenty more minutes to go before we would have a winner. The pressure-cooker tension was palpable. If we could feel it, what must it have been like for the players? Mehrtens cut into the atmosphere with a massive 55-metre penalty kick from in front of the posts. With eighteen minutes left it was 12–9. Soon Small was then free on the right and a try was on, but he gave a forward pass inside to Van der Westhuizen. The South Africans were still hungry; they wanted this final more. At the end of the third quarter, Stransky obliged with his third penalty goal. He was fast becoming the surprise success story of the whole tournament. It was 12–12 and there were ten minutes left. One fatal mistake would decide the game.

And then it happened. Stransky dropped his second goal to give South Africa the lead again. Unlike Rob Andrew's goal which wrapped up England's semi-final against Australia, however, it was not a last-ditch effort – there were still an excruciating seven minutes to go. It was nerve-tingling stuff. New Zealand continued to play to their strengths and ran the ball, though sadly Ellis was guilty on too many occasions of coming in from the wing when staying out would have been the better option; furthermore, he knocked on twice when it must, it seemed, have been easier to catch the ball. Time was running out for the Blacks. South Africa had one more chance to stretch their lead when Kronfeld went offside, but Stransky missed the penalty. It mattered little. Two minutes later it was finally all over.

François Pienaar sank to his knees and said a prayer. How long would it be before he appreciated what he had accomplished over those previous five weeks? The crowd, understandably, were completely delirious. The Springboks did a lap of honour to thank their supporters, which was made possible by the tight security at the ground. Red fences had been erected to prevent spectators from running on to the field. The team were received rapturously by the home fans. There was going to be the party to end all parties across the nation tonight. We stood in wonderment. Three more sky-divers arrived carrying three different messages. One said: 'Jo'burg, Sports Centre of Africa'; another, 'Congratulations South Africa'. The last slowly descending diver waltzed in front of us spreading the message 'See You in Wales 1999'. Neat touches to an amazing afternoon.

President Nelson Mandela was next onstage. The crowd roared his name. The whites were gradually coming to love this truly outstanding man. He took off his Springbok cap and acknowledged their cheers again – the politician in him milking it for all it was worth. While we were waiting for the presentation of the William Webb Ellis trophy, SABC, who had cornered François Pienaar and were interviewing him, relayed the interview over the PA system so that we could all hear what he had to say. It was another pleasing touch. 'This has been the greatest six weeks of my life,' declared the South African captain. 'It's been very tough; the All Blacks played superbly.'

'What about the crowd?' asked the interviewer.

191

'The crowd? There were not sixty-three thousand cheering us on out there. There were forty-three million.' His answer was so apt that it was difficult to believe that it was delivered off the cuff and hadn't been carefully rehearsed. 'It went down to the wire. We had to keep calm. Joel Stransky, you beauty,' he added.

A beaming Mandela handed the cup to Pienaar, two different people wearing the same shirt. Long may it last. The lap of honour to display their prize began. The All Blacks, some of whom had trooped off, rallied and, led by Zinzan Brooke, went across to the large contingents of Kiwi supporters to thank them. It was a brave gesture from a beaten side who would struggle for some days to understand how they had contrived to lose the third World Cup.

It came as no surprise that the press conferences were packed to the rafters. New Zealand, as the losers, were first up. Sean Fitzpatrick was surprisingly upbeat, and even managed to raise a laugh. He had become one of the great captains in the history of the game and had also established himself as a mean competitor and a flashy scorer of tries. On the field he talked non-stop to the referee and frequently gained yards with penalties by placing the ball some way in front of the referee's divot. Even today, there was one occasion on which Ed Morrison had been obliged to move the ball back to its rightful place. Laurie Mains masked his disappointment; Colin Meads looked glum and miserable and said nothing. Brian Lochore appeared to have aged ten years. The truth was that New Zealand had lost a final they should have won comfortably. They had been rocked by the solid tackling of the two wing forwards, Ruben Kruger and François Pienaar, and the two centres, Japie Mulder and Hennie le Roux.

South Africa's press conference was, of course, dominated by the golden boy, François Pienaar. 'Seeing Nelson Mandela wearing my shirt was the biggest thrill of my life,' he said. 'He came into the changing room before the match and saw that we were calm. He thanked us for what we had done for South Africa; we returned the compliment. We may have been calm, but we were tense, too.' Kitch Christie put the win down to 'defence. In the semi-finals we didn't let in a try, nor did we in the final. That's why we won. Lomu? He's a giant. I had no idea how big he was until I saw him in the tunnel before the game.'

'I'm the happiest man in the world,' concluded Pienaar.

And so to the post-mortem dinner, which was a curious affair. The players or captains trooped up, some wrongly called, to accept their medals for first, second, third and fourth places. François Pienaar, still overcome by the whole thing, gave speech number 16 and everyone thought, hooray, we can start supper – or at least the main course. But nobody had counted on a gatecrasher, some guy called Louis the Lip, who wanted to hog the show. He took the podium.

Before I speak I would like one man to come up here, Riaan Oberholzer. Ladies and gentlemen, of course for us South Africans this is a great day. This is what we have been waiting for for so many years. We boasted in '87 that the real World Cup was not won by New Zealand because we were not there. Then in '91, we boasted again. We were not there. Then in '95, we proved that if we had been there, we would have won.

I want to say one thing. So much has been said about Rugby World Cup. If ever one man made all this possible, one man who worked round the clock, one who did everything for South Africa, it was Riaan Oberholzer.

Riaan Oberholzer just happened to be Luyt's son-in-law. Luyt continued:

I heard that my coach, Kitch Christie, today told his players he was not available henceforth. I want to tell you, you haven't spoken to me yet, pal [pointing at Christie from the podium]. You will be available. So will you, Morné du Plessis [gesticulating again]. You will be available. We build the perfect team around a perfect manager. The manager, Morné, the coach, Kitch, and the team.

I heard that Murdoch's name was mentioned here. Sir Ewart Bell said we must never lose the rugby culture. Sir Ewart, we today assure you we would never lose it. Rugby Union is part of our culture. And this is the way to show League that we are there.

I thank you for your support and I thank you for coming here. I thank you for supporting this country. We went through very tremendous periods, tumultuous periods. There was a time when the rugby World Cup could have been removed from South Africa. We fought for it, we kept it here, and we showed the world that we can host it, and host it in a way that will be very difficult, may I say to Wales, to emulate.

It was incredible, and in absurdly bad taste. Luyt then gave a gold watch to Derek Bevan (which he later auctioned, such was his embarrassment), who wasn't the right referee, and forgot to thank Ed Morrison and his two linesmen. He was like a cross between Marlon Brando's Godfather and, more uncomfortably, Robert Maxwell.

Within five minutes, the New Zealand team had packed their bags and cleared the site and they were followed by the English and the French teams. The evening had been sullied; there was a nasty smell and for once it wasn't the old farts. Was this modern rugby? Perhaps, in Luyt's defence, it could be pointed out that his speech was off the cuff, and it was clear, too, that English was not his first language. There were repercussions that evening: Mike Brewer apparently had a few choice words for Luyt, and Tom Kiernan, too, gave the South African supremo a piece of his mind.

The following morning, as everyone began to wind down from this terrific month-long rugby extravaganza, the SARFU called a hurried press conference to try to spin Dr Luyt's speech into a positive. Edward Griffiths spent the day doing his level best to persuade the media that one speech shouldn't spoil the party. There was some talk of Luyt resigning, but that seemed unlikely. The English, too, were giving a final farewell conference, and the French were holding a debriefing at Club France in Pretoria. Club France was in a beautifully civilized setting. The French Fédération de Rugby had decided that as they were in Pretoria for the opening pool games, they needed a place to entertain the players, their partners, administrators and embassy officials. It was easily the best party in town. The gathering was addressed by Bernard Lapasset, the last president of the IB under the existing pattern of Buggins' turn for a year at a time. In September 1995, the IB meeting in Tokyo would decide a new structure, to be examined by a committee of Lapasset, Syd Millar of Ireland, John Jeavons-Fellows of England and Alan Sharp of Canada. By the time this book is published you will have read about the outcome. Lapasset said that the generally favoured option was to have a president for three years, and yes, the favourite was Vernon Pugh of Wales. When pressed on whether there would be a chief executive for the IB and a chief executive for RWC '99, he would not be drawn, but his smile suggested that something of this order was likely.

And what of amateurism, the sole item on the agenda of the August IB meeting in Paris? 'I think it is accepted, even by Ireland and Scotland, that the days of amateur rugby are over,' said Lapasset. 'We must now move to a non-professional scenario, a life between going truly open. The French have had such a system in place this past year, and it has worked very well. I favour it. The new regulations are out with all the presidents of the board members and we should have a resolution in August.' And, indeed, at this meeting rugby union went, if not totally professional, at least open and more honest.

Bernard Lapasset has spent his life in public service as a civil servant in Customs and Excise. He is a thoroughly decent sort of chap. He was honest and straightforward and, on the subject of Berbizier, resolute that the French coach should continue in his role and that his selection policy for the semi-finals had not been faulty. Lapasset was almost too nice to be immersed in the cut-throat world of rugby politics. However, he would soon be involved in the cut-throat world of politics proper. The French were due to entertain the New Zealanders for a two-Test series in November. The trouble was that a different sort of test was going to be taking place before then. President Jacques Chirac of France had given the go-ahead for a nuclear test in the Pacific Ocean. Prime Minister Jim Bolger in New Zealand had vowed to stop it and had threatened to pull the tour. This was a double blow for Bernard Lapasset because, after the *Rainbow Warrior* affair in which French secret agents had sunk the Greenpeace boat in Auckland Harbour, he had helped found the French–New Zealand Society in Paris to foster stronger relationships between the two countries. It was just his luck that he was president of this organization too in 1995.

The day of World Cup final hangovers concluded with the Famous Grouse Awards dinner. The prizes went to Jonah Lomu for best player; to Josh Kronfeld for best try, against England; and to Italy, for best non-seeded team. This exhilarating but exhausting tournament was over, and it was time to go home.

Epilogue

The three years preceding the third rugby World Cup were given over to the discussion of two major questions. The first was, when would the game at last go open? On the Friday morning before the final between South Africa and New Zealand we were given the answer to that when the presidents of South Africa, New Zealand and Australia respectively announced their ten-year US$550 million television rights deal with Rupert Murdoch's Newscorp.

The second matter was whether the third World Cup would in fact take place in South Africa. On that score, I was deeply opposed to the Republic being awarded the tournament in the first place. It was a mistake, and one that will come back to haunt the organizers of future World Cups. South Africa should have paid her dues to the international rugby fraternity first. Marcel Martin was the most relieved man leaving South Africa at the end of June 1995. He and Louis Luyt had not seen eye to eye on most aspects of the management of the tournament, and had been on the receiving end of a great deal of hostility from the SARFU.

None the less, the tournament was an outstanding success for the hosts. Rugby Union united this new country, born out of such hatred and division, and this must be considered an extraordinary feat by any standards. Merle McKenna's magical opening ceremony brought such joy and such tears to the new nation that we were lucky the start of the opening game between South Africa and Australia wasn't delayed by flooding on the pitch. It was simply breathtaking just to be a part of it all. And then, to complete the day, South Africa defeated the world champions of 1991.

That win both made and destroyed the 1995 rugby World Cup. It meant that South Africa would, at least, make it to the semi-finals and, with a good wind, to the final as well – they had only to play the runner-up from the England pool, Western Samoa, to qualify for the semis. For England and Australia, on the other hand, things were much tougher. One of them would be on an early plane home after the quarter-finals. Their route to the final was the hardest in the tournament. England had to try to overcome Australia, then New Zealand, then South Africa in the space of fourteen days to win the competition.

The pool matches were fascinating. Teams which had not been able to threaten the old hegemony – Italy, Western Samoa (again) and Argentina – showed that they must now be treated with respect. Tonga, too, showed flashes of brilliance, and if both Pacific Islands sides could stop the drain of players to New Zealand and Australia, they would emerge in the second tier of countries, which now included Wales and Ireland. As to the overall standard of play, this was much harder to evaluate. For one thing, the laws were different in 1995 from those in force in both 1991 and 1987; for another the general levels of mental and physical fitness were much higher – witness the number of games that were only settled in the first, second or third minute of extra time. In 1987, New Zealand dominated the tournament because the threat from Australia failed to emerge. In 1991, it was team-work rather than individual brilliance that was to the fore – then, Australia and England were clearly the two best teams and in David Campese, that tournament had the most charismatic figure. The Wales–Ireland game in 1995 sunk rugby and the World Cup to new depths. Players could not think for themselves, couldn't give or take a ball and failed to appreciate some of the most basic of skills. But, overall, the standard of play was, I think, higher. Japan, despite their hammerings, were a much better side than they were in either 1987 or 1991 – it was just that everyone else had progressed at a faster rate.

The 1995 tournament brought before the world many new players, mainly All Blacks, who were to dominate the event. Jonah Lomu was formidable – his speed off the mark drew gasps from an excited crowd. Andrew Mehrtens was a sensation – his kicking out of hand was unreal – and Josh Kronfeld covered more ground than a Wilton carpet. Yet the team of the tournament was, unquestionably, South Africa.

Tactically, though, few teams developed during the competition. Only Scotland, New Zealand and South Africa demonstrated new thinking when confronting old adversaries. England, aside from the second-team outing against Western Samoa, were locked into 1991 mode. France took an age to combine discipline with flair, and in the end Berbizier lost the semi-final because of his commitment to Christophe Deylaud at fly-half. Yet, on the day, France were a better side than South Africa, even if both were affected by the dreadful conditions, and must count themselves unlucky not to have reached their second final.

New Zealand emerged during the pool rounds as the one team who had been brave with selection and with opting for the type of game necessary to win the World Cup. Bachop, Mehrtens, Little, Bunce, Wilson, Lomu and Osborne, with Ellis in reserve, were the most formidable set of threequarters gathered in one team since the British Lions of 1971. They pooh-poohed the current coaching concept that you cannot score tries from first-phase possession. They were the biggest breath of fresh air in the whole place. Given the brilliance of their games against Scotland and England, it was and is still hard to understand quite how they blew it in the final. Laurie Mains had taken much stick in New Zealand for the two years leading up to the World Cup, but his originality of thinking and in the preparation of his players was outstanding.

In the end, we all had to reassess South Africa on the world stage. Dr Luyt's memory was short when he suggested in that graceless speech that had South Africa been in the 1987 and 1991 World Cups (never mind that irritation called apartheid, to which he was a party) they would have won. In 1992 South Africa lost at home to both New Zealand and Australia and away to England. They drew a series in France and then lost series to France at home, and Australia and New Zealand (both away). The critical elements in South Africa's success were the management. Morné du Plessis was the key figure here. Despite his long absence from the game, his innate intelligence and catholicism was behind the team's thinking in terms of the larger society of which they had become a part in the 1990s. It would be difficult to overestimate his contribution. Ultimately, he was the real star of 1995. England had no separate manager – Jack Rowell doubled as coach-manager, a mistake in retrospect; New Zealand confused the picture by having both Colin Meads and Brian Lochore in attendance alongside Laurie Mains; France needed someone in addition to Pierre Berbizier to moderate his tantrums. Along with Du Plessis, Kitch Christie, François Pienaar and Nelson Mandela were the constituents of South Africa's success, and how they deserved it. Let us hope that Edward Griffiths' fertile plans for redevelopment in the townships will bring more than just rugby balls and rugby pitches.

Twenty teams will assemble in Cardiff in September 1999. By then the Arms Park will have been rebuilt and we will have some idea of how the seedings will operate. I am against the existing pool competition that has so far been a part of every World Cup. As I have said, if the seedings are to have real worth, then the eight best teams should qualify automatically to a last-sixteen stage. That way many more than twelve other teams could qualify for the pool stage. As matters currently stand for 1999, there will be a plate competition for those knocked out of the pool stage, which means that every side will be able to stay on for a final. That in itself is a major innovation. The question of the opening game also needs addressing. Should Wales lose to South Africa in the first match of 1999, they can virtually say goodbye to any further involvement in the tournament. An opening ceremony of Olympic quality staged separately from the matches themselves would dispense with the requirement for a 'big' game to kick off the tournament, and Wales might stand a better chance of qualifying for the quarter-finals and beyond.

The management of world rugby is a mess. There has always been too much petty bourgeois, even mean-minded, politics in rugby. Far too many men who are undistinguished in their own careers have used the game as a way of soothing their own mid-life crises. This has suffocated rugby. The IB need to appoint a chief executive to run the sport and part of his or her domain should be the rugby World Cup. Running rugby and the World Cup as separate entities has been greatly to the detriment of the sport.

The players themselves now need their own world players' organization on the lines of the USPGA. Perhaps Grant Fox, Brian Moore and Nick Farr-Jones would be the appropriate figures to kick-start this for the current generation of players.

Sport has a bad name. Its senior institutions have been neither publicly accountable nor democratically organized; indeed, they have too frequently become the fiefdom of one man. Rugby must be the candle that lights the world.

The desire of the three senior southern hemisphere countries – Australia, New Zealand and South Africa – to force the majority of the senior northern hemisphere nations, of which Wales and France were the leaders, to create a professional game at international level was embodied in rugby lore in Paris in August 1995. At that meeting the IB announced that rugby was to go open, and would thus embrace professionalism, something with which, as we have seen, it had struggled to come to terms for the previous thirty years.

The most critical decision in the history of the modern game was made without a formal vote. Had one been taken, the sport would not have gone open: such is the state of the body that governs world rugby.

The game is now challenged as never before. The southern triumvirate does not have to contend with club rugby. These countries all share a similar set-up – that is, a pyramid of national and regional or provincial sides. Their northern brothers, by contrast, have a national and club structure. Indeed, club rugby has become the talk of the City of London. Leading clubs like Saracens, Richmond, Newcastle and Harlequins have found fairy godfathers; others, such as Bath and Wasps, hope to launch themselves on the unlisted securities market to raise the £5 million needed to compete in this open world. The rest will struggle, and ultimately go to the knacker's yard unless they can find their own unique solution. This was never the intention of the August 1995 IB meeting, but within six months it had become the new reality.

The IB, lacking judgement, did not take cognizance of the success of the salaries-for-caps scenario that dominates American and some elements of Australian professional sport. Nor did they commission a report, as New Zealand had done from the Boston Consultancy Group, to analyse the potential impact of their decision. They truly are an amateur lot.

In England, professional club Rugby League had been rescued from near oblivion by the television money of Newscorp. In its fresh, vibrant incarnation as a summer game, it now has a chance to develop a new audience. Among other consequences, this has led to a number of players signing professional forms for both League and Union sides, such as English and Australian cricketers have done down the years.

When the Wigan Rugby League club creamed the élite of the Rugby Union competition in winning the Middlesex Sevens at their first attempt in May 1996, such was the fascination of the spectacle of a fully fledged professional side playing that the Twickenham car parks, normally buzzing throughout the afternoon, emptied. The best of the Union players now knew how far they still had to go to match their counterparts. It was a salutary lesson which had been hinted at earlier that week when Wigan's thirteen-a-side team put over eighty points past English League and Cup double-winners Bath in a rather pointless game of Rugby League. Nothing had changed in this respect since the two codes were last pitted against one another, at international level under Union rules at the end of the Second World War.

The logical conclusion to all this is that there will be only one code covering both sports before the fourth rugby World Cup in 1999. It will depend on how much the media moguls are prepared to throw at the game to make it truly global. The amalgamated code might keep proper scrums and line-outs but use only thirteen players, while doing away with rucks and adopting the League tackle law.

This scenario will prove the leap of faith in Paris to have been a costly error, one of such magnitude that from the professional ashes, now inextricably linked to the media barons, will rise a new game with its own separate administration, made up of fifteen players a side, called amateur Rugby Union. I would be its first member.

Statistics

THE WORLD CUP 1987

POOL A

	P	W	D	L	F	A	Pts
AUSTRALIA	3	3	0	0	108	41	6
ENGLAND	3	2	0	1	100	32	4
USA	3	1	0	2	39	99	2
JAPAN	3	0	0	3	48	123	0

23 May, Sydney

AUSTRALIA 19
Tries: Campese, Poidevin
Con: Lynagh
PGs: Lynagh (3)

ENGLAND 6
Try: Harrison
Con: Webb

24 May, Brisbane

UNITED STATES 21
Tries: Purcell, Nelson, Lambert
Cons: Nelson (3)
PG: Nelson

JAPAN 18
Tries: Taumoefolau (2), Yoshinaga
PGs: Yoshinaga, Kutsuki

30 May, Sydney

ENGLAND 60
Tries: R. Underwood (2), Rees, Salmon,
    Richards, Simms, Harrison (3),
    Redman
Cons: Webb (7)
PGs: Webb (2)

JAPAN 7
Try: Miyamoto
PG: Matsuo

31 May, Brisbane

AUSTRALIA 47
Tries: pen. try, Smith, Slack, Leeds (2),
    Papworth, Campese, Codey
Cons: Lynagh (6)
PG: Lynagh

UNITED STATES 12
Try: Nelson
Con: Nelson
PG: Nelson
DG: Nelson

3 June, Sydney

ENGLAND 34
Tries: Winterbottom (2), Harrison, Dooley
Cons: Webb (3)
PGs: Webb (4)

UNITED STATES 6
Try: Purcell
Con: Nelson

3 June, Sydney

AUSTRALIA 42
Tries: Slack (2), Tuynman, Burke (2),
     Grigg, Harthill, Campese
Cons: Lynagh (5)

JAPAN 23
Tries: Kutsuki, Okidoi, Fujita
Con: Okidoi
PGs: Okidoi (2)
DG: Okidoi

POOL B

	P	W	D	L	F	A	Pts
WALES	3	3	0	0	82	31	6
IRELAND	3	2	0	1	84	41	4
CANADA	3	1	0	2	65	90	2
TONGA	3	0	0	3	29	98	0

24 May, Napier

CANADA 37
Tries: Stuart, Frame (2), Vaesen (2),
     Palmer (2)
Cons: Wyatt (2), Rees
PG: Rees

TONGA 4
Try: Valu

25 May, Wellington

WALES 13
Try: Ring
PG: Thorburn
DGs: Davies (2)

IRELAND 6
PGs: Kiernan (2)

29 May, Palmerston North

WALES 29
Tries: Webbe (3), Hadley
Cons: Thorburn (2)
DG: Davies
PGs: Thorburn (2)

TONGA 16
Tries: Fiela, Etaiki
Con: Liava'a
PGs: Amone, Liava'a

30 May, Dunedin

IRELAND 46
Tries: Bradley, Crossan (2), Spillane,
     Ringland, McNeill
Cons: Kiernan (5)
PGs: Kiernan (2)
DGs: Kiernan, Ward

CANADA 19
Try: Cardinal
PGs: Rees (3), Wyatt
DG: Rees

3 June, Brisbane

WALES 40
Tries: I. Evans (4), Bowen, Devereux,
      Hadley, A. Phillips
Cons: Thorburn (4)

CANADA 9
PGs: Rees (3)

3 June, Brisbane

IRELAND 32
Tries: McNeill (2), Mullin (3)
Cons: Ward (3)
PGs: Ward (2)

TONGA 9
PGs: Amone (3)

POOL C

	P	W	D	L	F	A	Pts
NEW ZEALAND	3	3	0	0	190	34	6
FIJI	3	1	0	2	56	101	2
ITALY	3	1	0	2	40	110	2
ARGENTINA	3	1	0	2	49	90	2

22 May, Auckland

NEW ZEALAND 70
Tries: pen. try, Jones, Kirk (2), Taylor,
      Green (2), McDowell, Kirwan (2),
      Stanley, A. Whetton
Cons: Fox (8)
PGs: Fox (2)

ITALY 6
PG: Collodo
DG: Collodo

24 May, Hamilton

FIJI 28
Tries: Gale, Naiviliwasa, Nalaga, Savai
Cons: Koroduadua (2), Rokowailoa
PGs: Koroduadua (2)

ARGENTINA 9
Try: Travaglini
Con: Porta
PG: Porta

27 May, Christchurch

NEW ZEALAND 74
Tries: Green (4), Gallagher (4), Kirk,
      Kirwan, pen. try, A. Whetton
Cons: Fox (10)
PGs: Fox (2)

FIJI 13
Try: Savai
PGs: Koroduadua (3)

28 May, Christchurch

ARGENTINA 25
Tries: J. Lanza, Gomez
Con: Porta
PGs: Porta (5)

ITALY 16
Tries: Innocenti, Cuttitta
Con: Collodo
PGs: Collodo (2)

31 May, Dunedin

ITALY 18
Tries: Cuttitta, Cucchiella, Mascioletti
PG: Collodo
DG: Collodo

FIJI 15
Try: Naiviliwasa
Con: Koroduadua
PGs: Koroduadua (2)
DG: Qoro

31 May, Dunedin

NEW ZEALAND 46
Tries: Kirk, Z. Brooke, Stanley, Earl,
      Crowley, A. Whetton
Cons: Fox (2)
PGs: Fox (6)

ARGENTINA 15
Try: J. Lanza
Con: Porta
PGs: Porta (3)

POOL D

	P	W	D	L	F	A	Pts
FRANCE	3	2	1	0	145	44	5
SCOTLAND	3	2	1	0	135	69	5
ROMANIA	3	1	0	2	61	130	2
ZIMBABWE	3	0	0	3	53	151	0

23 May, Auckland

ROMANIA 21
Tries: Paraschiv, Toader, Hodorca
PGs: Alexandru (3)

ZIMBABWE 20
Tries: Tsimba (2), Neill
Con: Ferreira
PGs: Ferreira (2)

23 May, Christchurch

SCOTLAND 20
Tries: White, Duncan
PGs: G. Hastings (4)

FRANCE 20
Tries: Sella, Berbizier, Blanco
Con: Blanco
PGs: Blanco (2)

28 May, Wellington

FRANCE 55
Tries: Charvet (2), Sella, Andrieu,
      Camberabero, Erbani, Laporte,
      Lagisquet (2)
Cons: Laporte (8)
PG: Laporte

ROMANIA 12
PGs: Bezuscu (4)

30 May, Wellington

SCOTLAND 60
Tries: Tait (2), Duncan (2), Oliver,
      G. Hastings, Paxton (2), Jeffrey,
      Tukalo (2)
Cons: G. Hastings (8)

ZIMBABWE 21
Try: D. Buitendag
Con: Grobler
PGs: Grobler (5)

2 June, Auckland

FRANCE 70
Tries: Modin (3), Dubroca, Rodriguez (2),
    Charvet (2), Camberabero (3),
    Laporte, Esteve
Cons: Camberabero (9)

ZIMBABWE 12
Try: Kaulbach
Con: Grobler
PGs: Grobler (2)

2 June, Dunedin

SCOTLAND 55
Tries: Tait (2), Jeffrey (3), Duncan,
    G. Hastings (2), Tukalo (2)
Cons: G. Hastings (8)
PG: G. Hastings

ROMANIA 28
Tries: Murariu (2), Toader
Cons: Alexandru, Ion
PGs: Alexandru (4)

QUARTER-FINALS

6 June, Lancaster Park

NEW ZEALAND 30
Tries: A. Whetton, Gallagher
Cons: Fox (2)
PGs: Fox (6)

SCOTLAND 3
PG: G. Hastings

7 June, Sydney

AUSTRALIA 33
Tries: McIntyre, Smith, Burke (2)
Cons: Lynagh (4)
PGs: Lynagh (3)

IRELAND 15
Tries: McNeill, Kiernan
Cons: Kiernan (2)
PG: Kiernan

7 June, Sydney

FRANCE 31
Tries: Lorieux, Rodriguez (2), Lagisquet
Cons: Laporte (3)
PGs: Laporte (2)
DG: Laporte

FIJI 16
Tries: Qoro, Damu
Con: Koroduadua
PGs: Koroduadua (2)

8 June, Brisbane

WALES 16
Tries: Roberts, Jones, Devereux
Cons: Thorburn (2)

ENGLAND 3
PG: Webb

SEMI-FINALS

13 June, Sydney

FRANCE 30
Tries: Lorieux, Sella, Lagisquet, Blanco
Cons: Camberabero (4)
PGs: Camberabero (2)

AUSTRALIA 24
Tries: Campese, Codey
Cons: Lynagh (2)
PGs: Lynagh (3)
DG: Lynagh

NEW ZEALAND 49
Tries: Kirwan, Shelford (2), Drake,
    A. Whetton, Stanley, Brooke,
    Cowden
Cons: Fox (7)
PG: Fox (1)

WALES 6
Tries: Devereux, Thorburn

THIRD–FOURTH PLACE PLAY-OFF

18 June, Rotorua International Stadium

WALES 22
Tries: Roberts, P. Moriarty, Hadley
Cons: Thorburn (2)
PGs: Thorburn (2)

AUSTRALIA 21
Tries: Burke, Grigg
Cons: Lynagh (2)
PGs: Lynagh (2)
DG: Lynagh

FINAL

20 June, Auckland

NEW ZEALAND 29
Tries: Jones, Kirk, Kirwan
Con: Fox
PGs: Fox (4)
DG: Fox

FRANCE 9
Try: Berbizier
Con: Camberabero
PG: Camberabero

THE WORLD CUP 1991

POOL A

	P	W	D	L	F	A	Pts
NEW ZEALAND	3	3	0	0	95	39	9
ENGLAND	3	2	0	1	85	33	7
ITALY	3	1	0	2	57	76	5
USA	3	0	0	3	24	113	3

3 October, Twickenham

NEW ZEALAND 18
Tries: M. Jones
Con: Fox
PGs: Fox (4)

ENGLAND 12
PGs: Webb (3)
DG: Andrew

5 October, Otley

ITALY 30
Tries: Barba, Francescato, Vaccari,
    Gaetaneillo
Cons: Dominguez (4)
PGs: Dominguez (2)

USA 9
Try: Swords
Con: Williams
PG: Williams

8 October, Gloucester

NEW ZEALAND 46
Tries: Earl, Wright (3), Purvis, Timu,
    Tuigamala, Innes
Cons: Preston (4)
PGs: Preston (2)

USA 6
PGs: Williams (2)

8 October, Twickenham

ENGLAND 36
Tries: R. Underwood, Guscott (2), Webb
Cons: Webb (4)
PGs: Webb (4)

ITALY 6
Try: Marcello Cuttitta
Con: Dominguez

11 October, Twickenham

ENGLAND 37
Tries: R. Underwood (2), Carling, Skinner,
    Heslop
Cons: Hodgkinson (4)
PGs: Hodgkinson (3)

USA 9
Try: Nelson
Con: Williams
PG: Williams

13 October, Leicester

NEW ZEALAND 31
Tries: Z. Brooke, Innes, Tuigamala,
    Hewett
Cons: Fox (3)
PGs: Fox (3)

ITALY 21
Tries: Marcello Cuttitta, Bonomi
Cons: Dominguez (2)
PGs: Dominguez (3)

POOL B

	P	W	D	L	F	A	Pts
SCOTLAND	3	3	0	0	122	36	9
IRELAND	3	2	0	1	102	51	7
JAPAN	3	1	0	2	77	87	5
ZIMBABWE	3	0	0	3	31	158	3

5 October, Murrayfield

SCOTLAND 47
Tries: S. Hastings, Stanger, Chalmers, pen.
    try, White, Tukalo, G. Hastings
Cons: G. Hastings (5)
PGs: Chalmers, G. Hastings (2)

JAPAN 9
Try: Hosokawa
Con: Hosokawa
PG: Hosokawa

6 October, Dublin

IRELAND 55
Tries: Robinson (4), Geoghegan,
    Popplewell (2), Curtis
Cons: Keyes (4)
PGs: Keyes (5)

ZIMBABWE 11
Tries: Dawson, Schultz
PG: Ferreira

9 October, Dublin

IRELAND 32
Tries: O'Hara, Mannion (2), Staples
Cons: Keyes (2)
PGs: Keyes (4)

JAPAN 16
Tries: Hayashi, Kujihara, Yoshida
Cons: Hosokawa (2)

9 October, Murrayfield

SCOTLAND 51
Tries: Tukalo (3), Turnbull, Stanger, Weir,
       White, S. Hastings
Cons: Dods (5)
PGs: Dods (2)
DG: Wyllie

ZIMBABWE 12
Tries: Garvey (2)
Cons: Currin (2)

12 October, Murrayfield

SCOTLAND 24
Tries: Shiel, Armstrong
Cons: G. Hastings (2)
PGs: G. Hastings (3)
DG: Chalmers

IRELAND 15
PGs: Keyes (4)
DG: Keyes

14 October, Belfast

JAPAN 52
Tries: Horikoshi, Yoshida (2), Masuho (2),
       Kutsuki (2), Tifaga, Matsuo
Cons: Hosokawa (5)
PGs: Hosokawa (2)

ZIMBABWE 8
Tries: Tsimba, Nguruve

POOL C

	P	W	D	L	F	A	Pts
AUSTRALIA	3	3	0	0	79	25	9
W. SAMOA	3	2	0	1	54	34	7
WALES	3	1	0	2	32	61	5
ARGENTINA	3	0	0	3	38	83	3

4 October, Llanelli

AUSTRALIA 32
Tries: Campese (2), Horan (2), Kearns
Cons: Lynagh (3)
PGs: Lynagh (2)

ARGENTINA 19
Tries: Teran (2)
Con: Del Castillo
PG: G. del Castillo
DGs: Arbizu (2)

6 October, Cardiff

WESTERN SAMOA 16
Tries: Vaega, Vaifale
Con: Vaea
PGs: Vaea (2)

WALES 13
Tries: Emyr, I. Evans
Con: Ring
PG: Ring

210

9 October, Pontypool

AUSTRALIA 9
PGs: Lynagh (3)

WESTERN SAMOA 3
PG: Vaea

9 October, Cardiff

WALES 16
Tries: Arnold
PGs: Ring (3), Rayer

ARGENTINA 7
Try: G. Simon
PG: G. del Castillo

12 October, Cardiff

AUSTRALIA 38
Tries: Roebuck (2), Slattery, Campese,
    Horan, Lynagh
Cons: Lynagh (4)
PGs: Lynagh (2)

WALES 3
PG: Ring

13 October, Pontypridd

WESTERN SAMOA 35
Tries: Tagaloa (2), Lima (2), Bunce,
    S. Bachop
Cons: Vaea (4)
PG: Vaea

ARGENTINA 12
Try: Teran
Con: Arbizu
PGs: Laborde, Arbizu

POOL D

	P	W	D	L	F	A	Pts
FRANCE	3	3	0	0	82	25	9
CANADA	3	2	0	1	45	33	7
ROMANIA	3	1	0	2	31	64	5
FIJI	3	0	0	3	27	63	3

4 October, Beziers

FRANCE 30
Tries: pen. try, Saint-André, Roumat,
    Lafond
Con: Camberabero
PGs: Camberabero (4)

ROMANIA 3
PG: Nichitean

5 October, Bayonne

CANADA 13
Try: S. Stewart
PGs: Rees (3)

FIJI 3
DG: Serevi

8 October, Grenoble

FRANCE 33
Tries: Sella (2) Lafond (3), Camberabero
Cons: Camberabero (3)
PG: Camberabero

FIJI 9
Try: Naruma
Con: Koroduadua
PG: Koroduadua

211

9 October, Toulouse

CANADA 19
Tries: MacKinnon, Ennis
Con: Wyatt
PGs: Wyatt (2)
DG: Rees

ROMANIA 11
Tries: Lungu, Sasu
PG: Nichitean

12 October, Brive

ROMANIA 17
Tries: Ion, Dumitras, Sasu
Con: Racean
PG: Racean

FIJI 15
PGs: Turuva (2)
DGs: Rabaka (2), Turuva

13 October, Agen

FRANCE 19
Tries: Lafond, Saint-André
Con: Camberabero
PGs: Camberabero, Lacroix (2)

CANADA 13
Try: Wyatt
PGs: Wyatt, Rees
DG: Rees

QUARTER-FINALS

19 October, Murrayfield

SCOTLAND 28
Tries: Stanger, Jeffrey (2)
Cons: G. Hastings (2)
PGs: G. Hastings (4)

WESTERN SAMOA 6
PG: Vaea
DG: Bachop

19 October, Paris

ENGLAND 19
Tries: R. Underwood, Carling
Con: Webb
PGs: Webb (3)

FRANCE 10
Try: Lafond
PGs: Lacroix (2)

20 October, Dublin

AUSTRALIA 19
Tries: Campese (2), Lynagh
Cons: Lynagh (2)
PG: Lynagh

IRELAND 18
Try: Hamilton
Con: Keyes
PGs: Keyes (3)
DG: Keyes

20 October, Lille

NEW ZEALAND 29
Tries: Timu (2) McCahill, Brooke, Kirwan
Cons: Fox (3)
PG: Fox

CANADA 13
Tries: Tynan, Charron
Con: Wyatt
PG: Wyatt

SEMI-FINALS

26 October, Murrayfield

ENGLAND 9
PGs: Webb (2)
DG: Andrew

SCOTLAND 6
PGs: G. Hastings (2)

27 October, Dublin

AUSTRALIA 16
Tries: Campese, Horan
Con: Lynagh
PGs: Lynagh (2)

NEW ZEALAND 6
PGs: Fox (2)

THIRD–FOURTH PLACE PLAY-OFF

30 October, Cardiff

NEW ZEALAND 13
Try: Little
PGs: Preston (3)

SCOTLAND 6
PGs: G. Hastings (2)

FINAL

2 November, Twickenham

AUSTRALIA 12
Try: Daly
Con: Lynagh
PGs: Lynagh (2)

ENGLAND 6
PGs: Webb (2)

THE WORLD CUP 1995

POOL A

	P	W	D	L	F	A	Pts
SOUTH AFRICA	3	3	0	0	68	26	9
AUSTRALIA	3	2	0	1	87	41	7
CANADA	3	1	0	2	45	50	5
ROMANIA	3	0	0	3	14	97	3

25 May, Cape Town

SOUTH AFRICA 27
Tries: Hendriks, Stransky
Con: Stransky
PGs: Stransky (4)
DG: Stransky

AUSTRALIA 18
Tries: Eales, Kearns
Con: Lynagh
PGs: Lynagh (2)

26 May, Port Elizabeth

CANADA 34
Tries: Snow, Charron, McKenzie
Cons: Rees (2)
PGs: Rees (4)
DG: Rees

ROMANIA 3
PG: Nichitean

30 May, Cape Town

SOUTH AFRICA 21
Tries: Richter (2)
Con: Johnson
PGs: Johnson (3)

ROMANIA 8
Try: Guranescu
Con: Ivanciuc

31 May, Port Elizabeth

AUSTRALIA 27
Tries: Tabua, Roff, Lynagh
Cons: Lynagh (3)
PGs: Lynagh (2)

CANADA 11
Try: Charron
PGs: Rees (2)

3 June, Stellenbosch

AUSTRALIA 42
Tries: Roff (2), Foley, Burke, Smith,
    Wilson
Cons: Burke (2), Eales (4)

ROMANIA 3
DG: Ivanciuc

3 June, Port Elizabeth

SOUTH AFRICA 20
Tries: Richter (2)
Cons: Stransky (2)
PGs: Stransky (2)

CANADA 0

POOL B

	P	W	D	L	F	A	Pts
ENGLAND	3	3	0	0	95	60	9
WESTERN SAMOA	3	2	0	1	96	88	7
ITALY	3	1	0	2	69	94	5
ARGENTINA	3	0	0	3	69	87	3

27 May, East London

WESTERN SAMOA 42
Tries: Lima (2), Harder (2), Tatupu,
    Kellett
Cons: Kellett (3)
PGs: Kellett (2)

ITALY 18
Tries: Marcello Cuttitta, Vaccari
Con: Dominguez
PG: Dominguez
DG: Dominguez

214

ENGLAND 24
PGs: Andrew (6)
DGs: Andrew (2)

ARGENTINA 18
Tries: Noriega, Arbizu
Con: Arbizu
PGs: Arbizu (2)

30 May, East London

WESTERN SAMOA 32
Tries: Harder, Leaupepe, Lam
Con: Kellett
PGs: Kellett (5)

ARGENTINA 26
Tries: Crexell, pen. try
Cons: Cilley (2)
PGs: Cilley (4)

31 May, Durban

ENGLAND 27
Tries: R. Underwood, T. Underwood
Con: Andrew
PGs: Andrew (5)

ITALY 20
Tries: Vaccari, Massimo Cuttitta
Cons: Dominguez (2)
PGs: Dominguez (2)

4 June, East London

ITALY 31
Tries: Vaccari, Gerosa, Dominguez
Cons: Dominguez (2)
PGs: Dominguez (4)

ARGENTINA 25
Tries: Martin, Corral, Cilley,
    pen. try
Con: Cilley
PG: Cilley

4 June, Durban

ENGLAND 44
Tries: Back, R. Underwood (2), pen. try
Cons: Callard (3)
PGs: Callard (5)
DG: Catt

WESTERN SAMOA 22
Tries: Sini (2), Umaga
Cons: Fa'amasino (2)
PG: Fa'amasino

POOL C

	P	W	D	L	F	A	Pts
NEW ZEALAND	3	3	0	0	222	45	9
IRELAND	3	2	0	1	93	94	7
WALES	3	1	0	2	89	68	5
JAPAN	3	0	0	3	55	252	3

27 May, Bloemfontein

WALES 57
Tries: I. Evans (2), G. Thomas (3), Taylor,
    Moore
Cons: N. Jenkins (5)
PGs: N. Jenkins (4)

JAPAN 10
Tries: Oto (2)

27 May, Johannesburg

NEW ZEALAND 43
Tries: Lomu (2), Bunce, Kronfeld, Osborne
Cons: Mehrtens (3)
PGs: Mehrtens (4)

IRELAND 19
Tries: Halpin, McBride, Corkery
Cons: Elwood (2)

31 May, Bloemfontein

IRELAND 50
Tries: Corkery, Francis, Geoghegan,
    Halvey, Hogan, pen. tries (2)
Cons: Burke (6)
PG: Burke

JAPAN 28
Tries: S. Latu, Izawa, Hirao, Takura
Cons: Y. Yoshida (4)

31 May, Johannesburg

NEW ZEALAND 34
Tries: Little, Ellis, Kronfeld
Cons: Mehrtens (2)
PGs: Mehrtens (4)
DG: Mehrtens

WALES 9
PGs: N. Jenkins (2)
DG: N. Jenkins

4 June, Bloemfontein

NEW ZEALAND 145
Tries: Ellis (6), Rush (3), Wilson (3),
    Osborne (2), R. Brooke (2), Loe,
    Ieremia, Culhane, Dowd, Henderson
Cons: Culhane (20)

JAPAN 17
Tries: Kajihara (2)
Cons: Hirose (2)
PG: Hirose

4 June, Johannesburg

IRELAND 24
Tries: Popplewell, McBride, Halvey
Cons: Elwood (3)
PG: Elwood

WALES 23
Tries: Humphreys, Taylor
Cons: N. Jenkins (2)
PGs: N. Jenkins (2)
DG: A. Davies

POOL D

	P	W	D	L	F	A	Pts
FRANCE	3	3	0	0	114	47	9
SCOTLAND	3	2	0	1	149	27	7
TONGA	3	1	0	2	44	90	5
IVORY COAST	3	0	0	3	29	172	3

26 May, Rustenburg

SCOTLAND 89
Tries: G. Hastings (4), Walton (2), Logan
    (2), Chalmers, Stanger, Burnell,
    Wright, Shiel
Cons: G. Hastings (9)
PGs: G. Hastings (2)

IVORY COAST 0

26 May, Pretoria

FRANCE 38
Tries: Lacroix (2), Hueber, Saint-André
Cons: Lacroix (3)
PGS: Lacroix (3)
DG: Delaigue

TONGA 10
Try: T. Va'enuku
Con: Tu'ipulotu
PG: Tu'ipulotu

30 May, Rustenburg

FRANCE 54
Tries: Lacroix (2), Benazzi, Accoceberry,
    Viars, Costes, Techoueyres, Saint-
    André
Cons: Lacroix (2), Deylaud (2)
PGs: Lacroix (2)

IVORY COAST 18
Tries: Camara, Soulama
Con: Kouassi
PGs: Kouassi (2)

30 May, Pretoria

SCOTLAND 41
Tries: Peters, G. Hastings, S. Hastings
Con: G. Hastings
PGs: G. Hastings (8)

TONGA 5
Try: Fenukitau

3 June, Rustenburg

TONGA 29
Tries: Tu'ipulotu, Latukefu, 'Otai, pen. try
Cons: Tu'ipulotu (3)
PG: Tu'ipulotu

IVORY COAST 11
Try: Okou
PGs: Dali (2)

3 June, Pretoria

FRANCE 22
Try: Ntamack
Con: Lacroix
PGs: Lacroix (5)

SCOTLAND 19
Try: Wainwright
Con: G. Hastings
PGs: G. Hastings (4)

QUARTER-FINALS

10 June, Durban

FRANCE 36
Tries: Saint-André, Ntamack
Con: Lacroix
PGs: Lacroix (8)

IRELAND 12
PGs: Elwood (4)

10 June, Johannesburg

SOUTH AFRICA 42
Tries: Williams (4), Rossouw, Andrews
Cons: Johnson (3)
PGs: Johnson (2)

WESTERN SAMOA 14
Tries: Nu'uali'itia, Tatupu
Cons: Fa'amasino (2)

217

11 June, Cape Town

ENGLAND 25
Try: T. Underwood
Con: Andrew
PGs: Andrew (5)
DG: Andrew

AUSTRALIA 22
Try: Smith
Con: Lynagh
PGs: Lynagh (5)

11 June, Pretoria

NEW ZEALAND 48
Tries: Little (2), Lomu, Mehrtens, Bunce,
    Fitzpatrick
Cons: Mehrtens (6)
PGs: Mehrtens (2)

SCOTLAND 30
Tries: Weir (2), S. Hastings
Cons: G. Hastings (3)
PGs: G. Hastings (3)

SEMI-FINALS

17 June, Durban

SOUTH AFRICA 19
Try: Kruger
Con: Stransky
PGs: Stransky (4)

FRANCE 15
PGs: Lacroix (5)

18 June, Cape Town

NEW ZEALAND 45
Tries: Lomu (4), Kronfeld, Bachop
Cons: Mehrtens (3)
PG: Mehrtens
DGs: Z. Brooke, Mehrtens

ENGLAND 29
Tries: R. Underwood (2), Carling (2)
Cons: Andrew (3)
PG: Andrew

THIRD–FOURTH PLACE PLAY-OFF

22 June, Loftus Versfeld

FRANCE 19
Tries: Roumat, Ntamack
PGs: Lacroix (3)

ENGLAND 9
PGs: Andrew (3)

FINAL

24 June, Ellis Park

SOUTH AFRICA 15
PGs: Stransky (3)
DGs: Stransky (2)

NEW ZEALAND 12 (a.e.t.)
PGs: Mehrtens (3)
DG: Mehrtens

SOUTH AFRICA: A. Joubert; J. Small (B. Venter), J. Mulder, H. le Roux, C.
Williams; J. Stransky, J. van der Westhuizen; J. du Randt, C. Rossouw, I. Swart (G.
Pagel), J. Wiese, J. Strydom, F. Pienaar (c), M. Andrews (R. Straeuli), R. Kruger
NEW ZEALAND: G. Osborne; J. Wilson (M. Ellis), F. Bunce, W. Little, J. Lomu;
A. Mehrtens, G. Bachop (A. Strachan, temp.); C. Dowd (R. Loe), S. Fitzpatrick (c),
O. Brown, I. Jones, R. Brooke, M. Brewer (J. Joseph), Z. Brooke, J. Kronfeld

Index

219